ARGYLE

ARGYLE

THE IMPOSSIBLE STORY OF AUSTRALIAN DIAMONDS

STUART KELLS

MELBOURNE
UNIVERSITY
PRESS

MELBOURNE UNIVERSITY PRESS
An imprint of Melbourne University Publishing Limited
Level 1, 715 Swanston Street, Carlton, Victoria 3053, Australia
mup-contact@unimelb.edu.au
www.mup.com.au

Cover design by Peter Long
Cover photograph by Paul Williams/Science Photo Library
Typeset in 12/15.5pt Adobe Garamond Pro by Cannon Typesetting
Printed in Australia by McPherson's Printing Group

 A catalogue record for this
book is available from the
National Library of Australia

9780522877250 (paperback)
9780522877267 (ebook)

For Ewen Tyler, Bill Leslie and Alan Jones—
without whom the diamonds would not have been
mined, and this book would not have been written

FOREWORD

GEOFFREY BLAINEY

T HIS IS THE history of Argyle, one of the most surprising mines
in the world. In its heyday it produced a higher annual tally of
diamonds than any African mine, and it is still famous as the treasure
house of the rare pink diamond. And yet the first diamonds were
discovered in an isolated corner of Australia that was renowned for its
fierce summers and an annual 'monsoonal assault of high humidity
and torrential rain'.

As a historian I first visited this north-west corner of the nation in
1961. In that year no politicians or geologists would have predicted
that it would become, in the next thirty years, one of the world's
richest and most diverse producers of minerals. I spent two days in
sleepy Port Hedland. You could hardly call it a harbour, but it was to
become one of the biggest cargo ports in the world and the hub of
a huge iron ore province. Nearby was Marble Bar, a struggling gold
town seemingly close to extinction, and yet 400 kilometres away was
the Great Sandy Desert where eventually the Telfer mine became the
nation's second-largest gold producer.

Back in 1961, in an aircraft travelling further north, I sat next to
a man who told me that he was about to be a lighthouse keeper at
lonely Cape Leveque. There he would be in radio contact with only
a few small ships each month; today two new ports nearby send away

a procession of big ships carrying liquefied natural gas and iron ore to cities in East Asia. It was in this same dynamic region that Argyle's diamonds were unexpectedly discovered in 1979, almost at the close of the remarkable burst of mineral discovery.

A hero of this fascinating and lucid history is Ewen Tyler. At the age of twelve he had chanced to see tiny diamonds in the jungle of Sarawak, but he became intrigued by the geology of diamonds when he was a university student in Perth where his lecturer, Rex Prider, possessed that rare gift: an original mind.

At first Tyler's livelihood was in goldmines in Tanganyika (today's Tanzania), and it was not until 1968 that he and his wife, Aldyth, returned to Western Australia, which was then in the midst of an exploration boom. Before long he was in charge of the little Kalumburu syndicate and searching for diamonds in rocky terrain. It is a common myth that the quest for a buried mineral deposit is usually a simple short-term task, calling only for a four-wheel drive and a tough pair of boots. However, an intensive mineral search is now a branch of science, and high finance. A revolutionary geological theory had to be shaped, and accepted knowledge overthrown, before the first pipe of diamonds was discovered in a peculiar volcanic setting that had seemed worthless to scientists fresh from southern Africa, the traditional home of diamonds. And the buyers in Amsterdam and jewellers in Paris and Los Angeles had to be persuaded of the worth of these distinctive gems.

In this isolated region where the towns and big mines were far apart, and remoter from the nearest capital city, efficient transport was crucial and costly. Even the discovery team employed a helicopter in the daily collecting of rock samples that provided clues to the hidden presence of diamonds. A bold decision was made to abandon the idea of building a large township for the workforce, and to experiment instead with the novel fly-in and fly-out system. Soon the typical employees arrived by special planes, worked long hours for two or three weeks, and then flew perhaps half the length of the continent for a time of leisure at home.

By the time hydro-electricity arrived from the Ord River Dam, the open-cut mine was working on a large scale. We imagine a diamond mine will not be large, but a mountain of rock has to be mined in order to recover the scatter of diamonds. Today this gigantic quarry-hole, though mostly quiet, is an eye-opener. If it chanced to lie in the Blue Mountains instead of several thousand kilometres to the north-west, and if it could be easily reached by day-tourists from Sydney, the visitors would marvel at its size and symmetry, the steep terraces and the varied rock-colours. But back at Argyle, as this book explains, the Aboriginal people were not sure that they themselves were the gainers.

Stuart Kells, the author, has a background that aided him. Though young, he has been a senior official in government, a director at one of the Big Four accountants, a dealer in antiquarian books, an editor, and a participant in financial change: he once worked for the sharebroker and investment bank Potter Warburg. Originally a country boy, he does not have that unease towards mining that tends to characterise each big Australian city except Perth and now permeates even the primary schools and their teachers. This book is a valuable insight into an industry once widely praised but now undervalued by a nation that relies on it so strongly.

CONTENTS

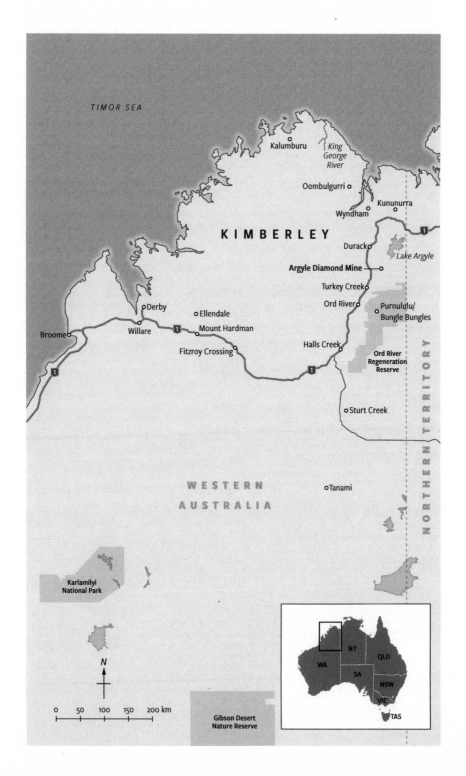

ABBREVIATIONS

AAPA	Aboriginal Affairs Planning Authority
ADEX	Australian Diamond Exploration NL
AIDC	Australian Industry Development Corporation
AMPLA	Australian Mining Petroleum Law Association
AO	Anglo Oriental (Australia) Pty Ltd
APR	advance purchases reserve
ASX	Australian Stock Exchange
AWU	Australian Workers' Union
BCG	Boston Consulting Group
cpht	carats per hundred tonnes
CRA	Conzinc Riotinto of Australia
CSIRO	Commonwealth Scientific and Industrial Research Organisation
CSO	Central Selling Organization
CZC	ConZinc Corp
DAA	Department of Aboriginal Affairs
DiCorp	Diamond Corporation (Switzerland) Limited
DMS	dense media separator
DTC	Diamond Trading Company
FIFO	fly-in fly-out
FIRB	Foreign Investment Review Board
HMS	heavy media separation

IPO	initial public offering
JV	joint venture
KB	Kleinwort Benson
KDC	Kimberley Diamond Company NL
MIM	Mount Isa Mines
MMC	Malaysia Mining Corporation Srn Bhd
NL	no liability
RTZ	Rio Tinto Zinc
TBE	tetrabromoethane
TWU	Transport Workers' Union
UMAL	Union Minière Australia Limited
UNIMIN	Union Minière Mining and Exploration Limited
UWA	University of Western Australia
VEL	Van Eck and Lurie
WADC	Western Australian Development Corporation
WADT	Western Australian Diamond Trust
WMC	Western Mining Corporation

AUTHOR'S NOTE

All monetary amounts are in Australian dollars unless otherwise indicated.

PROLOGUE

I F YOU SQUEEZE a diamond in a vice, in all probability the vice and not the diamond will be scarred. Forty times stronger than ruby and sapphire, diamond is the hardest naturally occurring substance on earth. The etymology of 'diamond'—along with sister words 'adamant' and 'adamantine'—refers to hardness and implacability. (The Sanskrit word for diamond is *vajra*, 'thunderbolt'.)

Historically, many diamonds were used in industry as abrasives and for grinding and drilling. They are tough enough to cut through stone and steel and concrete. But diamonds are also brittle. If you whack one hard enough with a hammer, the diamond and not the hammer will shatter. In the storied history of diamonds, the ability to smash them is surprisingly important. In one tale from ancient India, a clever con man fools diamond finders into thinking they've found worthless crystals. 'Look,' the trickster says. 'I can break them easily, so they mustn't be diamond.' The despondent finders walk away while the swindler gathers up the crystalline 'rubbish'.

Under the focused flame of a blowtorch, a diamond will glow red-hot. And if enough oxygen is nearby, the heated gem will disappear in an astonishing puff of carbon dioxide. Diamonds, it seems, aren't really forever. The puff of CO_2 is a nightmare scenario for owners of antique diamond jewellery and modern diamond engagement rings, especially

1

those purchased (according to a pseudo-tradition that mainly benefits the diamond industry) with a quarter of the purchaser's annual income. Fortunately for fiancés and fiancées, the puff scenario is rare. Nearly all the jewellery-grade diamonds ever discovered and marketed are still out there, unsmoked and unsmashed.

Diamond is a crystalline form of carbon, the fourth most abundant element in the universe. A stable and versatile substance, carbon comes in a variety of states that differ depending on how the atoms are organised and bonded. In diamonds, the atoms are attached to each other in an especially regular way, forming a tight lattice. Coal and graphite are carbon in different, less well bonded forms. Diamonds don't conduct electricity well, but they usually fluoresce, which makes them easy to spot with X-rays. They repel water but usually adhere to grease. These and other properties are important for processing diamond-bearing ore.

For carbon atoms to organise themselves into diamond, the surrounding temperature and pressure must reach extreme levels: more than 1000 degrees Celsius and 45 kilobars. Intense conditions such as these occur deep below the earth's surface: more than 150 kilometres below, in the mantle—the thick layer of hot rock between our planet's crust and its core. (These temperatures and pressures also occur on other rocky planets, and most of those planets also contain carbon. So somewhere, not too far away, in all probability there are extraterrestrial diamonds. Meteors, too, occasionally contain diamonds, or create them at the point of impact.) The precise crystalline form of diamonds is important: it affects their hardness, brittleness and colour. If the diamond lattice is twisted or tilted, for example, it can capture and refract light differently, imparting colours such as blue, violet and yellow.

Carbon might be common, but diamonds are rare on the earth's surface. Yet they can sometimes be found there. Certain types of volcano carry diamonds up from the mantle and through the crust. When those volcanoes cool, they form vertical plugs or 'pipes' that stretch as far as 200 kilometres, topping out at the surface. Diamond hunters have long known that diamonds can be found in the blue, green and yellow volcanic rock called kimberlite.

Diamond mines process massive quantities of ore—quantities that are measured in millions of tonnes. Diamonds, though, are weighed at tiny scales. Their weight is expressed in carats. A carat is a fifth of a gram. A diamond weighing just six-tenths of a carat is still regarded as a respectably sized gem, and a marketable one. (Some diamonds are spectacularly large. The famous Excelsior Diamond weighed 995.2 carats before it was cut up. The Cullinan Diamond, from the Premier Mine in South Africa, was almost three times larger, weighing 3106 carats or 680 grams. That's a single diamond with the mass of two-thirds of a litre of milk.)

Diamond people use a wonderful and arcane language. Malformed diamonds are 'bort'. Smashed fragments are 'grits'. A 'naat' or 'knot' is a flaw or irregularity. A 'gletz' or 'feather' is a cleft or fracture. Rock in which diamonds are found is 'diamondiferous'—a splendiferous word if ever there was one. The coloured diamonds most prized by connoisseurs are called 'fancies'. Untouched stones are referred to as 'rough diamonds', or simply as 'rough'. When released from their surrounding rock, rough diamonds look like the dull and blocky fragments of a smashed windscreen. There are thousands of rough diamond categories, ranging from cheap industrial stones to the uppermost gem-quality ones. The value of polished diamonds has traditionally depended on an alliteration of factors: carat weight, cut, clarity and colour. Before they are sold, diamonds are expertly classified according to these four dimensions of quality and desirability.

The market value of diamonds is a delicate balance. On the plus side, they are hard to find; they have an intrinsic beauty and a special glamour; and people group them with other precious commodities such as gold, platinum and emeralds. Even the word itself is glamorous, suggesting perfect geometry, echoing *demimonde*, and evoking modernity and hedonism. Diamonds, in short, are sexy. (In the Middle Ages, some people believed diamonds could mate and produce offspring. For three decades, diamond mines in India were closed to allow the stones some private time in which to pair off and breed.)

On the other hand, new mines come on stream from time to time, some of them large. And then there is the looming, ever-present 'overhang': the enormous quantum of all the diamonds previously found and sold—each one readily transportable and potentially saleable. Another problem for diamond values: the extreme temperatures and pressures of the earth's mantle can be replicated in factories. In 1953, the Swedish electrical manufacturer ASEA made the first synthetic diamonds. Two years later, the first diamond patent was granted. These milestones were for industrial-grade synthetics, but in 1969 America's General Electric began making artificial diamonds of gem-quality. Today, manufactured diamonds represent more than 70 per cent of the world's diamond output.

Throughout the twentieth century, a unique, cartel-like entity wielded an exceptional degree of control over the international market for natural diamonds. Founded by Cecil Rhodes in 1888, the De Beers Group used its power in hard and soft ways across the production, distribution and marketing of diamonds. The group had a stake in nearly all of the world's major diamond mines. It dominated diamond sales through its Central Selling Organization (CSO) and a network of tied distributors. And it stoked demand for diamonds by paying for stylish advertising—featuring words such as 'forever' and 'everlasting'—and glamorous product placement. (Philadelphia advertising agency NW Ayer & Son came up with the De Beers slogan 'A diamond is forever' in the 1940s. Half a century later, the pitch of De Beers' millennium campaign was 'Show her you'll love her for the next thousand years.')

An example of the power of diamond advertising, and the CSO's role in it: in 1967, fewer than 5 per cent of Japanese fiancées received a diamond ring as an engagement or wedding ring, but by 1981, some 60 per cent of Japanese brides wore diamonds. A CSO marketing campaign had dramatically changed what was an entrenched Japanese tradition, and Japan became the second-largest market for diamond engagement rings, behind only the United States.

(Running counter to restrictive trade practices rules, the centralised model of diamond marketing regularly attracted official interest. In 1943, Britain considered reforming the market for gem diamonds. An investigative report recognised the merit of price maintenance but recommended the CSO be restructured, bringing it under the control of the most important producers and their respective governments. The report was put to John Maynard Keynes in Treasury, but ultimately the government followed Keynes' advice that the market arrangements should be left 'undisturbed'.)

Using all the tools at its disposal, De Beers sought for many years to manage the delicate balance of diamond values. The dangers it confronted were many. Apart from action by anti-monopoly regulators, there was the risk that consumers' preferences would change: diamonds could become unfashionable, or at least less fashionable; and people could revise their perceptions of what diamonds might be worth. There were risks, too, on the supply side. At any moment, a plethora of new diamonds could flood the market. And the burdensome overhang of old diamonds was ever-ready to fall from the sky and crush the market. (A core message of diamond advertising is that people should hold on to their gems.)

In the face of these dangers, De Beers largely succeeded in its mission. Diamonds continued to be seen as a desirable luxury, and continued to fetch reliably high prices. As further proof of De Beers' success, people went to extreme lengths to steal diamonds. The owners of diamond mines had to adopt extraordinary security measures, including scanning mine workers with X-rays, spying on them in their quarters, and manually searching their bodies. (An early attempt to prevent diamond theft involved spreading the rumour that diamonds were poisonous if swallowed. The thieves quickly saw through this stratagem.) Diamond mines typically operate with strong security powers, even paramilitary ones.

Diamonds may be glamorous in the showroom, but very unglamorous things go on behind the scenes. Diamond miners blast, smash and crush rock. They run the broken ore and gravel over grease belts or through X-ray beams. And they search their personnel with rubber gloves. The largest diamond mines recover stones directly from kimberlite ore. Kimberlite volcano pipes were first discovered in South Africa in the 1860s. Initially called 'blueground', the pipes came to be known as kimberlites after Kimberley in South Africa's Cape Province, which in turn was named after a British colonial secretary, Lord Kimberley. The town of Kimberley grew around the famous

'Big Hole': an enormous, hand-dug kimberlitic diamond mine. The novelist Anthony Trollope visited the district in 1877. He was impressed by the hole, but thought the town itself—with its flies and heat and dust—was among the worst he'd visited. Despite that judgement, the name 'Kimberley' has long had magical connotations in the world of diamonds.

An average mineable diamond deposit will have around 60 carats in every 100 tonnes of rock. That's around eight parts per million, or the weight of a metal staple in a tonne of rock. Some viable diamond mines have concentrations as low as one part in 100 million. So mining diamond ore is hard work. There are other ways, too, to find diamonds. At the moment of eruption, volcanic diamonds can be shot into the air before settling over a large area. They are then washed into creeks and rivers, and alluvial diamonds can be gathered from loose gravels or from 'conglomerate' (ancient alluvial deposits). Kimberlites can also release diamonds through erosion.

Because of the low concentrations, you can't just walk around and hope to find a mineable deposit of diamonds, and because of their composition, you can't use a metal detector. You have to do something much cleverer and more difficult: you have to search for tiny chemical clues. When the diamonds ride the volcanoes to the surface, they travel with more abundant and less valuable minerals—such as garnets, ilmenites, zircons and chrome diopsides—that were formed at the same depths inside the earth. Members of this family of red, green, yellowish and lilac-coloured minerals are known as 'indicator minerals' because, when found, they hint that fellow-travelling diamonds might be nearby. In Russia they are referred to as *sputniki*, 'little satellites'.

Diamonds and indicator minerals have more in common than their deep origins. Collectively, they are called 'heavy minerals' because their specific gravity (also known as relative density) is greater than 2.9, meaning they are more than 2.9 times heavier than an equivalent amount of water. They also share chemical properties. These facts are very useful for diamond hunters, who accumulate and guard specialist knowledge about the particular minerals that travel with diamonds. By finding indicator minerals in a stream, diamond searchers can sometimes follow the trail to a kimberlite pipe. Samples of gravel are collected and scrutinised for indicators. These days, most of the scrutiny takes place in laboratories. But not so long ago in Africa, the scrutiny happened in the field using sieves and a process of 'hand jigging'. In the eye of the jig the *sputniki* would congregate, if they were present at all. Sometimes, tiny diamonds would be found this way.

Though finding a diamond is exciting, it is usually a dead end. Discovering even a large gem doesn't mean you've found where it came from. Diamonds are tricky prey. They are small and robust, and this makes them especially mobile. Left to their own devices, they can travel a long way. When a prospector finds a diamond, they may be hundreds of kilometres from the gem's source: for example, the diamonds that make up the rich beach deposits of Namibia travelled there from a source some 950 kilometres to the east. And even if you're lucky enough to find the source, it might not be mineable. The yield may be too low, the source may be inaccessible or, for any one of a thousand other reasons, the diamonds might remain out of reach. Mineral exploration often culminates in the word 'no'. The risk is often too high, the benefits too meagre. Searching for diamonds is the riskiest of all types of mineral exploration. The raw statistics are firmly against the prospector. According to one estimate, less than one-tenth of 1 per cent of kimberlites that are discovered will have a high enough yield to justify a diamond mine. That's a failure rate of 99.9 per cent.

1

BREAKING OUT OF THE CONGO

M ODERN ADVENTURE TOURISTS seek out remote places for
exotic and energising experiences. Sometimes there is danger,
oftentimes adrenaline. But the tourists' adventure quotient is nothing
like what was possible in the nineteenth century at the height of the
British Empire. In those days, you could go to a place, raise your own
army, forge your own artillery, take the place over, subjugate its people,
appropriate their natural wealth and set them to work in extracting
it. Between 1870 and 1902, Cecil Rhodes made an extraordinary
transition from scrounging businessman to a kind of king. Looked
at through today's eyes, many of Rhodes' accomplishments were
appalling. But in his day, schoolchildren throughout the Empire
were served up stories of his deeds as examples to emulate.

Founded in 1899 as part of Rhodes' African realm, the company
Tanganyika Concessions Limited served multiple purposes. It held
monopoly mineral rights that broadened and deepened Rhodes'
mining portfolio. It gave him an audacious foothold in a part of
Africa that was claimed by King Leopold of Belgium. And it was a
way to remain in the good graces of the Prince of Wales, Britain's
future monarch. Rhodes installed the prince's glamorous mistress
the Countess of Warwick as a founding shareholder of the company,

whose name was self-consciously exotic and which everyone shortened to 'Tanks'. (The countess herself was known as 'Daisy'. She inspired the popular music-hall song, 'Daisy, Daisy', which the HAL 9000 computer famously sings in Stanley Kubrick's *2001: A Space Odyssey*.) Rhodes is believed to have manipulated Tanks' assets and share price to ensure a handsome return for its owners, and particularly for the countess. In the words of the Congo historian Enrico Carisch, Rhodes 'always ensured that the Prince's girlfriend was doing well'.

The enterprise had begun soon after Rhodes' geologist, George Grey, found 'scandalously rich' copper fields in the Katanga Province during a clandestine expedition into King Leopold's territory in the *Congo belge*. The company's first leader and 'founding father' was Sir Robert Williams, a mining entrepreneur and trusted confidant of Rhodes. Williams mounted the prospecting expeditions that discovered the African Copperbelt. He had a ship built that was carried in pieces across Africa, then reassembled to provide the first commercial service on Lake Tanganyika. His mineral exploits inspired the film *King Solomon's Mines*, and his maritime ones *The African Queen*.

Rhodes and Williams first met in 1885 at the De Beers diamond mine in Kimberley, South Africa. Standing at the edge of the legendary Big Hole, Rhodes expressed the fear that the edges might cave in, taking with them much of the town of Kimberley. Williams, then a young mining engineer, assured Rhodes that all would be well. His assurance was good for the better part of a century. (In the mid-1970s, 1.5 million tonnes of rock collapsed into the pit.)

Claiming the Katanga deposits naturally led to conflict with the Belgians. However, after Rhodes' death in 1902, a compromise was reached. In 1906, in cooperation with the powerful Belgian group Société Générale, Tanks founded the Union Minière du Haut Katanga—the Mining Union of Upper Katanga—as the vehicle for joint ownership of the Belgian mines. A major shareholder in Union Minière, Tanks was also the principal manager of its assets. When Williams died in 1938, Tanks' main investments were the Katanga mines and a railway in Angola. These investments made the company one of the world's top producers of copper, as well as zinc and germanium (at Kipushi) and uranium ore (at Shinkolobwe), from which Union Minière extracted radium for radiotherapy and other medical uses.

(Apart from the small quantities that were used for making yellow glass, the uranium 'yellowcake' was an unmarketable waste product. Or it was until the 1940s, when the US Secret Service searched the world for uranium to use in the Manhattan Project. Union Minière's managing director at the time, Edgar van der Straeten, made a revelation that was as helpful as it was unsettling: the company had stockpiled tonnes of yellowcake in a waterside warehouse on Manhattan Island. Those supplies were used to make the first atom bombs.)

In the decades after World War II, Tanks was full of former naval and military men. At the company's London head office, the room containing the mineral maps was referred to as 'the chart room'. (The company's affairs were diligently recorded in handsome leather-bound ledgers and journals, which are now in the University of Manchester Library.) Some of the company's leaders supported African independence and self-determination and were appalled by the Mau Mau executions in Kenya and the Sharpeville massacre in South Africa. But Tanks' chairman, Capt. Rt. Hon. Charles Waterhouse, led a group of directors and senior staff who were aligned with the right wing of the Tory party and who were 'quite against' independence. (During the Suez Crisis, Waterhouse had led the ultra-conservative 'Suez Rebels' in Britain's parliament. They believed Britain should never have left the Suez Canal.)

Harold Macmillan was Britain's relatively moderate Conservative prime minister. In February 1960, he delivered in Cape Town his landmark 'Wind of Change' speech, in which he telegraphed Britain's support for African independence and self-determination. Back at Tanks, Waterhouse was appalled. The company's boardroom lunches (at which Waterhouse was the designated chief salad tosser) were typically scenes of great political debate. Once news of the prime minister's speech reached the directors, the dominant feeling at lunch was 'Macmillan has to go'.

Entangled in multiple ways with the British monarchy, the British Government and Britain's overseas possessions, Tanks was very much a creature of the Empire. And in the postwar decades of imperial decline, the company was very much in trouble. In Africa, the death throes of the colonial era were manifested in war, apartheid, nationalism and revolution. Some mines closed and some investors fled. On the ground, the major players fought to hold on to assets, or to carve out a share of the spoils. In the Congo, businessman Moise Tshombe became leader of the Katanga province. On 11 July 1960, he declared the southern part of the Congo independent from the newly created Congo Republic. For two-and-a-half years his Katanga rebels fought for independence, aided by military support from Belgium and financial support from Tanks and Union Minière.

Backing the rebels in this way was a gamble that didn't pay off. The United Nations sent in peacekeeping troops, just as it had done in Egypt during the Suez Crisis, the secession movement collapsed, and the rich mineral deposits of the Katanga moved out of Belgian control. Union Minière lost its main investments, including mines that were producing a quarter of the world's copper output.

In 1966, Ewen Tyler was a youngish director and technical consultant at Tanks' London headquarters. With his Australian wife, Aldyth, he'd moved to London from Geita in Tanganyika (now Tanzania) on a one-year contract—and ended up staying for ten. A geologist, Tyler came from a mining family. His mother, Ethel Matthew, grew up in Hoyland, a Yorkshire village where the 'knocker-up' would go from cottage to cottage before dawn and wake the coalminers for their early shift. His father, the geologist Harold Tyler, had worked in Burma, then in Africa for Tanks and later in Australia and Sarawak for Rio Tinto. At Tanks, Harold got to know Sir Robert Williams. (Williams' family estate was in Scotland on the river Spey. Ewen has a boyhood memory of large fresh salmon arriving at his home in white wooden boxes from 'Speyside'.) Through this connection, Harold was just one degree of separation from Cecil Rhodes and the seminal moments of South Africa's diamond industry.

Aldyth Tyler came from a political family in Western Australia. Her father, Arthur Watts, led for many years the Country Party there. Through his career Watts held numerous portfolios, including deputy premier, minister for north-west, and minister for industrial development—a portfolio he passed on to the state's future premier

Charles Court. Before Ewen's decade in London, he'd spent a decade in Africa for the Tanks Group. He and Aldyth were married in Kenya, and their three children were born in the mine hospital at Geita. Initially as assistant geologist (with no senior geologist to assist) and ultimately as underground manager, Ewen's main role in Africa was to oversee the prospecting and mining of gold from banded ironstone at Tanganyika's Geita Gold Mine, the largest goldmine in East Africa.

Now at Tanks in London, Ewen worked alongside knights and lords and baronets who were invested in a version of England and Empire that pre-dated the world wars. The atmosphere at Tanks was like a gentlemen's club, and much of the company's work was conducted in actual gentlemen's clubs, such as Boodle's, Buck's, the Gresham and the Cobden. Moderate of height and slight of build, Ewen looked every bit the Englishman, and was in fact English by birth. But he'd gone to secondary school and university in Australia and saw himself very much as an Australian. In the debate about Africa's future, he was on the side of independence. 'An independent Africa would be better for Africans,' he said. In Tanzania and Australia, he'd worked alongside people of all races. Now in London, the work was fascinating and important but he was shocked by the retrograde and even racist attitudes around him. His father had received his nickname in the Royal Australian Engineers: 'Wat' or 'Watty' Tyler, after the leader of the fourteenth-century English peasants' revolt. Ewen got his own nickname at Tanks. On account of his Australianness and his independence of mind, he was referred to as 'the Colonial', or 'the Mad Colonial'.

For the directors of Tanks and Union Minière, the defeat of the Katanga rebellion and the loss of the Katanga assets was a major setback, and one that took a while to sink in. Pressing issues confronted them in Africa, such as potential compensation for nationalisation, questions of engineering and technical management, and the ownership of US$400 million of copper stockpiled outside the Congo (by now called Zaire). But Ewen Tyler felt there was a lot of 'wistfully longing for the old days' on the boards of both companies. Just hoping that somehow the Katanga mines would come back into their control wasn't helping anyone. Overall, the mining assets and prospecting activities of Tanks and Union Minière were heavily weighted towards Africa. From London, Tyler had a good view of the group's assets and exploration programs, and he could see it needed to do something quickly. It had to find or buy mines in other parts of the world. In particular, he believed, it had to look to Canada. And Australia.

Tyler thought the group's directors, especially the Belgian ones, weren't sufficiently international in their outlook. And he felt they lacked a sense of urgency. In 1966, however, there was change at the top. Waterhouse retired and Lord Colyton became chairman of Tanks. Before his appointment, Colyton had already had careers as a diplomat and a politician. In Winston Churchill's second and last government, he served as secretary for overseas trade and then as minister of state for colonial affairs. He maintained strong personal relationships with leaders in Africa and elsewhere in the former empire. In 1955 British Prime Minister Anthony Eden had offered him the choice of becoming governor-general of Nigeria or high commissioner in Australia; Colyton declined both posts and instead went to the House of Lords.

In 1966, three years after the Katanga rebellion had collapsed, Tanks hosted a dinner party at London's Ritz Hotel to farewell Waterhouse and honour Tshombe. Tyler was invited ('7.45 p.m. for 8.15 p.m.,' the invitation read, 'Piccadilly entrance … No black tie necessary') and at the party he pitched his idea to the new chair. Lord Colyton had an eye to the future. He was an internationalist in spirit and in practice. With much of Africa still in turmoil, he supported Tyler's vision: the idea of establishing a presence in the New World; the ambition, if it paid off, of restoring Tanganyika Concessions to its former glory.

In 1967 and with Colyton's imprimatur, Tyler took a team of Union Minière executives to Australia. Out of professional and national pride, he devised a gruelling itinerary for the visitors, determined to show them everything Australia might offer. They would make contact with the federal and state governments and the local and overseas companies that were active in Australia. And they would inspect mining assets and prospects in every corner of the continent.

As soon as the visitors arrived, the leaders of Australia's mining sector embraced them. Those leaders, who believed they were building nothing less than the country's future, were hungry for international knowledge and capital. 'It was immediately apparent', Tyler said, 'that Union Minière's money and expertise would be most welcome.' Apart from copper and zinc, Union Minière knew a great deal about the mining and processing of uranium. 'It was natural that in Australia they should be invited to participate in uranium exploration and mining.'

Belgium's steel industry relied on low-quality European iron ore. At the time of the visit, iron ore resources in the Pilbara were being opened up. Charles Court, then minister for industrial development in Western Australia, sought to interest Union Minière in the Robe River iron ore deposits. An American, Bill Dohnal, was seeking to reduce his interest in those deposits. As the responsible minister, Court was eager to see the ore mined. Through Arthur Watts, Tyler and the Belgian team met with Minister Court to discuss the potential for Union Minière to invest. Other opportunities, too, were presented to the Belgians. All the lights were green. At the end of the 1967 visit, Union Minière decided to establish an Australian holding company, Union Minière Australia Limited (UMAL), and a Victorian subsidiary of UMAL, Union Minière Mining and Exploration Limited (UNIMIN). The Belgians were finally breaking out of the Congo.

2
A DUAL ROLE

E WEN TYLER WAS appointed as a London-based director of UMAL and UNIMIN. In Australia, a handsome, likeable, well-dressed Franco-Belgian was appointed as the subsidiaries' local director. Very soon, Serge Fontainas was driving the straitlaced mine managers and geologists mad. But in antipodean social circles he was a huge hit. Lady Mary Fairfax introduced him to the fashionable set in Sydney. His job was dull and the miners were mostly boring, but he knew all the best people and the best restaurants, and when he saw his merry friends in the street he would call out and greet them extravagantly.

In 1968, Tyler took his whole family, now including three teenage children, to Australia by sea. Aldyth's parents were living in Perth, as was Ewen's mother, Ethel. (Harold Tyler had died in 1951.) The Tyler children would see their grandparents, and Ewen would see what Fontainas and Union Minière were up to. The situation was immediately clear: the subsidiary was too far away for the Belgians to keep a proper eye on it, and in that vacuum a playboy was managing the Belgians' affairs in Australia—perhaps, Tyler thought, because Union Minière couldn't handle him in Brussels. The Australian Government and the Australian mining industry had laid out a smorgasbord of opportunities before the company, but Tyler was disappointed to learn it had not taken them up. Union Minière's first visit to Australia had been a success, but its first Australian subsidiaries were failing.

The problems were deeper than Fontainas' recreational enthusiasms. In Tyler's view, the Belgians had a peculiar mindset: they were fixated on how things had been done in Africa, and wanted to replicate African mining models elsewhere. Tyler could see that that mindset, along with the Belgian corporate culture, was going to bring clashes: 'Conventional wisdom in Belgium didn't think Australian uranium prospects would be as good as Shinkolobwe in the Congo. The Robe River iron ore deposits wouldn't suit the Belgian steel industry. There was too much iron ore in the world. Who wanted Australian iron ore?'

These were just some of the philosophical challenges confronting Union Minière in Australia. The Belgians' expertise was in copper, zinc, uranium and diamonds, along with germanium and other scarce elements. 'They had no experience in nickel,' Tyler said, 'but rapidly, because of Western Mining Corporation's success in the discovery of nickel in Kambalda [near Kalgoorlie] in the mid-1960s, their exploration focused on nickel. It's amazing how sheep-like corporate culture can be.'

Tyler was a director of the two Union Minière companies in Australia, but his ideas and ambitions for that country extended well beyond the confines of the Belgian entities. Once back in London, he pushed for Tanks to do its own thing in Australia, separately from Union Minière. Tanks people had, after all, discovered the copper mines of the Katanga, and Tanks had its own tradition of mining. Lord Colyton again supported Tyler's plans. Other Tanks directors were also supportive. But the support wasn't universal. The group's Belgian directors tended to be against establishing a second presence in Australia. Nevertheless, after much pushing and shoving, it was agreed that Tanganyika Holdings, a Tanks Group subsidiary based in London, would set up a branch in Australia, separate from Union Minière.

If Tanks was to launch an Australian venture, then Tyler was determined to lead it. There were pull factors drawing him and his family to the antipodes. Apart from grandparents, the potential for Australian mining was a strong inducement. And there were also push factors from London: Tyler had had enough of the office clock, he'd had enough of Tanks' Tory politics, and he'd had enough of London itself. The English weather was a burden, especially in winter, as was the bleak ordeal of travelling to the city by train. Ewen Tyler was a 'son of Empire' but not a 'man of Britain'. He'd spent ten years in Africa and ten years in London. He was ready for a new phase of life.

Tyler knew much of the technical side of geology and mineralogy. He knew about looking for valuable minerals. He knew about mine financing and mine management. And he was Australian. Within the Tanks Group, he was the obvious choice as head of the new venture. He petitioned Tanks' leaders to base him in Australia as the group's representative there. They agreed on condition that the new branch wouldn't compete with Union Minière. Tyler would therefore take on a dual role: as director of the Union Minière companies in Australia he would support their activities, and, wearing his Tanks hat, he would establish and lead the Australian branch of Tanganyika Holdings. The London directors of Tanks gave their new Australian branch a limited mandate and a modest budget: just £65,000 per year for five years. The branch would have three roles: it would act as a listening post, it would make investment recommendations, and it would carry out low-key exploration investigations.

Tyler left England in July 1969. He passed all his directorships in the London companies to a colleague, Dr Vivian Wadsworth, who boasted that he'd spied for MI6 in Rhodesia. Wadsworth promised to ensure continuing support in Britain for Tyler's activities in Australia.

3

THE ALLURE OF DIAMONDS

WITHIN THE LIMITED scope of Ewen Tyler's antipodean mandate, the Australian branch of Tanks would look for copper and platinum. And diamonds.

For most of the twentieth century, very few people thought Australia could ever be a serious diamond producer. A proper, kimberlitic diamond mine was as elusive as Lasseter's mythical reef. But that's not to say the southern continent was free of homegrown diamonds, or that no-one sought them there. The idea of finding diamonds in Australia had long been a bewitching dream and, for some, an all-consuming quest.

The first people to arrive on the continent came very early in the timeline of modern humans. (According to one theory, a massive volcanic eruption some 75,000 years ago created vast natural rafts of pumice, which people rode from the Indonesian archipelago to northern Australia.) Indigenous Australians probably found diamonds in creeks and rivers and just lying about on the ground. The sparkling stones were incorporated into their rich library of Dreaming stories.

During the Australian gold rush of the 1850s, treasure-hunters found diamonds by accident at places such as Beechworth, Bathurst and near Harrow in western Victoria. The gold-seekers mostly used pans and sluices and other simple equipment to search alluvial gravels for riches. Occasionally they found diamonds in their pans, and there are stories of old-timers wandering into remote missions and homesteads with handfuls of gems, not entirely sure what they were or what they might be worth. In New South Wales, a diamond was reported as early as in 1851. In that state, tin was being recovered from so-called 'deep leads' (actually paleo-river gravels) on a large scale. Sluices were used to concentrate the tin. Hard diamonds—a mystery and an anomaly in the mining process—sometimes rolled off the ends of the sluices.

By the 1870s, miners were extracting alluvial diamonds at a number of sites in the New England region of north-eastern New South Wales. The most important of those fields were at Copeton and Bingara, about 400 kilometres north of Sydney. Copeton was the larger of the two fields. There, from 1875 to 1915, a total of 300,000 carats were produced. One of the largest mine sites at Copeton, the Star of the South, produced in one good year 25,477 carats, nearly a tenth of the region's output from the four decades. The gravel was reached by a vertical shaft 27 metres deep. The stones were small but the yield was high, averaging between 3 and 4 carats per tonne. The largest stone from Copeton was 6.25 carats. Bingara was mined from the mid-1870s to around 1902. Its diamonds were even smaller, from 5 per carat down to 20 per carat, though the quality was better. At Copeton much tin was also found, enhancing the total marketable yield; around 4 kilograms of cassiterite (SnO_2 or tin oxide) per tonne of wash. At Bingara it was gold that helped lift the yield.

The family name of Joris is intertwined with the history of Australian diamonds, and especially with the New South Wales diamond fields. Jules Joris came from a line of Antwerp diamantaires—specialist diamond dealers—who migrated to Australia. He worked with Copeton and Bingara diamonds, which were notoriously hard and therefore difficult to cut: they were known as 'Can-ni-faire', 'hard to make'. In 1948, Joris formed the Southern Cross Diamond and Tin Mining Company, which raised money to search for the source of the Copeton diamonds.

Where were they coming from? Had the diamonds travelled to Copeton and Bingara on ancient glaciers from Antarctica, or by rivers from some other source? Perhaps they'd come from an even more distant source, by riding a meteorite, or following an exotic, non-kimberlitic route that brought them up from deep underground. (The New South Wales Geological Survey has shown that diamonds sometimes originate from the ocean floor. Colliding tectonic plates can compress organic carbon, from fish and other marine life, to form diamonds. This can happen at depths as shallow as 80 kilometres.)

Joris searched hard and far but never found the source of the alluvial deposits. (The terminology for this is 'headless placer deposit'.) Other companies, too, including the Belgian diamond outfit Sibeka, and Stockdale Prospecting, a subsidiary of De Beers, would search without success for the elusive source. In recent years, geologists have studied the internal structure of the Copeton stones and found that the diamonds fall into two groups. The first are very old and were formed deep in the mantle. The second group 'were probably formed much later, as Australia drifted eastwards over subducting Pacific plates and [were] then brought to the surface by some magma other than kimberlite'. Together, the two groups of diamonds remain one of the greatest mysteries of Australian geology.

Ewen Tyler had had some experience with diamonds.

As a boy growing up in England, he went to school at Coombe Hill House preparatory in South London, and then Whitgift School in Croydon. These were years of indelible moments. At Coombe Hill: lessons in Latin and French, plus a detention in which the headmaster gave six strokes of the cane to another boy, Rasmussen. 'I resolved this was not for me,' Tyler remembered. At Whitgift: History and English Literature. Cadets and the smell of cordite. The declaration of war. And a Messerschmitt 109 flying over the school at the height of the Dunkirk evacuation. 'For a time we had a Jewish German housemaid, Bertha Myer. She would listen to Hitler's broadcasts and shout at the wireless.'

Soon, other indelible moments were laid down in Tyler's memory, including the moment of leaving Britain to escape the war:

> Sea trunks had to be bought. We were limited in what we could take, and because 'careless talk costs lives' I wasn't even allowed to say goodbye to friends or even to tell the school that I was leaving. On the Thursday morning, after breakfast, we asked our then Irish maid, Kitty, to wash up, close the house and give the key to a neighbour.

With his mother and brother he sailed from Liverpool in a convoy of warships and merchant ships. The cruisers and destroyers honked and hooted and flashed at each other. A U-boat had recently sunk a passenger vessel bound for Canada and with many children on board. The atmosphere was tense, but the Tylers safely reached Sarawak via Singapore. There was no school for Ewen to attend in Borneo. Instead, the plan was for him to go to Western Australia for the start of the 1941 school year. In the meantime, he was attached to the Sarawak Museum in Kuching, where the curator taught him how to prepare and paint plaster casts of snakes and fish for exhibiting in the museum:

> There were some European children, mainly girls, and a Eurasian family, whose birthday parties I was asked to attend, but my principal friends were two Malay boys, Sinawie and his younger brother Sibawie, sons of the museum's principal taxidermist.

Ewen and Sinawie and Sibawie became an inseparable trio. They went to the Saturday matinees to see the Spider and Hopalong Cassidy in action. They made wooden pistols and staged hold-ups in the bazaar.

Sarawak was where Tyler had his first direct exposure to mineral exploration, and to mining, and diamonds. With his father he went on a week-long trip into the jungle, travelling by boat and on foot up to the mercury deposits. (The jungle's leeches were abundant and aggressive, and Ewen learnt how to use his father's lit cigarette to remove them.) Adits were being driven into the hills. Creeks were being panned for cinnabar, the ore of mercury, which the military needed for detonators.

A Chinese prospector, Ah Gin, was the proprietor of some mineral claims under offer to Mineral Properties Investigation, a Rio Tinto subsidiary. One morning, he was teaching Ewen how to use a *dulang*, a conical pan not unlike a rice hat, to look for cinnabar. Ewen was washing gravel in the *dulang* when Ah Gin told him to stop. '*Tuan Kitchie*,' Ah Gin said. 'Little master, that is a diamond.' Nestled in the coarse sand at the bottom of the *dulang* was a shiny octahedron about the size of the nail on Ewen's pinkie finger. It was the first natural diamond he'd seen. He was twelve years old. He was enchanted.

After five years of boarding at Guildford Grammar School, near Midland Junction just outside Perth, Tyler spent four years at the University of Western Australia:

> Chemistry was to be my major subject, with physics my second. In the first year I had to study five subjects. I could find four with two maths subjects, but what to do for the fifth one? There were all the 'ologies': psychology, zoology, geology, etc. With no real interest, I chose geology, because my father was a geologist.

Professor Edward de Courcy Clarke, Dr Rex Prider and Dr Curt Teichert were the principal faculty members in the UWA Geology Department. They wrote the main textbook and were major figures in the wider discipline.

Each of the top scholars had his own style and philosophy. Prider believed attention to detail was paramount. A petrographer, he was fascinated by the processes by which different rock types were formed. He inspired curiosity and meticulousness, teaching his students petrography and mineralogy and how to prepare detailed mineralogical maps. When Professor Clarke retired, Prider secured the chair. In 1948, Tyler's third year at UWA, he had Prider for hard rock geology. Tyler remembered the lessons vividly. He was impressed by Prider's scrupulous methods: 'We used chains and compasses, plane tables and levels, to create our own maps and cut our own rock slices.'

When Teichert left the Geology Department he was replaced by Rhodes Fairbridge, son of Kingsley Fairbridge, the famous founder of Farm Schools in Africa and Australia. Rhodes had different ideas about how to teach geology. To interest his students in the geological 'big picture', he gave classes in continental drift and the make-up of the entire planet. His macro view was in healthy tension with Prider's micro one. Tyler admired both men, but it was Prider's meticulousness that would shape his approach and, ultimately, his career.

Prider taught Tyler about reading the land: how a good geologist working in the field could read the landscape and understand what had happened going back deep into geological time. Even the smallest details were important. 'He interested me in mineral grains,' Tyler said. 'I spent my honours year on an almost impossible research topic, of my own choosing, seeking to separate and differentiate the Ordovician and Silurian rocks by their heavy minerals collected from rocks at the Captains Flat lead and zinc mine, where my father was general manager. As a result, I knew something about the recovery of heavy minerals from rocks and sands and gravels.'

Prider had made important contributions to the study of Western Australia's geology, and particularly its volcanoes. In 1907, a geologist had visited the state's wild and remote Kimberley region and noticed the existence of many volcanic vents in the West Kimberley. 'The volcanics are obvious,' Tyler later said. 'The vents and plugs rise conspicuously above the surrounding plains.'

In 1920, RA Farquharson wrote about Western Australia's 'ultra-mafic' (dark-coloured and volcanic) rocks and leucite 'lamproites' (former volcanoes consisting of mantle-derived rock). A decade and a half later, Prider was at Cambridge University studying a suite of volcanic rocks for his PhD research. Arthur Wade had collected the rocks in the West Kimberley. 'What an unimpressive lot they were,' Prider later said of those rocks. 'Mostly weathered, difficult to section.' But he noticed something important about them: they contained minerals similar to those that had accompanied the diamonds in South Africa. Prider hypothesised that the leucite lamproites of the West

Kimberley were mantle derived from a magma similar to the South African kimberlites. (At the time, kimberlites were believed to be the only host rock for diamonds.) He asked a critical question: could the Kimberley lamproites be similar to and occur with kimberlites? (The word he used was 'consanguineous'.)

In South Africa, the diamond pipes are the tops of volcanoes rooted deep in the earth's crust, probably as deep as 200 kilometres. Prider concluded that the West Australian Kimberley rocks were similar to but not the same as the diamond-bearing rocks of South Africa. With Wade, he wrote a paper that appeared in 1940 in the *Quarterly Journal of the Geological Society of London*, 'Leucite-bearing pipes of the West Kimberley'. The paper was a good gamble for a young scholar, as Prider later remarked: 'There were many, I believe, who thought my ideas on the origin of these rocks were crazy, but I always said, "If they find a diamond in these rocks it will prove I was right, and if they don't find a diamond in them it won't prove I was wrong."' Published as it was during wartime, the paper and its hypothesis went largely unremarked and uncontested by the diamond world. But they wouldn't be ignored forever.

4

TYLER'S MINING START-UP

IN AUGUST 1969, the Tyler family arrived in Melbourne and Ewen opened Tanganyika's Australian branch in the new Stock Exchange building at 351 Collins Street. (Having escaped London's weather, he was shocked to see a light fall of snow outside his office window.) Tyler met with banks and brokers and businessmen. He watched developments in Australian mining, and brushed up on what he knew about the local geology, diverse as it was. He hosted visits from principals of the Tanks and Union Minière companies, and sent regular reports back to London.

The goals of Tanganyika Concessions in the southern continent were highly speculative. Australia was a major producer of gold, as well as silver, opals, sapphires and many other precious commodities. But neither diamonds nor platinum had been mined there on a very large scale. And compared to Africa, Australia was a high-cost location. The new branch of Tanganyika had limited resources. Against the background of Australia's high costs and speculative prospectivity, the outpost had to make the best of those resources. Its investments had to be astute, and its exploration program had to be agile, focused and super-efficient. Under the last plank of its triple role, the branch could be involved in commodities of Tyler's choice, while preferably not clashing with the activities of Union Minière. On that basis, the branch quickly secured a stake in a platinum venture based at Coopers Creek in Gippsland, Victoria. Quickly, too, the branch was into copper.

Tanganyika Concessions had close dealings with the London Tin Corporation, one of the world's largest tin producers. Both groups were major international mining enterprises, and they had a director in common: Lord Colyton. In London, Colyton discussed the possibility of the two groups doing something together in Australia.

Around the same time that Tyler returned to Australia, Alan Jones did, too. Jones had worked with London Tin in Malaysia during that country's transition from British colony to independent nation. His background was in accounting—he'd studied Commerce at the University of Melbourne—but a chance meeting with a mining engineer and former prisoner of war had interested him in a different career path: mine development. 'So instead of going to London to become an accountant, I went to Malaysia and became a miner,' he said. 'It was one of the best decisions of my life.' In all, Jones spent nineteen years in Malaya and Malaysia. Then, in 1969, he and his wife came back to Melbourne (their children were already at boarding school there) and he took charge of the local subsidiary of London Tin: Anglo Oriental (Australia) Pty Ltd. Among other things, the subsidiary had started looking for tin and copper deposits in Australia.

London Tin Corporation was well known to Ewen Tyler from his decade in England, and it was through London Tin and Lord Colyton that Tyler met Jones. The two men immediately hit it off. They had a lot in common, including similar values and outlooks, and similar backgrounds in the old empire.

Tyler knew something about copper mining and exploration from his Africa and London days. He told Jones that he wanted to link up with trustworthy partners for the Kimberleys copper rush. His plan was to search for commercial quantities of copper in Western Australia's far north, and to investigate the viability of establishing an African copper model there. Jones said he was interested, and suggested that Tyler contact Jennings Mining Ltd. That business, a subsidiary of the iconic Australian home builders AV Jennings, had been established in answer to the 1960s mineral boom. This was an

era of diversified conglomerates, well before today's doctrine of corporate specialisation. In those days, shareholders didn't mind if a tract
housing builder also searched remote country for rare minerals. In the
mining sector, Jennings Mining was seen as a cashed-up and aggressive
explorer. Jones and AO (Australia) had been working with Jennings
in a search for ilmenite and rutile, ores of titanium, near Eneabba in
Western Australia. Now, Jennings and AO joined Tanks' Australian
copper investigation. (Union Minière chose to stay out of the copper
venture, instead continuing to focus on nickel in Australia.)

Tyler's branch therefore had irons in the fire for copper and
platinum. What about diamonds? When Tyler was working in Tanzania
in the 1950s, the nearest mining neighbour to Geita was Williamson's
large and rich diamond mine at Mwadui, some 180 kilometres away.
The mine had only recently gone into production. A Canadian geologist, Dr John 'The Doc' Williamson, had discovered the kimberlite
pipe that was mined at Mwadui. Tyler had met diamond explorers
and prospectors who worked for the Doc and had talked to them
about exploring for diamonds and searching for indicator minerals
such as pyrope garnet, chrome diopside, zircon and picroilmenite.
Now, many of South Africa's diamond mines were ageing, as was clear
from their declining yields. Could the diamond industry's centre of
gravity move from southern Africa to Australia? The pendulum had
swung before—from India to Brazil, and then to Africa. Maybe it
could swing again.

Of all the Australian states, New South Wales had produced the
largest quantity of diamonds. But, being a graduate of UWA, and
remembering Rex Prider's hypothesis about the relationship between
the leucite rocks of the Kimberleys and the host rock for diamonds,
Tyler decided to base his diamond endeavours not in New South
Wales but in Western Australia.

◆

A remote and exotic region about 2400 kilometres north-east of Perth,
the Kimberleys are bordered to the north by the Timor Sea, to the west
by the Indian Ocean, to the south by the Great Sandy and Tanami

deserts, and to the east by the Northern Territory. Like the town of
Kimberley in South Africa, the West Australian Kimberleys were
named after John Wodehouse, 1st Earl of Kimberley and secretary
of state for the colonies. The region is sparsely populated and there
are few roads. A single main highway skirts the southern and eastern
fringes of the rugged interior. An unsealed track runs north–south
through the centre of the region, and a mostly unsealed road, the 660-
kilometre-long Gibb River Road, runs from the centre to the port of
Wyndham in the east.

The geography of the Kimberleys is unique. Known for its ancient
Indigenous rock art, it is a region of wide plateaus, deep gorges and
sharp cliffs that have an eerie beauty. The surreal Jurassic landscape
of Purnululu (the Bungle Bungle Ranges), south of Lake Argyle,
is perhaps the best example of mysterious Kimberley country. The
climate is hot all through the year. In summertime, 'the wet'—a
monsoonal assault of high humidity and torrential rain—turns some
of the dry Kimberley creeks into class-five rapids.

George Grey, a British army officer (not the discoverer of the
Katanga copper deposits), was one of the first Europeans to explore
the region. His expedition of 1837–38 searched for the fabled inland
sea. In the twentieth century the region was home to missions, large
pastoral properties and a Benedictine monastery, which the Japanese
attacked catastrophically in World War II. It was a land of fugitives
and runaways and bushrangers; a region of grand dreams and failed
schemes, such as the proposal, considered in the 1930s and '40s,
to settle a million Jewish refugees in the East Kimberley, near the
Northern Territory border.

From the 1950s, the Kimberley coast hosted a vibrant pearling
industry. And in the 1960s, people began looking inland for
diamonds. Why this place? Though the Kimberleys account for only
a small proportion of Western Australia as a whole, they are still an
enormous area, extending to more than 400,000 square kilometres—
nearly double the size of the diamond-yielding area of the South
African central plateau, which was home to nine diamond-producing
mines. Little was known about the precise geology of the Kimberleys,
but surely, in that largely unexplored area, there would be deposits

worthy of scrutiny? There was already much mining interest nearby, in the Pilbara, mainly focused on iron ore. What secrets might the Kimberleys hold?

There were hints that diamonds might be found there. George Stansmore, a member of a party led by the explorer David Carnegie, died near Halls Creek (440 kilometres east of Derby) in 1896 after accidentally shooting himself. Stansmore had reportedly found a 25-carat diamond. In 1967, nine small diamonds were allegedly found at Police Camp Pool on the Lennard River in the West Kimberley, not far from Prider's leucite rocks. Representatives of three 'no liability' mining companies (Exoil, Transoil and Petromin) claimed to have extracted those diamonds from just 1 tonne of alluvial gravel. Another corporate, the French group BRGM, had also decided to explore in the Kimberleys, as had Stockdale Prospecting, the Australian exploration arm of De Beers. (De Beers' head office in Kimberley, South Africa, was on Stockdale Street.)

De Beers had come to Western Australia as part of a continent-wide diamond hunt that began around 1965. The company's searchers found no diamonds in the Kimberleys, but at Orroroo in South Australia they found diamond indicator minerals (1968), and at Terowie, not very far from Orroroo, they found Australia's first known kimberlite (1970).

Soon after the Melbourne office was established, Tanks opened a second Australian office, in Perth. Ewen Tyler employed Mick Paltridge, a New Zealander who'd worked in the Zambian Copperbelt, as Tanks' West Australian general manager. When Tyler scrutinised Paltridge's CV, his African experience leapt out. It meant the Kiwi was adventurous and resilient and enterprising. In keeping with that picture, Paltridge sailed diamond-class yachts at the Royal Perth Yacht Club. He was also eccentric: prone to becoming obsessed with gadgets (such as his ever-present map dividers and scientific calculator) and to other quirks (such as conversing with his New Zealander wife in Bahasa).

Paltridge would soon persuade Tyler to look for Zambian-style copper deposits in the Teronis Member of the Kimberley group of rocks. And he would write a crucial document: a report on the opportunities the Kimberleys presented for diamond hunters. Completed in October 1969, the report mentioned the nine diamonds of Police Camp Pool and Western Australia's ultramafic leucite lamproites. Prider's hypothesis about the diamondiferous potential of lamproitic rocks hadn't been proven, and there were fundamental differences between Australian lamproites and African kimberlites, but the geology and structure of the Kimberleys resembled parts of southern Africa. Prider had probably hit on something important. The report also mentioned the paucity of reliable evidence on the prospects of finding Kimberley diamonds, and emphasised the need for thorough research.

For Tanks, the report was a landmark: the group's first report on diamond exploration in the southern continent. Tyler read it with enthusiasm. In light of the report and Tyler's reaction, Paltridge engaged another person with a background in African mining: Chris Smith of Mineral Investigators. An ever-positive Englishman and consultant geologist, Smith had spent eight years with De Beers in Africa looking for diamonds. Thanks to that exposure, he'd become a guru in the mineralogy of diamonds and kimberlites. From his experience in Malawi and South Africa and Zambia, he had assembled a priceless body of knowledge about indicator minerals. For Tanks, Smith now set to work on a proposal that answered the question: how might Tanks best look for diamonds in the Kimberleys? In 1970 he finished his audacious proposal: a sophisticated plan to spend $100,000 on a year-long Kimberleys search program that was unprecedented in its scope, ambition and methods.

Given the ability of diamonds to travel great distances, and given the shortage of previous systematic work in the Kimberleys, the diamond search had to be carried out over an enormous area. Smith's proposal required the collection of 1600 eight-kilogram samples from some 190,000 square kilometres of country, on what is referred to as the Kimberley Block. The area, three times the size of Tasmania, was almost as large as the Australian state of Victoria, and the whole of Great Britain.

Tyler and Paltridge were attracted to the proposal, except that its scale was a lot to swallow. On its own, Tanganyika lacked the capacity to mount even a preliminary investigation in the Kimberleys. And then there was the cost. The proposed program far exceeded the permitted exploration expenditure of Tyler's 'listening post'. His maximum spend was $20,000 for any given exploration deal. This meant Tanks couldn't be the sole funder of the diamond program as Smith had conceived it. Tyler had to find joint venture (JV) partners who would share the costs. Ideally there would be four other partners so that the investment amounts were equal. If no-one had a bigger share than Tanks, there was less of a risk that another party could dominate the JV, or seize control of it.

Apart from being necessary, the JV model was also useful. It offered risk-sharing and risk-spreading among the participants, and a way to bring together different expertise and approaches. (The concept of a joint venture dated from the seventeenth century, when producers and merchants entered 'joint adventures' to import coffee and sugar.) Tyler believed Smith's diamond proposal could be used to attract other parties to the search, and convince them to stake the additional $80,000. On paper, the opportunity sounded compelling and the team hoped it would be a drawcard. But who might the four partners be? The choice of JV participants would later prove to be extremely important, but these were early days and the search for fellow travellers was more opportunistic than strategic. Nevertheless, it would still take a frustratingly long time to identify the parties and get them to sign a suitable JV agreement.

The identification of possible partners followed multiple trains of thought. Adding some Australian entities to the mix would make sense, as would introducing international mining groups that had relevant expertise and existing commercial connections with Tanks. In that last category, London Tin was an obvious choice. Tanks was already in a JV with London Tin's local subsidiary, AO (Australia). Tyler promptly put a diamond proposal to Alan Jones, who agreed to advise his board to participate at 20 per cent.

If AO was going to be in the venture, it was only natural to turn to Jennings Mining as well. Jennings was the other participant in Tanks' copper JV with AO, and the three businesses had established a good working relationship. 'I was looking for diamond hunters,' Tyler recalled, 'and AO and Jennings seemed obvious choices. Alan said yes, as did Len Brown from Jennings. All they had to do now was persuade their boards.'

◈

Important nickel discoveries had made Western Mining Corporation the darling of the Australian stock market. The company's future looked bright, and more than one competitor tried to emulate its success. In 1970 a stockbroker friend persuaded Ewen Tyler to take an interest in a newly formed company, Northern Mining Corporation, which had similar ambitions to Western Mining. The stockbroker introduced Tyler to Northern's managing director and principal promoter, Rees Towie. Towie had worked in the Canadian oil industry; he spoke like an American and came across as an old-style, hard-nosed Texas oilman. In reality, though, he was a West Australian and, like Tyler, an Old Guildfordian. For Tyler, that fact had special significance.

Early in 1941, aboard the MV *Gorgon*, Tyler had sailed with his mother and brother from Singapore via Broome to Fremantle. Unaccustomed to Australian conditions and especially to Australian beaches, at Broome he gashed his heel on the sharp coral. 'I had a fear of the ship's doctor,' he remembered. 'Foolishly I said nothing to anyone. The wound eventually healed.' In Perth, a Tyler family friend known as 'Aunty Billy' had a brother, Arthur, who'd gone to Guildford Grammar School. Aunty Billy enrolled Tyler there, too. He started at Guildford in February 1941, as a boarder in St George's House. One of the boys in his dorm was Harvey Barnett. At that time, Barnett was a marvellous mimic; in the future he would head Australia's main spy agency, ASIO. George Beere was Tyler's housemaster. Beere was determined to transform Tyler into an Australian.

When Japan entered the war, the Americans entered Australia. Guildford Grammar School became an American Army hospital, and the boarders were evacuated to the Fairbridge Farm School, near Pinjarra, around 100 kilometres south of Perth. The farm school's South African founder, Kingsley Fairbridge, had had a vision. Impoverished English children, many of them orphans, would benefit from a rural upbringing, far from England's slums. To bring his vision to life, he established two farm schools, one in Southern Rhodesia, the other at Pinjarra.

By 1942, many of the permanent students had left the Pinjarra school. As a result, its cottages could easily accommodate the 150 relocated Guildfordians. Each of the Guildford houses was split across two or three cottages, and each cottage housed around fifteen occupants. In a military convoy the US Army moved the students, lab equipment and anything else that was portable. (Tyler was put in charge of a 5-tonne International truck.) During his two years at Pinjarra, Tyler learned to love the bush and science, and especially explosives. One day, he created an enormous explosion in the school's laboratory by mixing potassium chlorate with antimony sulphide. The science master, 'Pug' Milne, was umpiring a cricket match when he heard the explosion. Fearing the whole lab had been destroyed, he raced to the scene and found Tyler stunned and singed. Tyler was banned from the laboratory for some time.

The school's gym master, Jock Woolgar, taught Tyler to pan for gold in the creeks of the Darling Ranges at the back of the farm. Tyler later wondered how close he'd come to finding 'Boddington', the major gold deposit in those ranges. In 1944, the tide of war turned in the Allies' favour and Tyler returned to Guildford.

Apart from Barnett, Tyler met Rees Towie at Guildford. 'He was a couple of years older than me,' Tyler later recalled, 'but I remembered him well, as "Tracker Towie", reading the lessons in the school chapel. He was a day boy and didn't go to Fairbridge in 1942. He ended up reading engineering at the University of Western Australia.'

In 1970, a mania for Australian mining shares had lured Towie back to Western Australia from North America. Tyler thought he could be trusted: 'At school I'd had almost no contact with him, but the fact that he was an Old Guildfordian made him OK.' Tyler was also attracted to the diversified portfolio of mining assets that Towie was assembling in Northern Mining. 'He had several appealing things in his bag. Some iron, some gold, copper.'

Towie's copper was in South Australia, but his main game was West Australian iron. Northern Mining was hoping to develop the

Weld Range as an alternative to the Pilbara as a source of iron ore. To Tyler that made good sense: in 1971, shipping Weld iron ore out of Geraldton looked like a better prospect than further developing the Pilbara in the cyclone belt.

Towie was new to the mining industry and knew little about iron ore. But he was a good advertiser. He and his fellow Northern Mining co-founders had adopted a similar-sounding name and a similar-looking logo to Western Mining. Thus armed, they promoted their company with vigour. To many investors and mining industry insiders, Northern Mining looked like a good starter. Adding to the respectable picture of Northern, a London-based business had already invested in the company. The Mitchell Cotts Group was an international conglomerate with diverse investments in plantations, engineering and merchandising. Tyler knew the group from Africa as well as from London. In Australia, it had invested in engineering businesses and saw an opportunity to participate in mining through Northern.

Tyler therefore encouraged Tanganyika Concessions to take a 10 per cent stake in Northern Mining Corporation. The directors agreed and Tyler, as the local representative of a substantial shareholder, joined Northern's board in 1971. As a result, Northern was now associated with two substantial London-based groups.

Not everyone agreed that Northern was respectable or credible. One observer described it as a tin-pot company. But to Tyler, inviting Northern to participate in the diamond program seemed a logical next step. The company had relationships with Tanks and Mitchell Cotts, Tyler was a director of Northern, it seemed well backed, and it was Australian owned and directed. Towie accepted the invitation, and Northern joined the diamonds JV as the second Australian participant with a 20 per cent share. There were now four participants: Jennings and Northern from Australia; and two foreign groups, Tanganyika Concessions and London Tin / AO.

However, there was a big problem in the list of participants: none of the four was specifically a diamond business, and none of their staff knew anything about the diamond world. It seemed appropriate to find someone who did. Tanganyika Concessions and the Union

Minière group were both parts of the Belgian mega-group Société
Générale de Belgique. Also within that group was the major African
diamond producer Sibeka. Through its subsidiary MIBA, Sibeka
ran the world's largest diamond mine (in volume terms): the Mbuji
Maya mine in Zaire (now the Democratic Republic of the Congo).
Effectively, Sibeka was the diamond arm of Union Minière.

Economic nationalism had seen Sibeka's interests in the Zaire
diamond mines fall to 25 per cent. Mining there was becoming
more and more difficult. The company needed to find a new diamond
field. Would Sibeka, Tyler wondered, be susceptible to Australian
advances? Would the company be willing to join the search? Via
contacts in Union Minière, he put out feelers about Sibeka joining
the JV. In February 1972 he flew to Brussels and presented a proposal
to the company's principals. For Sibeka, a $20,000 investment was
modest to say the least. Politely and with some amusement, the
company's representatives met the young Australian and considered
his quaintly audacious proposal. Yes, they answered. Yes, they would
be willing to participate.

Ewen Tyler now had the partners he needed. He named the joint
venture Kalumburu, after the Benedictine mission at the top of the
Kimberleys. 'That obscure name was an ideal choice', he said, 'for
what was of necessity a clandestine activity.'

In 1972, representatives of the five participants signed an agreement to bring the Kalumburu Joint Venture officially into being.
(The legal structure relied on precedents from British maritime law.)
Tanganyika Australia was the JV's manager. By any measure the JV was
a mixed bag: three major overseas companies—Sibeka, London Tin
and Tanganyika Concessions—along with the well-known Jennings
and the little-known Northern Mining Corporation. But there was a
strong sense of camaraderie and shared purpose among the venturers.
They were doing something interesting and important, they enjoyed
each other's personalities, and they were embarking on an adventure.
Finalising the JV team felt a bit like assembling an exploration party,
and a bit like forming a rock band.

5
LOOKING FOR DIAMONDS IN AUSTRALIA

Ewen Tyler and his Tanks team had the money, authority and support they needed to kick off their ambitious search program. The team had spent the 1970 and 1971 field seasons searching the Kimberleys for copper. Mick Paltridge had again retained Chris Smith and Mineral Investigators to help steer that search. Now, in early 1972, the members of the Kalumburu JV had signed up and the wet season was over. The JV sent crews back out into the field, this time to look for diamonds—or at least for tiny hints and traces of them.

Though the focus of Tanks' 1970 and 1971 field seasons had been on copper, those seasons were extremely helpful for Kalumburu's diamond plans. The Tanks team had learnt a lot about the logistics and practicalities of using helicopters to collect samples over vast areas. (The use of helicopters was still novel. Not too long before, explorers had been travelling through this country by horse and camel.) With the benefit of that experience, the JV's people set about collecting the 1600 eight-kilogram samples from creek sites spread across 190,000 square kilometres of Australia. Hopefully, in one of the sample bags, there would be indicators of diamonds.

The use of geologists in the sample collecting process was an important innovation. It added to the cost: geologists were more expensive than general 'fieldies'. But Tyler thought this approach would be cost-effective in the long run. He knew geologists were better able to read the landscape, and perhaps better able to collect samples from areas where diamonds and indicators were more likely to have become trapped ('trap sites'). He hoped that with geologists there would be less wasted time in the field, and the time there would be spent on finding the most useful trap sites from which to collect samples.

Apart from being astute, the use of geologists was opportunistic. In September 1969, at a time of surging demand for nickel, prospector Ken Shirley had made a promising nickel discovery in Western Australia. Shirley had been in the field for Poseidon NL ('NL' stands for 'no liability'). When news of his find spread, Poseidon's share price rose from 50 cents to an extraordinary $280. The rise also lifted other mining stocks. Chancers rushed to launch businesses and investment funds that had dubious prospects, but the music soon stopped. 'People saw through the hollow promises of the new businesses,' finance journalist Alan Kohler later wrote, 'and Poseidon itself was shown to be much less of a prospect than first thought. Its nickel was of a lower grade than originally thought, and the extraction costs were higher.' (Mineral Securities Australia Ltd or 'Minsec' had invested heavily in Poseidon and was among the many casualties when, in 1971, the mining investment bubble burst.)

In 1972, a 24-year-old English geologist arrived in Perth. Maureen Muggeridge had tried and failed to get a government-assisted passage to Australia. 'In 1972 it was the end of the nickel boom,' she later said, 'and there were lots and lots of geologists out of work.' Two of her uncles had agreed to pay her passage. (One of the uncles was the writer and broadcaster Malcolm Muggeridge.) She arrived in Australia 'with nothing more than £10 and a degree in geology' from Scotland's St Andrews University and reportedly spent her first night sleeping under a palm tree in Perth's Kings Park. Soon she was working as a barmaid, and she responded to a newspaper advertisement for a geologist. Paltridge interviewed her and offered her a job with the Kalumburu JV. She thought he was joking. 'Australia was famous for gold, base metals and iron ore,' she recalled, 'but not diamonds.'

Muggeridge had lived in Africa: she spent much of her childhood in Nigeria and Cameroon where her father worked for Crown Agents, paving the way for independence. This experience was important for Paltridge and meant Muggeridge immediately had much in common with other members of the Tanks team. Very soon she was 'flying over the outback in a helicopter looking for diamonds'. Rob Mosig joined the JV team, too, on secondment from Northern Mining. Chris Smith trained Muggeridge and Mosig in the mineralogy of diamonds and indicators. 'It all had to be hush-hush,' Muggeridge later said. 'You couldn't say you were looking for diamonds because that would spark too much interest. I felt like a character in a James Bond movie or a Wilbur Smith novel.'

With set-up and downtime, the helicopter sampling took up all of the 1972 field season. It was difficult work for the crews of pilots and geologists and field assistants, their shirts soaked with sweat, their pores clogged with dust. They described themselves as 'gravel gatherers', but the reality was much more sophisticated than that sounds. As Smith described, helicopter sampling was a major logistical exercise involving remote base camps, fuel dumps and landing sites:

> We would put out fuel dumps along the tracks to extend helicopter range. But there were large 200-kilometre sections without any access, especially in the west, that were going to be a problem and would require fuel drums to be airlifted in by helicopter.

From the choppers, the pilots and geologists and fieldies selected promising sites, many of which were hard to reach: 'The rugged terrain meant that you could not always land next to them. Lots of walking and even cliff climbing were still required to get to them and carry heavy samples back out to the chopper.' Each sample of gravel was carefully collected from a creek-bed trap site. The collected samples were meticulously tagged and recorded. To cover the search area efficiently, the teams adopted a leapfrog system. A single chopper would carry two geologists and two fieldies, along with the pilot, and, as Smith described,

> One geo and one fieldie would be put down at the first trap site; the other two would then go on to be put down at the second

site. The chopper would return to the first party, who would use
a signalling mirror to ensure the pilot saw them, and they would
be moved on to a third site when the chopper would return to
the second pair.

In the north-west Kimberley, there were no roads or airstrips: the
region had to be supplied from the sea. To access this area, Tanks
made an arrangement with Japanese pearlers to set up a camp site
at the Kuri Bay pearling station. The explorers' helicopter fuel and
camping gear were brought in from Broome on the pearlers' supply
ship. Another remote base for the diamond search was a camp site on
the Durack River, near the crossing of the Gibb-River-to-Wyndham
track. Smith related a story of how, at the end of hot days, the field
crews would swim in the clear water of the large river pool:

> Then we noticed it was full of crocodiles, but they didn't seem to
> mind us and nor did we them. We received a camp cook, a young
> Welshman who had just arrived in Australia. In the morning we
> all flew off in the chopper, leaving the cook to settle in. He was
> horrified to see an enormous reptile several feet long coming into
> his kitchen tent; in terror he fled to his own tent and hid himself
> inside, where we found him cowering on our return later in the
> day. From his description we realised it was one of the enormous
> goannas that lived there, which we would occasionally feed with
> some food scraps; they are quite harmless. But there was no meal
> ready for us and the cook took some convincing about his safety
> before he nervously emerged, still half believing that it was a
> crocodile that had come for him.

The anxiety about crocodiles was well placed. The Kimberley population of freshwater crocs numbered in the hundreds of thousands. In
Kununurra alone, there were at least as many crocs as people. During
a later stage of the diamond search, geologist Frank Hughes would be
badly bitten on the forearm by a middle-sized freshie.

In this first season, the diamond program was enormous in its
extent but modest in its goals. All that the 'gravel gatherers' sought

to prove was the existence of a single indicator-mineral grain in the Kimberley region. Such a grain would be an important encouragement, a first step towards showing that north-western Australia had diamond-bearing kimberlites.

The fieldwork program had one major complication, as Maureen Muggeridge pointed out: the entire search, and indeed every other aspect of the whole enterprise, had to be conducted in secret. If people outside the JV learnt what Kalumburu was up to, in one way or another they would try to cash in. They could attempt their own piggyback exploration or, even worse, they might try to 'jump the claim' once a promising site was found. And there was a fear that even mentioning diamonds could prompt a diamond rush on a colossal scale.

Tight security was therefore essential, and the JV agreement was established on that basis: a condition of the agreement was that the partners had to keep secret the search for diamonds. The agreement and other corporate documents gave no indication that the JV was interested in mineral title or looking for diamonds. In correspondence, the word 'diamond' was never used. Instead, the participants used the code word 'baryte'. (Baryte is a low-value mineral used in drilling mud, mainly in the oil industry.)

The earlier copper exploration program provided a cover for the JV's activities, as did diamond drilling for copper in the Bindoola Dome in the central Kimberleys. There was another cover, too. Whenever someone asked Mick Paltridge if there was truth to the rumours that Tanganyika might be looking for diamonds, he would reply with a roar, 'I *sail* diamonds!'

In Ewen Tyler's university days, he'd painstakingly removed heavy minerals from samples. He knew how to use heavy liquids to produce a heavy concentrate, and how to remove mineral grains from the concentrate for identification. 'I spent my fourth year at the university doing just that,' he said. During Tyler's decade in Africa, he got to know the diamond prospectors who'd worked for Dr Williamson. He knew how 'the Doc' had found the Mwadui diamond pipes, and he knew the importance of pyrope garnets as indicator minerals in that discovery. Now, for the Kalumburu JV, the careful processing and

observing of the Kimberley gravel samples began. On the ground in
Perth, Chris Smith steered the technical side of looking for indicator
minerals such as pyrope, chrome diopside, zircon and picroilmenite.

Indicator minerals can be identified under the microscope.
To get to that point, a multi-stage process must be followed. The
samples collected in the field have to be screened and separated,
before being carefully scrutinised. For Kalumburu, some aspects of
the processing could be farmed out to a commercial laboratory. At
Sampey's lab in the Perth suburb of Midland, the 1600 samples of
gravel from the Kimberley creek system were separated by immersion
in tetrabromoethane or 'TBE'. (Liquid at room temperature, TBE
is heavy and toxic with a pungent, chloroform-like odour. Low-
density minerals such as quartz and feldspar float in it, but heavy
minerals sink.)

At Sampey's, Darian Sampey and Don Zimmerman carried out the
separation using plastic rubbish bins in the open air. They skimmed
off the 'floats' with plastic kitchen strainers. In this way, they recovered
mineral grains between 0.87 millimetres and 0.177 millimetres
in diameter with a specific gravity of more than 2.9. Once washed
and dried, the processed heavy grains were packaged and delivered
to the Tanks office in a Victorian-era cottage on Emerald Terrace in
West Perth.

The next stage, mineral observing, involved the more detailed work
of examining the concentrates and, hopefully, picking out indicator
minerals with a fine paintbrush. Correct investigation of the heavy
mineral concentrate is even more important than correct collection
of samples in the field. It is a specialised skill; no lab in Australia was
capable of carrying it out. In the compact kitchen of the cottage, the
JV established and equipped its own mineral observing laboratory.
Smith trained people in the fastidious work of identifying indicator
minerals by peering down binocular microscopes and turning over
every visible mineral grain. He shared with the mineral observers his
technical knowledge: what indicator grains to look for, their chemical
and optical properties, and how they appeared under the microscope.

'Imagine examining an eggcup full of pinpoint-sized sand-grains
by turning the grains one by one with a fine brush,' Tyler said. 'That's

what the mineral observers had to do.' The first concentrates were difficult to examine. While in theory the concentrated minerals were to be examined visually on a grain-by-grain basis, in reality many of the samples were flooded with limonite, an iron oxide. There was so much limonite that it had to be separated by various methods. 'The observers resorted to whatever worked,' Tyler said. 'Heavy liquids, methylene iodide, Clerici solution. All these were used to reduce the volume of the concentrates prior to observing.' After all the effort to clean up the flood, the sample results were slow to come through. The whole process—of collecting gravel samples from remote bush sites and then separating out tiny grains—was meticulous and onerous. Tyler described it as a hard slog.

6
M109

Towards the end of 1971, negative energy began to gather around Northern Mining. Tensions were building within the company and among its principal corporate relationships. There were strains with Tankanyika Concessions because Rees Towie wanted Tanks to exercise its options to buy more Northern shares. There were strains with Mitchell Cotts, which in Towie's eyes was treating Northern as a wayward subsidiary and not as a strategic investment or respected peer. There was Towie's fear that Mitchell Cotts or someone else might try to buy him out. And there was his tactic of playing off Mitchell Cotts against Tanks. He would say one thing to Mitchell Cotts and another to Tanks; and in London the two groups would compare notes. None of this gave them confidence in Towie, or in Australian mining more generally. (During Ewen Tyler's London days, a common definition of an Australian mine was 'a hole in the ground with a liar sitting on top'.)

Sir Louis Loder, a respected engineer, was chairman of Northern Mining. Late in 1972 he died, and the appointment of a new chair became another source of tension. 'Where', Tyler's London directors asked, 'are we going to get a chairman for Northern?' Towie favoured Sir Lenox Hewitt for the role or, better still, himself, but the London groups didn't want Towie or anyone he suggested. Towie looked to

Tyler with his UK experience for support. He also pressured Tyler to back what he was telling Mitchell Cotts and Tanks. Tyler for his part was eager to stay on good terms with Towie and not to be an irritant in the joint venture. Tyler supported Towie in some of his arguments.

'The upshot', Tyler said, 'was that my chairman in London was writing to the chairman of Mitchell Cotts in terms of what to do about Northern. I was supportive of Towie and this became a major issue. My chairman became irritated with me.' That chairman was new to Tanks. Ronald Medlicott, a banker, had joined the group from British investment bank Kleinwort Benson. 'He was an eccentric Englishman,' Tyler said. Known in London as 'Ronny Muddle Cock', his claim to infamy was that he'd left the D-Day orders—the most sensitive document in the world—under a bed in a London hotel. When he went back to find them they were still there, and the invasion and his bacon were saved. From that day on, whenever he left a hotel room, he would exhaustively search every cupboard and every drawer.

Medlicott visited Australia in January 1973. (His special dark glasses, with fine mesh round the sides, were apparently 'suitable for shooting bustards in India'.) Initially he'd been a keen supporter of Tyler's Australian activities, but on this visit he discussed with Tyler the idea of closing down the branch the following year. Soon Medlicott was back in England, and in March 1973, the London committee of Tanganyika Concessions (by this time ostensibly based in the Bahamas, for tax reasons) resolved to run down the Australian branch 'in an orderly manner'. The branch had just eighteen months of its five-year life still to run. Tyler could see the writing on the wall for his Australian vision.

In accordance with the March 1973 close-down instructions, at the end of 1974 Tyler would have to let go all of the Tanks employees who were not part of the Kalumburu JV. Instinctively he'd always known how difficult it would be to maintain London interest in Australian affairs once he was no longer present day-to-day in England. His concerns were well founded. The person who'd promised to look after Tyler's interests didn't. Tanganyika had formed an oil and gas subsidiary to focus on North Sea oil, and the group's attentions were focused in that direction. 'Australia was now considered entirely 'expendable,' Tyler said. Overall, it was for him a time of considerable gloom. Northern Mining wasn't the only business under a cloud:

> Union Minière in Australia was going nowhere, my investment recommendations were a source of concern. The stock market was in the doldrums following the collapse of the Poseidon boom and the Minsec debacle. Australia was going nowhere and had elected a 'socialist government'.

The Towie problems in particular had been poorly received at Tanks in London. Tyler's correspondence with Medlicott reflected irritation that was mutual and growing.

> 6 John Street, London
> 14th May, 1973

> Dear Ewen,
> A brief reply to your letter of 7th May ... Regarding investment in Australia generally, we have been over most of this before. Your mining blue chips do not stand up to international comparison, your currency is over-valued, your Government is being objectionable—UM were recently denied the opportunity even of entering an exploration project with an Australian company. As far as research & development is concerned, the Belgians have, of course, always been extremely depressed by the outcome of investment in exploration companies, such as GME, NM, Coopers Creek, etc., but the really important factor is that if we do the North Sea deal it is going to result in such big exploration expenditures that we shall have no room for anything else whatever, and even our existing stake in UMICAN and Thierry may have to be reviewed. I hope, however, that we do not have to part with that because it is the only exploration project which has clearly proved successful.
> Yours ever,
> Ronny Medlicott

The 'Mad Colonial' had no intention of returning to London to pick up where he'd left off, even if the British mining barons wanted him back, which was far from certain. 'My chips were at a low ebb,' Tyler said. All this, though, was about to change.

◈

In April 1973, at a meeting in Melbourne of the Kalumburu JV parties, Chris Smith presented a small vial containing what he said was a grain of chrome diopside, an indicator mineral for diamonds. The grain came from the Charnley drainage in the West Kimberley. As the vial was passed around, some participants were surprised, others disbelieving. The grain was so small it was hard to see with the naked eye. More than one person was certain Smith was joking and the little pot was empty. But it wasn't. Though the object in question was tiny, it represented major progress. The JV had achieved its first goal.

A few months later, the news would be even better. In August 1973, on the eve of Tyler's forty-fifth birthday, Rob Mosig was examining a portion of concentrate from a sample called 'M109': M for Maureen, not Messerschmitt. Maureen Muggeridge had taken the sample in 1972 at a remote creek that was subsequently given the prehistoric-sounding name 'Pteropus Creek'. (The team named the creek after the genus of the flying foxes that were abundant in the trees along its bank.) Mosig was with Muggeridge in the lab when he asked her to look at some strange-looking mineral grains under his microscope. What were these grains? Were they chrome diopside? Muggeridge looked down the microscope. 'No,' she said. The mysterious minerals were mega-crystal zircons that had formed in the low-velocity zone at the base of the lithospheric mantle. They weren't *sputniki*.

Smith was also in the lab. After overhearing the conversation, he, too, had a look down the microscope. Almost immediately he noticed something marvellous in the top of the field: a little grain, about the size of a pinhead, with unmistakable triangular bumps on its white surface. A shimmering diamond. 'My heart leapt,' he later said. From that moment, everything changed.

The Tanks team named their first diamond 'D1'. It was tiny, just 0.008 of a carat or about 1 millimetre long, but it was crucially important as evidence and encouragement in the diamond search. And sample M109 had still more to give. After further examination it was shown to contain a full suite of indicator minerals. Each of the fractions contained pyrope, picroilmenite, kimberlitic zircon, and lots of chromite (a type of spinel).

Smith, now employed full-time as chief geologist in the Tanks branch, telephoned Tyler from the lab to say sample M109 contained not only a suite of indicators but also a diamond. Smith was buzzing. 'We've found the lot,' he said. 'Pyrope, picroilmenite, chromite, kimberlitic zircon, and a diamond!' Again there was surprise, and incredulity. After a long and digestive pause, Tyler replied, 'Are you sure?' He asked Smith to test and confirm the diamond. Smith said he didn't need to, as he later explained: 'I said I knew it was definitely a diamond, but he insisted the joint venturers would require separate proof.'

'It was hard to believe,' Tyler said, 'and we didn't. We thought someone in the sampling and processing chain was having us on.' The JV's discovery of a diamond was promising but not definitive. The stone could have travelled some distance from its source (though the set of indicators suggested the source was nearby). Whatever the case, there was one critical achievement: the JV had shown that diamonds did indeed exist in the Kimberleys. Tyler immediately ordered a re-sampling of the site. In September 1973, Smith and Muggeridge chartered a helicopter from Wyndham and flew to where M109 had been collected. (The meticulous tagging and record keeping made this possible, and efficient.)

Pteropus Creek is a classic Kimberley waterway. It flows through a gorge lined with palms and other trees that in the daytime are heavy with bats. From the creek and its banks, Smith and Muggeridge col-lected a series of check samples (weighing 35 kilograms each) and sealed them in tin trunks. The trunks were sent to Perth where, under Smith's supervision, they were processed and the mineral grains were prepared for examination. On 23 September, Tyler flew to Perth. He would oversee the process, reassure himself that it was conducted properly, and be present when the results of the check samples were available.

The check sampling failed to bag another diamond, but it verified the presence of the indicator minerals. This confirmed that the first lab result hadn't been a glitch or a fluke. The presence in one location of the full suite of indicators was very important. It strongly suggested that D1 had come from a kimberlite pipe, and that the pipe was nearby. Otherwise, the mineral clues would have been more dispersed, or absent altogether. 'We were elated,' Tyler said. 'There wasn't another diamond in the check samples, but the indicator matter was the same and we were certain we were looking at something having shed from a kimberlite that wasn't very far away.'

This was a breakthrough. The Tanks team now knew for certain that the Pteropus Creek catchment contained diamond-bearing pipes. In other words, they now knew there were kimberlites in the Kimberleys! The diamond project was on the right track. At the time of the check sampling, Mick Paltridge was in Angola looking at carbonatites as a source of rare earths. But the rest of the team—Tyler, Muggeridge, Mosig and Smith—went out for a celebratory lunch at a Mexican restaurant in West Perth. The celebrations continued well into the afternoon, and then on to a jubilant dinner—steak tartare, vegetable lasagne—at Perth's top restaurant in Matilda Bay.

7

OPPOSITE SIDES

T HAT SAME MONTH, on 29 September 1973, Tyler returned to Melbourne to share the good news with the Victoria-based participants of the JV. First he met with Alan Jones of AO (Australia) and Len Brown of Jennings. Jones and Brown would be the first people outside the Tanks team to hear about the discovery. Tyler walked into their meeting carrying the small vial that contained the tiny D1. 'Now we are in elephant country!' he declared. Brown was a mathematical person, a member of MENSA and very much a MENSA man. (He developed his own unique form of what his colleagues called 'single entry accounting'.) His sense of humour was as dry as the Tanami Desert but he was heartily amused by Tyler's elephant comment, and elated by the D1 news. Jones, too, was delighted. 'They were as excited as I was,' Tyler said.

Then it was Rees Towie's turn to hear the news. He was in London but would soon be back in Melbourne. Tyler arranged to meet him on 17 October for lunch at the RACV Club on Queen Street. The JV agreement had only recently been finalised, and Tyler felt deep reserves of goodwill towards Tracker Towie, who'd helped get Kalumburu off the ground and who now had a stake in its initial success. Over lunch, Tyler recounted the discovery: the small diamond, plus the complete set of indicator minerals that had been confirmed in the follow-up sampling. He outlined what would happen next in the exploration program, including further testing, and conveyed his excitement at the find while reiterating the need to keep the discovery secret. Towie's response was immediate, direct and dark. 'Now we are on opposite sides,' he said. Towie wanted to broadcast the news far and wide. He made clear that he would extract for Northern every bit of mileage the diamond discovery would permit. From this point on, he and the other JV participants would be at odds about confidentiality.

As a director of Northern Mining, and as a fellow Old Guildfordian, Tyler felt he knew Towie well. He'd seen the different shades of the big man's personality. He'd seen how his former schoolmate operated, and the games he played. 'He was mercurial, passionate, sometimes over the top,' Tyler said. 'A master of brinkmanship.' People would rail against Towie's obdurate style, his intermittent paranoia, and his sometimes questionable approach to business. But right now, at the RACV Club, Towie's views about confidentiality were understandable. He was a principal in a smallish listed company that depended on upbeat disclosures and positive sentiment. Without that, he couldn't raise money from outside investors. He therefore saw publicity as essential. Good news was his bread and butter.

The other participants in the JV were fearful of saying anything to the media or anyone else. But those participants didn't depend on outside sentiment or outside funds. They were entities within larger corporates that were fully able to raise funds internally. For them, there was no urgent need to announce the find. In fact, public release of the news at this point could be catastrophic.

The JV had overspent its budget of $100,000. The participants didn't yet have any mining rights or mineral title to show for it. They didn't have a diamond deposit, or any immediate prospect of finding one. And if Towie spread the news, many other people would go looking. Australia had just lived through a disastrous nickel boom. 'Diamond' is a powerful, evocative word, much more so than 'nickel'. If the D-word got out, the other participants feared, it could easily precipitate another boom, maybe one even more calamitous than the last. Inevitably a swarm of exploration companies would descend on the area. Any disclosure was patently against the JV's interests.

The whole enterprise, therefore, was finely balanced. The diamond search program depended on spending increasingly large sums of money, and the participants had to do this without any protection of the investment apart from the flimsy cloak of secrecy. And Towie now wanted to rip that cloak away. If he told too many people about the sampling results—and if he voiced the D-word too often—there was every possibility that the JV would see no dividends from its efforts and investment. There was a very real prospect that the end product of all the JV's toils would be a diamond mine owned by someone else.

Other more personal factors also appeared to be driving Towie's reaction. It was rumoured that in Canada he'd been at the centre of corporate machinations and corporate trouble. His company had been taken over, so the story went. He was unhappy with the process and the price, and was left feeling bitter and cheated, as if his business had been stolen. Not long after that, he'd returned to Australia hoping to make a fresh start, while at the same time almost expecting that others would again do him wrong. To the extent that Towie had dark thoughts, Mitchell Cotts and Tanganyika Concessions were often the focus of his fears. Tyler recalled: 'He became almost paranoid that Mitchell Cotts or one of the other investors would buy him out, and he'd be cheated again.'

For Tyler, the implications of Towie's response at the RACV Club were immediately clear and deeply disturbing. Even though Tyler was a director of Northern, he and Towie were now lined up on opposite sides of a matter that was central to Tyler's plans for Tanks, and for his life. Until now, there'd been rumours about what Kalumburu was up to, but no real secrecy problems among the parties themselves. But after he left the club that day, Towie would do what he could to breach the confidentiality. The partners urged him to keep to the agreement, but they soon suspected he was leaking information to the press.

(Because the parties were forced to be evasive, the more switched-on journalists sensed that a good story must be hiding somewhere nearby. John Byrne of the *Australian Financial Review* was one whose antennae were twitching. 'We were constantly being probed,' Tyler remembered. 'We lived in fear of John Byrne, who seemed to take a keen interest in our activities.')

One question was paramount: if Towie was determined to break confidentiality, how could the other participants curb his impulses? What could they do to keep him in the tent?

⬦

Apart from telling the local JV parties the good news, Tyler also had to tell the higher-ups at Tanks. In October 1973 he flew to London and gave with much satisfaction a major presentation to the directors. At Tanks, attitudes about Australia had been on a steep downward slope. There were deficits of trust and confidence. Now, though, the news about Pteropus Creek and sample M109 caused a rethink. Suddenly there was more than a little enthusiasm about the southern continent. Among the directors the discussion quickly turned to an important matter: how could Tanks make best use of the changed position? Options were thrown around, such as forming a new company, or wrapping Tanks' JV participation into Sibeka.

Tyler followed these deliberations with sharp attention. The UK directors might have been enthusiastic, but Tyler in London was overridingly pessimistic. He didn't see much to be gained from representing the old-style mining barons. They were too out of touch, too wedded to defunct modes and models. Sooner or later, he would have to leave the barons behind:

> I was looking for ways and means to transfer myself and my organisation into the hands of a group who would have more understanding of our Australian efforts. I was realising more and more that the task of converting a tired London company, with a historic mining tradition, into an organisation with a mineral future, could be beyond me. If Union Minière was unable to change, what hope could there be for Tanganyika, with directors who had no knowledge of mining and exploration? The vision of restoring Tanganyika Concessions Limited to its former glory, as envisaged by Lord Colyton and myself, had to be refocused. Now my energies had to be directed to diamonds in spite of Tanganyika.

8
THE PRICE OF SILENCE

TYLER WAS CONFIDENT that with the further application of money, the JV should be able to expand its discoveries. But the costs of the program were escalating: $750,000 was required in 1974, compared with around $150,000 during 1972 and 1973. Northern Mining alone was now faced with a contribution in the vicinity of $150,000, a substantial amount at that time for a smallish 'tin-pot' company.

After the 1973 discovery, the other Kalumburu JV partners were unanimous about keeping the find secret and continuing the search for the diamond's source. In Tyler's thinking, the continuing problem was how to keep Northern quiet and the joint venturers in a mood of confidence. The problem would be solved with money. Via a new document known as the Northern Mining Funding Agreement, the joint venturers agreed to fund Northern's share of the exploration costs for the next two years. This was effectively a loan: an advance against the day when the partners could announce they'd found something and it had been secured under title. In this way, Northern's position in the JV was radically altered, and so were the economics of the Northern stake. Buying Towie's silence brought a sharp reduction in Northern's costs and risk. To some of the other partners, especially the London-based ones, this felt like extortion. But it enabled them to keep the strategic advantage of confidentiality.

Under Australian law, the Crown owns all the minerals in the ground, whether on public land or private property. At the beginning of the twentieth century, most mining in Western Australia was for gold. In that state, the *Mining Act 1904* regulated rights to explore for and extract minerals. The Act had some important fans. President Theodore Roosevelt appointed the geologist AC Veatch to study Australian mining laws with a view to amending American ones. In 1906, Veatch observed:

> The Western Australian mining law, is, in short, a wonderfully symmetrical and carefully balanced enactment; and while one may not regard it as applicable in all its features to American conditions, it contains many suggestive provisions, all of which merit careful consideration.

The same Act, with amendments, governed mineral exploration and development up until 1983.

In the 1930s, Harold Tyler had gone to Australia in great secrecy on behalf of a subsidiary of the London-based mining group Rio Tinto. His mission: to evaluate the goldmining properties that had been part of the Claude de Bernales mining empire. Those properties came available after one of Britain and Australia's greatest financial scandals.

Brixton-born Claude de Bernales was a West Australian mining entrepreneur. He lived in Perth in a grand home in the ostentatious manner of a Spanish grandee. As a major supplier of mining equipment, he acquired mining leases at Kalgoorlie and Wiluna largely through defaults among his clients, and by taking equity as payment. In this way, he was able build a portfolio of mines with very little cash down; and he was able to weave a story that allowed him to raise millions of pounds in capital for his Wiluna Gold Mines company from investors in the City of London. By the end of the 1930s it had all come to a steaming end. De Bernales' mining empire unravelled, many of the investors were ruined, and de Bernales himself became a sad recluse.

Harold's mission in 1938 was to see what was left—to see if any of the Wiluna Gold Mines assets, or any other de Bernales properties, could be of use to Rio Tinto and its London-based associates. Once in Western Australia, he saw much potential but also many obstacles. Just one example: on Africa's Lupa goldfield he'd been impressed by the large-scale use of 'mechanical dry blowing', and he therefore investigated the possible use of that technique on the West Australian goldfields. But the state's legislative framework just wasn't what it needed to be. The *Mining Act* didn't allow for mining titles of sufficient size to permit operations on such a scale.

Now, in the 1970s, Ewen Tyler was coming up against the same legal obstacles. The Kimberley diamond search could succeed only under amenable legislation. The *Mining Act* worked well enough for small-scale mining but was otherwise inadequate, as lawyer Bill Leslie explained:

> Provisions for the issue of temporary reserves had been introduced into the Act to cover particularly exploration and evaluation for alumina, iron ore and coal, which gave temporary protection while a mining company proved up an already identified resource, but this was inappropriate for a diamond exploration program that covered a very large area and would take years before a discovery could not only be made, but be proven to be commercial.

The *Mining Act* didn't envisage the form of large-scale mineral exploration that Kalumburu had embarked upon. The legislation offered no protection, and nor did the common law, which was poorly developed in this area. There were some precedents: the Western Australian Government had previously granted temporary reserves for mineral exploration. The legislation limited their area to 200 square kilometres, but a review of the *Mining Act* had entertained the possibility of new rules about temporary reserves. And for iron ore exploration, the government had already granted temporary reserves that covered large areas of the state. Could this be a useful prototype, Tyler wondered, for Kalumburu's diamond search? Could the JV obtain a large-scale temporary reserve for diamonds?

(In 1971, the Western Australian Government established a committee of inquiry to review the 1904 Act. It concluded that the Act was positively archaic: 'The present Act is not only outmoded in its concept but it is ambiguous, vague and confusing. [It] is ill suited to the requirements of the mining industry as it exists today. The Act may well be described as a pick and shovel Act trying to fulfil the needs of a mechanised and sophisticated industry.')

Tyler had maintained contact with the West Australian MP Charles Court, and in 1973 Court was the state's leader of the Opposition. On 12 September, Tyler wrote to him seeking to discuss the possible implications of what could be the start of something big for the Kimberleys and Western Australia. 'Officially, no one outside the JV knew of what had been found,' Tyler said. 'I was apprehensive about disclosure to anyone, and especially to the state government.' Twelve days later, he met with Court and briefed him, in strictest confidence, on the discovery.

'What should I tell the government about the diamond discovery?' Tyler asked. 'Nothing,' Court said. 'For the time being, say nothing to anyone. Vamp in G.' Tyler had no idea what the Opposition leader meant. 'Vamp in G,' Court explained. 'That's what the pianist does whilst waiting for the Fat Lady to come on stage.' In other words, the JV should say nothing until the election in early 1974, at which time Court expected the government would change and he would be premier—and in a position to help. 'This suited my timing,' Tyler said. 'No more fieldwork was possible in 1973 because it would soon start to rain, and there was no money left in the budget for further work anyway.'

Early in 1974, the Court Government was indeed elected. Tyler contacted the premier, and a meeting was arranged with one of his ministers. A Hungarian by birth and a graduate of the University of Vienna, Andrew Mensaros now held important portfolios in the new government: Energy, Industrial Development and Mining. A story shared with amusement in Western Australia concerns the moment when Mensaros first met a Kalumburu JV delegation. One member of the delegation, by nationality a Belgian, was the Archduke Charles of Austria. On learning of this, Mensaros rose, clicked his heels, bowed deeply and said, 'Your excellency'. (When the archduke visited the head of Hamersley Iron at Dampier, he dazzled the miner's young daughter with pictures of the famous dancing horses of Vienna.)

At a subsequent meeting, Tyler proposed to Minister Mensaros that Kalumburu be granted a temporary reserve covering 196,000 square kilometres of the Kimberleys. That was almost a thousand times larger than the current maximum allowable area. 'Under the normal rules,' Tyler said, 'our annual rental for such temporary reserves would have been $1.96 million. We proposed a hundredth of that, which was $19,600.' The JV's argument depended on some simple prospecting mathematics. A mineable gold deposit might have a grade of one in 100,000, whereas the grade for a diamond deposit might be one in 100 million. According to this arithmetic, it might be a thousand times more difficult to find a diamond mine, and therefore a one-hundredth part of the associated rents might be a reasonable payment to the state.

Having presented this argument, Tyler attempted an audacious move. He tried to press into the minister's hand a cheque for $19,600 as an advance payment of the first year's rent. The minister sympathised, but he and his colleagues rejected the argument, and the cheque. 'The government tried to help,' Tyler said, 'but the *Mining Act* defeated them.' The tactic, however, wasn't a total failure. For the 196,000-square-kilometre search area, shown on a secret map that was kept in the safe of Joe Lord, the chief geologist, the Western Australian Government agreed not to grant to anyone else a temporary reserve for diamonds. This undertaking, made early in 1975, wouldn't prevent someone from staking a genuine mineral claim following an actual discovery. But it gave Kalumburu a weak form of protection: a pseudo mining right. The JV participants felt exposed, but this negative form of title would have to be enough for now.

9
TO OOMBULGURRI

As early as the seventeenth century, Indigenous Australians encountered Spanish and Dutch voyagers. The Yolŋu people, whose lands cover much of northern Australia, may have known about Europeans even earlier than that through their contact with Malay and Macassan traders from the East Indies. (The Yolŋu word for 'foreigner', *balanda*, is from 'Hollander'.) After those first contacts, Australia's Indigenous people saw waves of new arrivals with starkly different values, incentives and opportunities. The resulting history of Indigenous and European relations in the Kimberleys is full of terrible episodes. One particularly cruel event, the subject of a 1927 royal commission, took place in June 1926 and is known as the Forrest River massacre, or the Oombulgurri massacre. After a pastoralist was killed, two police constables joined a punitive expedition in which at least twenty Indigenous people were murdered. Other estimates put the death toll much higher.

In the early 1970s, there was a growing acknowledgement of past crimes and the rights of Indigenous people. But legally, politically and administratively, Indigenous affairs were a mess. There was a confusion of public agencies, including the federal Department of Aboriginal Affairs (DAA) and the West Australian Aboriginal Affairs Planning

Authority (AAPA), the latter of which, under 1972 legislation, had replaced the Native Welfare Department. Policy frameworks were ill-developed. Laws and programs were crudely conceived and they pushed in inconsistent directions. In the fight for fair treatment and the recognition of Indigenous ownership of land, there were at least as many opponents as supporters. Critically, there was no consistent legal recognition of Indigenous land rights or 'native title', as it became known.

Sample M109 was collected from within an 'A Class' Aboriginal reserve in 1972. At that time, entry into Aboriginal reserves in Western Australia was secured by a reserve entry permit, signed by the minister for native affairs. Exploration had to be carried out in accordance with the terms of the permit. 'The Aboriginal Affairs Planning Authority was a state government body that was able to grant entry permits', Tyler said, 'provided the Aboriginal people agreed.' In 1896, and again in 1913, the Anglican Church had established the Forrest River mission on the reserve. They'd since closed it down (in 1969), and by 1972, when the sample was taken, the property was unoccupied and a permit for that year's exploration program was given. But late in 1973, when the JV sought further access, the reserve was again populated.

This was an era in which the lives of Australia's Indigenous people were changing rapidly. There was a renaissance in Indigenous art and culture. Roads, planes and powerboats connected otherwise distant and divided communities. People suddenly knew a lot more about what others were doing, and what battles they were winning and losing, even in remote parts of the Northern Territory and the Kimberleys. There was growing contact with European outsiders, too, whom the local people called *kartiya* or *kardiya*. The outsiders came seeking knowledge, adventure, wealth, and other more personal prizes. Some of what the visitors sought was compatible with the aspirations and culture of the local people; much of it wasn't.

A resurgence in Indigenous land ownership was another striking trend. Through a combination of land purchases and land grants, and by reoccupying vacant traditional lands, Indigenous people re-established themselves on their own country. A variety of push and pull factors drove this return. A deep and sacred connection to land

is central to Indigenous culture. Celebrating and activating that connection helped strengthen family ties and rebuild cultural identity.
And returning to traditional lands helped Indigenous communities
better regulate the dangers and pitfalls of modern life. In particular,
it offered a way to reduce the disastrous role of 'grog' and other vices
in weakening Aboriginal culture.

In 1973, as part of the Indigenous land renaissance, fifty people
returned to the Forrest River mission and their surrounding ancestral
land, which they named Oombulgurri. The land was only accessible
by water or air, but the initiative enjoyed strong community support
and the population at the reserve quickly grew to around 200. Robert
Roberts led the movement to reoccupy and repopulate the reserve.
His motives were powerful. He and his wife had grown up on the
Anglican mission. When the mission closed, most of his people had
moved south-east to the coastal town of Wyndham. There, the perils
of urban living had taken a terrible toll on many of his friends and
peers. Something had to be done. Returning to Oombulgurri land
promised his people a better future.

Discussions with the AAPA made it possible for Ewen Tyler to go
to Oombulgurri and meet with elders and other leaders. On behalf
of the JV, he would seek to persuade the Oombulgurri to grant
further access.

During his student days in the 1940s, Tyler had met Indigenous
people in the Pilbara, and he was alert to their struggle for fairness
and respect. He was also alert to political and legal developments
in Indigenous affairs. He knew, for example, that Justice Edward
Woodward in the Northern Territory was writing a report on
Aboriginal land rights legislation, and that at the federal government
level, the Whitlam cabinet was talking about taking control of all
Indigenous reserves. In 1971, Yolŋu people at Yirrkala had sought
an injunction against Nabalco mining on traditional land. But in the
Gove land rights case, Justice Richard Blackburn of the Northern
Territory Supreme Court had ruled that Australia was *terra nullius*

before British occupation: the land had belonged to no-one. No concept of native title existed in Australian law.

When he arrived at the old Forrest River mission, Tyler was confronted by a busy scene. The reserve was home not only to Oombulgurri people but also to members of the Ecumenical Institute, a religious group from Chicago whose affiliates had established themselves as 'white advisers' to the Oombulgurri on matters of self-help. One morning at the reserve, Tyler overheard a voice with a strong American accent advising a group of Indigenous women on the mass production of didgeridoos, and how the women might obtain a monopoly on the sources of ochre for the instruments' decoration. He was struck by the cultural divide: the stark disparity between what the 'advisers' offered and what the Indigenous people might want and need. 'It seemed straight out of fairyland,' Tyler said.

In the middle of this clash between old and new, local and foreign, Robert Roberts saw the world through clear eyes. 'You whites must think we are mad,' he told Tyler. 'Why would a sane person hunt kangaroo with a boomerang if he could use a rifle?' He was justifiably sceptical of the motives of outsiders who were 'here to help'. But he and his team sat down with Tyler and John Toohey to work out a possible deal that would give Kalumburu access to Oombulgurri lands. Toohey was a respected lawyer in the West Australian Aboriginal Legal Service (and a future High Court judge). A strong advocate for Indigenous rights, he acted as counsel for the Oombulgurri.

The JV's efforts to maintain secrecy continued, including in the access negotiations. 'Because we had no mineral title in the A Class reserve,' Tyler said, 'it was impossible to disclose to anyone why we had continued to be interested in it. We had to describe our interest as being for minerals generally.' Tyler nevertheless felt he developed a good rapport with Roberts, though less so with Toohey. 'Toohey believed Oombulgurri lands should be left free of disturbance and exploration for 25 years, to allow the people time to adjust.' But Roberts and the Oombulgurri council of elders disagreed. For a $25,000 payment, they granted Kalumburu access for the 1974 field season.

Later that year, it became clear to Tyler that the JV needed to enter a longer-term arrangement with the Oombulgurri Association. He flew to Wyndham and made a second visit to the reserve, meeting again with Roberts and Toohey. On the basis of terms that were scribbled on a scrap of paper, the Oombulgurri agreed to give exclusive access to the 'Tanganyika Mining Company' (which, strictly speaking, did not exist). 'There was a traditional ceremony at which John Toohey and I were distinguished guests,' Tyler said, 'and it was made clear that Tanganyika would be welcome to explore the reserve.'

In more than one way, this was an important step for Tyler and Kalumburu: 'We thought that, with its exclusivity, the agreement would be almost as good as mining title, and in consideration we proposed a joint venture with the Oombulgurri.' That proposal envisaged a participation arrangement whereby the Oombulgurri Association would gain a stake in any mining activity on the reserve. It was the first agreement of its kind in Australia. But as Tyler later described, its future was doomed:

> Such an arrangement appealed to the Commonwealth Department of Aboriginal Affairs and to the local Aboriginal Affairs Planning Authority, but it was frowned upon by the state government. Negotiations proceeded amicably over several years with the people of Oombulgurri and the Aboriginal Lands Trust, but it became abundantly clear that we were offending the government.

Charles Court himself vehemently opposed the idea, as did some major mining companies who feared it could imply Indigenous people had a legal and economic interest in mineral resources, which of course they did. 'The idea', Tyler said, 'had to be canned.'

Tyler noticed that Indigenous access issues were a concern not just for the Western Australian Government but also for Kalumburu's international backers: 'Often reluctant contributors anyway, they now started to feel even less welcome in Australia.' He also noticed the racist and ignorant attitudes within Tanks' head office. Ronny Medlicott in particular couldn't understand what all the 'Aboriginal fuss' was about. 'They were cannibals a hundred years ago,' he wrote in a letter to Tyler.

Two decades later, Toohey would figure prominently in the Australian High Court's landmark Mabo judgement, in which the court recognised the traditional rights of the Meriam people to their islands in the Torres Strait. The court also reached a much broader conclusion: native title existed for all of Australia's Indigenous people prior to James Cook's declaration of possession in 1770, and prior to the process of colonisation that followed. The Mabo decision overturned the doctrine of *terra nullius*. Soon after the court's decision, the federal government would pass legislation that set out a framework for Indigenous people to seek recognition of their rights. The concept of native title became a pillar of Australian law.

10
STEEL BALLS

TANGANYIKA CONTINUED TO run its West Australian operations from a small house on Emerald Terrace in Perth. And it continued to operate its makeshift laboratory in that house's kitchen. But faced with the task of processing the 1974 samples, and with the role of supporting what Tyler now saw as a significant, multi-year gravel-sampling program, the team knew their makeshift lab wasn't going to cope. The JV had to build a proper, full-scale laboratory.

A geologist with AO (Australia), Wilfred 'Wilf' Jones, had extensive diamond experience from his time in West Africa with Selection Trust. Now in Perth, he helped Tanks design and build a new diamond search laboratory: an up-to-the-minute, state-of-the-art lab and workshop and corporate office, set up in a leased used-car showroom on Axon Street in West Perth. Mick Paltridge had the showroom's big windows painted over so nosy passers-by couldn't see the secret work that was going on inside. Designed and built to Tanks' specifications, the new diamond laboratory included a special mineral separation section that was refrigerated and fitted with extraction fans to control the TBE fumes, which otherwise would have been overpowering.

'That area was so cold it was quite impractical,' Tyler said. 'No-one could work in there for any length of time.' But overall Tyler was proud of Tanks' crucial new facility. The team installed X-ray equipment along with mineral-separation machines, which had been used with success by the heavy mineral miners at Eneabba. 'The new laboratory was divided into processing facilities', Tyler said, 'with lab-size Wilfley tables, the refrigerated TBE separating facility, a drying section and magnetic and electrostatic machines, an X-ray unit for crystallographic determinations, and an engineering facility for vehicle maintenance.'

The laboratory had to be highly capable and efficient. Chris Smith and Wilf Jones trained a pool of mineral observers who, under the supervision of mineralogists, would pick mineral grains from the heavy concentrate. 'Apart from a secretive De Beers laboratory in Melbourne,' Tyler said, 'we believed this was the only diamond laboratory in Australia in the 1970s. And the new one was more sophisticated, we thought. It was the first of its kind here.' (Tyler did some covert research on the De Beers lab: 'I used my own daughter, then a university student, to spy on their Melbourne facility by counting people going in and coming out, to obtain an idea of how many people were working there, and the distribution of the sexes.')

The Kalumburu JV's new laboratory became a vital facility. The work demanded patience and dexterity. At one stage, the JV had twelve mineral observers working at its unique laboratory—most of them women, many of them former nurses. But nothing spectacular emerged from the lab's work in 1974. There was a distinct feeling of unhappiness among the JV parties when Tyler asked for $800,000 for the 1975 program.

The flood of limonite meant that the processing of the original 1600 samples from 1972 was slow. In an important innovation, the lab team used hydrogen reduction to convert the limonite to magnetic hematite, which could then be removed with hand magnets. By 1974–75, all the results from the first 1600 samples were available. And they were encouraging. The sampling had identified not only the North Kimberley as a target but also the East Kimberley (Wilson River, June 1974) and the West Kimberley (Pigeon Creek, near Big Spring, January 1975). The 1974 and 1975 field programs confirmed that indicator minerals were widespread; Oombulgurri was by no means the only place of interest. Signs were found all over the Kimberleys.

Paradoxically, this represented further problems for the JV's backers. The potential target areas kept shifting and growing. The continuing definition of promising areas was an embarrassment of riches. It was a source of excitement for the Tanks team, but to some of the JV's funders it was a cause for doubt. The team were seeing diamonds everywhere and nowhere. They'd found hints and traces, but not an actual kimberlite pipe. Maybe, some participants feared, the whole enterprise was just a pipedream. The results were one more source of tension inside the JV.

For Tyler, these reactions were disappointing. 'It was as though only my technical team and I were encouraged,' he said. 'The parties contributing, including my own London company, would have preferred for there to have been only local success and no grand picture emerging.'

In 1974, a technical program and budget had been agreed. With these, the JV would carry out a follow-up program in the north-east Kimberley. By the middle of 1974, it was apparent that the 1975 work program would require a substantial investment in machinery and equipment. Special plant would have to be built to process hundreds of tonnes of gravel.

When Tyler was at Geita, there were initially three Australians on the mine: Tyler, Aldyth, and the mill superintendent, Norman Stansmore from Victoria (a descendent of the diamond finder George Stansmore). Then Norman left for South Africa, to work for Fraser & Chalmers. He was later asked to put in a modern diamond recovery process at Mwadui: a heavy media separation (HMS) plant, the first of its kind at the mine. (In Tanganyika, Norman asked Tyler for steel balls from Geita so Norman could use them to mill the kimberlite ore at Mwadui to extract the diamonds. Far from being a diamond expert, Tyler worried that the balls might crush the diamonds, but his fears were unwarranted. The steel balls worked well. The diamonds were unharmed.)

Tyler had kept in touch with Norman Stansmore over the years. Stansmore had moved to South Africa but would sometimes visit Australia; he and Tyler had met up in Melbourne several times. He was now part of the Mitchell Cotts group in South Africa, and Tyler met with him again, this time at Escargot, a French restaurant in South Yarra, where Tyler hoped to hear his advice on how best to process the bulk samples.

Tyler laid out what was needed. Stansmore understood the technical problems involved and knew who could solve them. He arranged for a follow-up discussion at which Tyler would meet with three of Stansmore's Mitchell Cotts colleagues, including Roger Falls. The Kalumburu JV partners were continuing to maintain the veil of secrecy over their activities, and this included speaking in code. During the follow-up meeting, which was held at Tyler's home, he spoke of 'barytes this' and 'barytes that'. Small ones, high-quality ones, high-value ones. And for much of this conversation, Falls and his mystified colleagues were certain Ewen Tyler had finally lost his marbles. Who in their right mind, the visitors wondered, would use a heavy mineral plant for something of such low value?

Stansmore, it seemed, hadn't told his colleagues about the code word. Eventually the confusion was cleared up, and Tyler ordered from Mitchell Cotts a Mark III HMS plant. Mitchell Cotts built the plant in Perth from South African drawings. The JV planned to set it up at a strategic point on the Drysdale River, midway between the Carson, King George and Drysdale drainages. There, the JV would establish a strategic base camp and airstrip, with a view to processing river gravel. By bulk sampling the drainages for commercial-sized diamonds, the JV hoped to solve the mystery of where the diamonds and indicators were coming from.

At Geita, Tyler had managed challenging logistics. Now, his team would do it all over again in the Kimberleys. The HMS plant had to be brought in from Wyndham by road—in two sections, trailer-mounted—to the Kalumburu mission. Then a new road was purpose-built from the mission to the base camp. Establishing the remote camp and the specialised plant was a major exercise that involved trucks and digging equipment to build the road and then the airstrip. In 1974, when the JV revisited Pteropus Creek, some supplies had to be brought from Wyndham by barge and on a work boat named *Robert Williams*, which made a perilous voyage up the Berkeley River. Afterwards, a commemorative medal was struck for the brave voyagers.

For the diamond venture, secrecy was still necessary, but it was becoming more and more difficult to maintain. When the JV established camps on the northern rivers, it was obvious to outsiders that Kalumburu was up to something. To provide some degree of protection, the JV gave the camps fictional and nonsensical names. Paltridge named the camp and airstrip on the Drysdale River 'Mumbo Jumbo'; another camp, on the King George, was called 'Geebung'. 'For years these names of airstrips appeared on the air navigation maps,' Tyler said, 'and people would nonchalantly say they were going to Mumbo Jumbo.'

The period from June to October 1975 was a difficult time for the Kalumburu Joint Venture. The Mitchell Cotts HMS plant arrived at Mumbo Jumbo in June 1975, but as soon as it was commissioned, it refused to perform to specification. To the great frustration of the field team, the machine didn't work. Mitchell Cotts didn't know what was wrong, and nor did anyone in the JV. An engineer came from South Africa to help. It turned out one of the channels had been installed backwards. This was rectified, but when the machine was eventually made to work, there were no diamonds in the samples. The team's morale was low and falling.

Representatives of Jennings and AO visited the site in September 1975. The end of the field season was fast approaching and the visitors were uncomplimentary about what they saw. In Tyler's words, the Australian JV investors thought the organisation was 'up the pole'. Tempers became frayed and the investors blamed the manager, Tyler, for the malaise. Standing on the edge of a Kimberley watercourse, he felt his credibility ebbing away. 'All parties had become instant exploration experts,' he said.

The widespread finds and activities meant continuing calls for cash from the JV partners. As the demands for more funding continued in 1974 and 1975, the five parties began to disagree among themselves. There was one thing, however, upon which most of them agreed: they wanted the cash to start flowing in the right direction. They wanted a return on their investment, and to some of them, collecting wild diamonds from rivers and creeks offered a quick way to do this.

Alan Jones and Tyler counselled the other parties to keep their eyes on the main game. 'Exploration is an expensive business,' Jones said, 'and people want quick results. But exploration often doesn't yield commercial results.'

'It's a common thing in mining,' Tyler said. 'As soon as people see positive signs, they want cash out right away. But it doesn't work like that. You need to put cash in to get cash out.'

Sibeka in particular, hearing more and more requests from the JV for cash, started to take an intense interest in the Kalumburu operation. From a base in Kinshasa, the geologist Bruno Morelli managed that company's mines in the *Congo belge* (now the Democratic Republic of the Congo). Tyler had previously met Morelli at Sibeka in Brussels. In the Sibeka camp he was Tyler's main technical contact. Now, the Belgian made a rare visit to Australia. He would take a look at the JV and its follow-up operation in the north-east Kimberley.

Morelli had some experience with kimberlites but mostly with alluvial diamond mines. He was no fan of kimberlite exploration, having been scarred by Sibeka's experience in the Congo, where productive pipes were hard to find and often the yields were too low to warrant a decision to mine.

Once in Australia, he made it clear that his preferred strategy for the JV was to search waterways for alluvial deposits that could generate an immediate flow of cash, some of which could then be used to fund a kimberlite search. The King George River had significant potential, he argued. The JV should establish an alluvial mining operation there. Putting his words into action, he took a pan, a pick and a shovel to a stretch of rapids on the King George. His efforts bore immediate dividends: he extracted from the gravel what appeared to be a small diamond. Morelli spoke French and Italian but only a little English.

Upon making this discovery, he exclaimed in French, '*Ah, nous avons le renard par la queue!*' 'Ah, we have the fox by the tail!' Chris Smith remembered the episode this way:

> [Bruno] spent some hours digging out crevices in the rapids and panning down the gravel. When we returned to pick him up, he proudly showed us the diamond he had found there. 'Now you see *la méthode belge*! The diamond is a slippery fellow, like a fox. When you have the fox by the tail, never let him go! There are diamonds here. Why don't you dig them up?'

From that point on, that stretch on the King George River would appear on maps and in the exploration literature as 'Morelli's Fox'.

Like Tyler, Smith believed there wasn't enough diamondiferous gravel to justify an alluvial mining operation. But Morelli demurred. 'Ah, Smith,' he said, 'you never find the kimberlite. And if you find him, he will have no diamonds.'

Morelli now started to promote the cause of alluvial mining among the JV participants. From Kinshasa and Brussels he was able to influence not only Sibeka but also Tanganyika Concessions and London Tin. The idea that alluvials might be richer in diamonds, and might generate an instant cash flow, was music to the ears of the overseas participants. But for Tyler and his team, the task had always been to find the source of the diamonds. For Tyler, the idea of focusing on alluvial mining was folly. 'It was a concept for which I held no conviction,' he said. 'I didn't see the North Kimberley as having any significant alluvial potential, and I regarded Morelli's intervention as a distraction. Its effect was to produce even more instability in the conduct of the joint venture, making my position as manager more difficult.'

But due to the pressure from Morelli and the international partners, the JV's field crews had to shift their emphasis. They began to explore the potential of an alluvial operation, while at the same time searching for mineable kimberlites. In the north-east of the Kimberleys, the JV tested alluvial gravels for diamond content.

11

A NEW PARTNER

I N 1974, THE outlook for the Kalumburu JV was bleak. There were
problems with money: the JV was burning through cash, and the
participants faced ongoing requests to cover rising exploration costs.
There were problems with site access and mineral title, or the lack
thereof. And there were problems in the exploration program itself:
the team hadn't found the source of the diamonds; there was no
immediate prospect of them doing so; and Bruno Morelli continued
to promote alluvials in preference to searching for pipes. In London
and Australia, the JV partners were nervous: about geology and
prospectivity; about Indigenous rights and access; and about Gough
Whitlam and the federal government's hostility to foreign investment.

A strident economic nationalist and former car dealer and local
councillor, Reginald Francis Xavier 'Rex' Connor was minister for
minerals and energy in the Whitlam Government. Under his influence, the government sought to limit the flow of foreign money into
Australia. It restrained overseas ownership and control of Australian
businesses and resources, enacted the *Foreign Acquisitions and Takeovers
Act 1975* and established a process to scrutinise international capital.
Foreign investment in major resources projects was not permitted
unless there was at least 51 per cent Australian ownership.

The Kalumburu JV had been established before there was such a thing as the Foreign Investment Review Board (FIRB), and before there were clear rules and guidelines about Australian ownership of minerals. But the nationalist views within the Whitlam cabinet meant that attracting foreign investment was now difficult. Even day-to-day international payments faced significant hurdles. 'At one stage,' Tyler said, 'it looked as though the overseas companies wouldn't be able to continue funding, and the project would collapse. A way around the problem was found, but only by jumping through all sorts of hoops. There were a lot of sleepless nights.'

At every turn there were problems, too, with Northern Mining and Rees Towie, about governance, money and strategy. Northern again made alarming requests to publicise the diamond program. Newspapers were starting to make observations about Tanganyika's activities, and the other parties suspected Towie was leaking information to journalists. 'The Kalumburu parties were losing patience with Northern Mining,' Tyler said. 'It interfered at every turn and with every document presented for signature. The other four parties could always agree, but Northern would always seek alteration.'

These are just some of the obstacles and difficulties that the Kalumburu Joint Venture faced throughout 1974 and 1975. Tyler was grappling with the difficulties of managing a diverse group of partners who were embarking on an innovative program with few signposts. Paradoxically, he thought part of the solution would be to introduce another participant. One that was well funded, and Australian. 'As if the problems of five parties had not been enough!' he said.

Early in 1975, the existing participants agreed to invite a major Australian company to join the JV, to make Kalumburu a six-party enterprise. Under strict confidentiality, and deeply nervous about the JV's lack of mineral title, Tyler began to make inquiries. He approached Sir Arvi Parbo of Western Mining Corporation. WMC declined to participate, but there was a more encouraging response from Peko-Wallsend, an Australian conglomerate that had interests in mineral exploration, mining and manufacturing. From around 1971, Tyler had served on a board with Peko's Sir John Proud and George Lean. When he approached them about the Kalumburu

JV, they sent Peko's head of exploration, John Elliston, to Perth. The JV team showed him what they were doing, and their results so far. 'Peko had considerable skill in geophysics,' Tyler said, 'which was something we were going to need, and it seemed that we would be a good match.' Elliston liked what he saw, and Kalumburu and Peko-Wallsend drafted a document that was called the 'Plateau Joint Venture Agreement'. According to the agreement, Peko would contribute $750,000 in exchange for a 25 per cent share in the diamond venture.

On 11 November 1975, a fateful day in Australian politics, the Kalumburu JV committee met in the Tanganyika Holdings offices to deal with the Plateau Agreement. The atmosphere was tense. Deep divisions had emerged over how to proceed with the project, how to raise more money, and whether the early results should be revealed to the public. Nevertheless, the majority of the JV participants wanted to sign up with Peko-Wallsend. In fact, in the lead-up to the meeting, all the parties with the exception of Northern had agreed to go ahead with Peko.

At the meeting, Tyler reported on the Plateau Agreement and the negotiations that had preceded it. Peko had accepted the invitation to participate at a level of 25 per cent. Documents had been prepared for imminent execution of the deal, which, helpfully for the federal government requirements, would have the effect of increasing the venture's Australian ownership from 40 to 55 per cent. 'I struck oil with Peko,' Tyler said. 'They were keen and we had an agreement drafted for signature. Their first payment of $250,000 was virtually in the bank.'

Rees Towie, though, declined to sign the agreement. Ever hungry for funding, he argued that the Peko contribution wouldn't be enough for the program that the JV envisaged. And he marshalled other arguments against the deal. Then, at the last minute, he announced he'd been in secret talks with other mining companies. Unbeknown to the JV manager or the other parties, Northern was seeking to introduce a company other than Peko. Towie had met with perhaps ten Australian and overseas exploration outfits, seeking to find a different source of capital for the diamond venture.

'Rees had been asking anyone and everyone,' Tyler said. 'So much for confidentiality!' The other parties had already consulted their lawyers as to what could be done about Northern. They knew there wasn't much they could do to force Towie to play by the rules. 'We did not see how we could make Northern sign up with Peko,' Tyler said, 'and there was a distinct chance that Peko, sensing a lack of joint venture cohesion, might walk away.'

At the 11 November meeting, Rees put forward a counterproposal. One month earlier, at a barbecue, he'd met John Collier, who had recently been put in charge of the exploration division of CRA, and the two had discussed CRA's participation in the Kalumburu diamond project.

CRA—Conzinc Riotinto of Australia—was half-owned by another major London-based mining group, Rio Tinto Zinc (RTZ). RTZ had been formed in 1873 to recommission an old copper mine in southern Spain. It was now a global force in the mining industry, especially in bulk minerals such as iron ore, copper and zinc. The group's Australian subsidiary, CRA, came from the marriage of RTZ with the Broken Hill zinc miner ConZinc Corp (CZC). As CRA executive Russel Madigan later said of that pairing, 'CZC had Broken Hill, the ideas and the prospects, and Rio Tinto, which had cashed in its Spanish interests, had the cash.' Under chief executive Sir Roderick Carnegie (formerly of McKinsey & Company), CRA became a mining powerhouse. The giant Hamersley iron ore project made the company one of the most important players in the West Australian economy.

Towie informed the other JV members that CRA was prepared to join with them in the diamond search, and in particular it was prepared to match the JV's estimated total expenditure to the end of 1975—some $1.6 million—in order to earn a 25 per cent stake.

During his London days, Tyler had had a lot of exposure to the RTZ Group. He knew the deputy chairman, Sir Mark Turner, and through him he'd met Carnegie. In some respects RTZ and CRA were ideal participants. 'They were big,' Tyler said, 'with plenty of muscle.' But their foreign ownership was a big issue, too, for the other foreign participants in the JV, and for the Australian Government. In addition to RTZ, CRA had other foreign shareholders. In aggregate, it was more than 70 per cent foreign-owned. The Kalumburu JV as it currently stood was 60 per cent foreign-owned. Introducing CRA would have increased the foreign share, in direct conflict with the wishes of the federal government and the existing foreign parties.

'Although I knew them well,' Tyler said, 'I'd avoided any discussion with CRA and RTZ because that would be averse to the foreign companies' preferred position.' And moreover, in Tyler's eyes the Peko deal was done and dusted:

> Their money was in the bank, and all the others had agreed, except Rees, and then the John Collier meeting took place. The others preferred Peko because CRA was an overseas company, and their participation would increase, undesirably, the overseas share. Had we simply wanted a funding participant, I would've selected Rio because they were all well known to me from my London days.

Apart from Turner (a merchant banker and one of the prime movers at Rio Tinto in the modern era), Tyler also knew Sir Maurice Mawby, a former CRA chairman. From London, Tyler had worked on exploration projects with CRA in north Queensland and with RTZ in Zambia. He would happily work with these men again. And he saw other benefits that could flow from the CRA option. 'It had been promoted by Northern,' he said, 'and presumably they would therefore have some commitment to it.'

The option had another benefit, too: it promised to reduce the role (and the voice) of Northern Mining in the diamond venture. Under the deal with CRA, Northern's interest would be diluted to 5 per cent. In contrast, under the putative Peko deal, Tyler had agreed to keep Northern's equity at around 15 per cent, mainly because Northern was Australian.

The question of whether to go with Peko or CRA was therefore finely balanced. Or it was until, that very afternoon, the Whitlam Government fell. From that moment, the foreign ownership calculus changed. A new government might very well bring a new attitude. Suddenly the idea of adding another Australian party seemed less important. By the end of the meeting, therefore, the JV partners decided to go with CRA. They wouldn't be signing the Plateau Agreement. On the face of it, and in the changed political environment, the proposed tie-up with CRA seemed like a better deal. The Kalumburu JV agreed to enter negotiations with CRA on its proposal.

Throughout these deliberations, Tyler had remained a director of Northern Mining. As with previous dealings with Towie, he had felt like the meat in the sandwich. But with the latest turn of events, his position as a Northern director had become utterly untenable, a source of embarrassment to him and his Kalumburu colleagues. He was gaining nothing from the association—if anything, it was wreaking damage. 'I was powerless to exert influence on Towie,' he said. 'None of us could tame him.' Tyler resigned from the Northern board.

12

A LONG-TERM PERSPECTIVE

T HE JV PARTNERS went into negotiations with CRA. Much of the deliberations took place in Melbourne between Ewen Tyler and John Harry, CRA's lawyer, at 95 Collins Street. There were also regular meetings in the CRA boardroom and the Melbourne office of Tanganyika Holdings. The Tanks office in particular was the scene of frequent arguments about the deal, some of them animated.

Sir Rod Carnegie and the CRA board might very well have said no to the proposed investment. CRA was focusing on building a bulk minerals business—how did diamonds fit into that? But Russ Madigan saw the potential, and from inside CRA he continued to speak for the tie-up. Madigan arranged for CRA's Carnegie and other senior executives to visit the Kalumburu field operation. They were impressed by what they saw. The CRA team also consulted RTZ in London, and the London owners suggested that the team seek advice on the venture's prospects from an international expert. Through Rio's South African office, they found the perfect adviser.

Robin Baxter Brown was a leading diamond geologist who knew all aspects of diamond exploration and extraction. He even had his own diamond mine, in Namibia. Rio Tinto asked him to visit Australia to look at what Kalumburu was up to, and report on the significance of the discoveries. Baxter Brown agreed and Rio engaged him as a consultant. He was optimistic about the possibility of finding new mines both within and outside Africa; the rich Venetia pipe, after all, had been discovered in a much-explored and much-worked part of South Africa just a few years earlier.

Tyler respected Baxter Brown as a diamond expert, and Baxter Brown in turn was complimentary of the team and how they were working. He was especially impressed with the Tanks lab in Perth, where he peered through his loupe and pored over samples and maps. The team by now had found many diamonds, but because of the way the samples were processed, none of the diamonds was of a significant weight. Baxter Brown set the team a new target. Previously, the goal had been to discover a single indicator grain. Now, it was to find a quarter-carat stone. That would demonstrate the presence of marketable diamonds in the Kimberleys.

The six-party JV negotiations continued from November into December and January. Along the way (on 5 December 1975), CRA's appropriations committee approved the investment. This was quickly ratified by the CRA board. A presentation from Collier was crucial to the board's decision. As general manager of exploration, he appreciated that the search for diamonds required a long-term perspective and a significant investment of money. Taking an optimistic view of the JV's potential, the board agreed to a 30 per cent increase in CRA's total exploration budget—to accommodate the substantial resources that would need to be committed to the Kimberley search.

With due prudence on behalf of its shareholders, the CRA board drove a hard bargain on the terms of the new JV. 'Collier beat us down,' Tyler said. 'But it was still a good deal, coinciding as it did with the departure of Mr RFX Connor and the election of Malcolm Fraser.' It was agreed that CRA would earn the 35 per cent interest by the expenditure of the $1.6 million, but there were arguments over what precisely that money would buy. Eventually the parties agreed to an escalating series of milestones and trigger points at which CRA would serve up slices of its contribution.

In the final agreement, one of the early milestones was the target set by Baxter Brown: the goal of finding a quarter-carat stone, and therefore demonstrating that 'commercial-sized stones' could be found in the Kimberleys. The next milestone in the agreement was the discovery of a diamond-bearing pipe. And the climax: a pipe with a diamond grade that was high enough to justify a mine.

The agreement also included a provision that would have a big impact on the future conduct of the diamond search venture. According to that provision, once all the points had been reached and the money spent, Tanganyika's role as manager of the JV would pass to CRA. The parties estimated that this would take from eighteen months to two years. When CRA assumed the role of manager, it would employ all of Tanganyika's Australian staff (about forty people) with the exception of Tyler. This included taking over the new diamond laboratory and its highly trained technicians.

As part of the deal, Northern Mining agreed to the radical reduction in its own equity in the venture, from 20 per cent to 5 per cent, but for Tyler and the other partners, the reduction of Northern's interests didn't mean the end of the Northern problems. Funding required for the diamond search program was substantial. Even at 5 per cent, Towie had the power to frustrate the program, with the goal of extracting a better deal. CRA and four of the original Kalumburu parties were willing to contribute to the projected program, but Northern wasn't. So in a side deal, CRA agreed to fund Northern's share of the costs of the exploration program in exchange for two-thirds of Northern's share of the JV. Northern thus continued the tactical pattern of not paying for its own investments. 'It was the Kalumburu Joint Venture funding arrangement all over again,' Tyler said, 'only this time CRA paid the bill.'

In February 1976, the Kalumburu Joint Venture ceased. The original five participants, plus CRA, formed the Ashton Joint Venture. Tyler and Harry chose the name 'Ashton' because it was the heading of the 1:250,000 map sheet that was more or less in the centre of the diamond searchers' target area.

In the specialised field of diamond exploration, CRA brought very little to the new JV. Its people knew next to nothing about diamond mineralogy or the Tanks lab technology. Their direct experience of diamond exploration was minimal. Only Peter Temby, a CRA geologist, had had some exposure to De Beers, and he now briefed CRA's geologist and field manager Frank Hughes, along with Warren Atkinson, the company's exploration manager in Western Australia. But the exploration program immediately benefited from a massive injection of money and resources. New equipment was installed, new staff were appointed. Mick Paltridge and Chris Smith had devised Tanganyika's chopper-based field-sampling techniques, and the Tanks field crews had been using those techniques since 1972. Paltridge and Smith immediately set about inducting Hughes into their methodology and training CRA's sampling crews, who were then deployed into the field.

The addition of CRA people thus strengthened the diamond exploration team. The new personnel were eager to learn all that the seasoned diamond searchers had to offer, but there were still hiccups, including inefficiencies and inaccuracies in sample collection. The different staff brought different corporate cultures. They were used to different mineralogy. They thought at a different scale, and took some time to match the old Kalumburu rhythm and precision.

'Inducting the new staff was not without its hassles,' Tyler said. 'They didn't follow Chris and Maureen's meticulousness.' But these were just teething problems. The new personnel came round to the old Kalumburu methods. Crucially, the new field crews continued to use geologists in sample collection.

Hughes of CRA became a key member of the Ashton JV team. In World War II he'd flown Lancaster bombers. He spoke with quiet humour and was superficially laid back, but underneath he was determined, precise and professional. Smith described him as 'a highly skilled field observer and geological mapper who loved nothing more than being out in the bush'. Thanks to these skills, Hughes had figured in several of Australia's major mining discoveries. He had played a decisive role in proving the Mount Tom Price iron ore deposit in the Pilbara, for example, as well as other CRA iron ore discoveries. 'He was an excellent geologist,' Tyler said. 'He could read the land. He had excellent eyes.'

Tyler and Smith quickly warmed to the idea of working with CRA. Crucially, Tyler hoped the company might become a powerful ally in the debate about alluvials versus pipes. In the search for alluvials, he felt that his diamond searchers had only been going through the motions: 'If I could persuade CRA of the technical correctness of the search for the pipes and to avoid the short-term alluvial nonsense, then my Australian diamond vision might still become a reality.'

Tyler was right about where CRA would land on this issue. Madigan was in charge of CRA's exploration activities, and he in particular supported Tyler's view. He understood the importance of finding the diamonds' source, not just the gems that had been washed downstream. From that point on, CRA as the majority partner in Ashton was adamant that the second milestone—discovery of a diamond-bearing pipe—should take precedence, and that they shouldn't be distracted by the alluvial discoveries. 'The emphasis on Kimberley gravels was very much reduced,' Tyler said.

Madigan came from an impeccable mining lineage. His father, Dr Cecil Madigan, a mining engineer, had been Douglas Mawson's meteorologist during the first Australian-led expedition to Antarctica. In 1939, while prospecting in Central Australia, Madigan senior crossed the Simpson Desert on a camel and named the desert after his sponsor, an Adelaide-based businessman. He surveyed Lake Eyre, and the southern part is now named Madigan Gulf in his honour. Russel 'Russ' Madigan studied Engineering at Adelaide University. After graduating he went straight to Broken Hill to work for ConZinc. When he left there, CRA appointed him to take charge of the Hamersley Iron development in the Pilbara. It would become the largest iron mine in Australia. Madigan led negotiations with the Japanese steel mills to secure long-term sales contracts. As lawyer and mining executive Bill Leslie noted, 'Broken Hill spawned many of Australia's great twentieth-century miners. When Russ joined the CRA board, he was one of five directors who'd been underground managers at Broken Hill.'

◇

Tyler was still the manager under the terms of the Ashton JV agreement, and CRA was funding the JV's activities. With Tyler and CRA in harmony, there would be no more disagreements about the focus of the search. The field crews had been disheartened by the earlier shift in emphasis towards alluvials. Now they were back searching for kimberlites, and they did so with a new energy and optimism.

Tyler might have warmed to CRA, but he was still furious with Rees Towie, whose obduracy and opportunism had threatened to destroy all that Tyler and the other partners had worked for. After the 11 November board meeting, Tyler and Alan Jones met Towie for coffee at Melbourne's Southern Cross Hotel. Tyler criticised Towie for his shenanigans around the introduction of Peko, and for not signing the Plateau Agreement. The pair argued, and to the astonishment of onlookers the argument became a shouting match. Both men rose to their feet. Towie threatened violence (not, according to Jones, for the first time) and in the heat of the moment the normally mild and unflappable Tyler lost his temper and considered throwing a chair at Towie, or clobbering him with one.

Beneath the bluster and the fireworks was an elemental battle between two opposing philosophies of mining and commerce. Tyler had strong ideas about how business should be conducted, and he felt Towie was hurting himself as well as his partners by playing too hard for short-term chances and fleeting scraps. Foremost in Tyler's mind was the fear that the diamond searchers were running out of luck, and that his Australian diamond vision was turning into an impossible dream.

13

THE GREAT EXPLORER

AFTER ALL THE effort to set up the HMS plant, the processing of bulk samples from Mumbo Jumbo on the Drysdale River produced nothing. However, early in 1976, before the ink was dry on the Ashton Joint Venture agreement, the laboratory results from all the sampling work of the previous four years became available. All the field crews' work started to pay off.

Following an agreement with the Indigenous owners for another year's entry permit, the team worked at Pteropus Creek. There, in February 1976, at a location just upstream from where sample M109 had been gathered, they discovered a volcanic pipe. (Among other things, this meant the JV participants now had a definite target, and they could apply for proper mineral title. There was finally something the participants could stick a stake into.) Then in May 1976, near the Big Spring Bore in the south-west, a JV crew followed a trail of chromite and phlogopite ('magnesium mica') up Pigeon Creek. At the head of the creek they found a total of six volcanic pipes.

Laboratory manager Wilf Jones was able to confirm from the samples gathered at Big Spring and Pteropus Creek that chromite was an indicator mineral for diamonds, although it had not been used as such in Africa, where it was not so prominent. In diamond exploration, this was a revolutionary discovery. Chromite profusion as a significant indicator was now a closely guarded secret inside Ashton.

The volcanic pipe that came to be known as Big Spring No. 1 was shown to contain diamonds. These diamonds were smaller than 0.25 carats, so the JV's second target had been achieved before its first one: they'd found a diamond-bearing pipe, but not a commercially sized diamond. In June 1976, there were further discoveries in the East Kimberley. Bulk sampling with a diamond pan in the Wilson River failed to locate any diamonds, but indicators were found. 'We realised we were close to more bodies,' Tyler said. (The Wilson River indicators would later lead to the discovery of elongate volcanic pipes, known as dykes.)

More than once, the King George River would feature prominently in the history of Australian diamonds. The 1974 sampling program (supplied from Sallyport on the Berkeley River) had found diamonds in that river's catchment at site M109. A second, smaller-scale bulk-sampling program was therefore planned, both to test the King George's alluvial potential, and to shed more light on where the diamonds were coming from. Early in the 1976 season, the Ashton team set up a trommel and Pleitz jig around 50 kilometres upstream from the King George Falls, near Morelli's Fox. With this equipment they began bulk sampling of gravel.

On 6 July 1976, CRA's top brass visited the site. They wanted to see what kind of operation they'd bought into. Sir Maurice Mawby, the recently retired chairman of CRA, was there, along with Russ Madigan as the CRA director responsible for exploration, plus John Collier, Warren Atkinson, and CRA's field manager, Frank Hughes. Mick Paltridge offered Collier the chance to pan for stones among the alluvial gravels. He was panning away with concentrate from the small jig when he suddenly whispered, 'I've got it.' To everyone's astonishment, he'd found an impressive-looking 0.4-carat diamond. This was the first diamond of that size to be found in the consortium's entire Kimberley operation. They'd smashed the goal of finding a 0.25-carat stone. There was jubilation among the visiting party and the exploration crew. And disbelief: was it a real discovery, or was the whole thing stage-managed, a stratagem to impress the eminent visitors? 'It seemed too good to be true,' Tyler said, 'and doubts were expressed. But Warren Atkinson and others believed it was a fair dinkum find. And an amazing coincidence.'

After this and other successful King George River sampling, the JV closed Mumbo Jumbo and moved the plant and equipment to Geebung on the King George. In September 1976, still in the North Kimberley, a Tanks crew discovered a kimberlite in the King George drainage. Maureen Muggeridge named it 'Skerring' because it was found between Scumble Creek and Red Herring Creek. The team began cutting trenches to examine the find. Sibeka and Bruno Morelli had continued to push for the JV to focus on alluvial diamonds; there was no chance, he'd said, of finding the actual source of the gems. But after the pipe was found at Skerring, Tyler and Chris Smith took Morelli there and showed him that such a discovery was possible. Morelli turned to Smith and bowed, before saying, '*Vous êtes le grand explorateur.*' 'You are the great explorer.'

Inexorably, Tyler was winning the argument with Morelli about the potential for pipes versus alluvials. And the argument would take a new turn after another find at Skerring. Muggeridge reported that she'd found a large gem while panning from one of the investigation trenches. The 2.5-carat stone was immediately dubbed not the Star of the South, but the 'Star of Skerring'. Maybe Morelli had been right all along. Based on this evidence, though, he wasn't. Tyler and Morelli were on a plane when Tyler opened a telex with news from the lab. Further testing of the 'Star of Skerring' showed the 2.5-carat 'diamond' had been misidentified. It was in fact a large zircon. Morelli's face fell. 'Morelli nearly had a fit with the news,' Tyler recalled. 'He was absolutely deflated.'

By November 1976, CRA had contributed well over $1 million to the Ashton JV. As a CRA explorer under Tanganyika's management, Hughes ran part of the 1976 field program. According to CRA policy, field geologists were responsible for receiving the analysis of laboratory samples and initiating any follow-up actions. But when checking lab records in Perth, Hughes noticed that a pyrope, reported in July 1975 at a remote site, hadn't been followed up. The site, Mount North

Creek, was near Mount Percy on the Lennard River sheet in the West Kimberley, around 360 kilometres east of Broome.

Pyrope is a deep-red garnet. It's an indicator mineral for diamonds. Hughes decided to go to where the pyrope had been found. Towards the end of 1976, he was at the site with a crew, exploring the creek. They soon found a diamond. The creek flowed over a 'strange-looking depression' that was several hundred metres wide, and in which indicator minerals were so plentiful that they could be seen with the naked eye.

'There was a gentle mound in the middle,' Hughes later recalled, 'and by getting down on your hands and knees, you could see the microscopic crystals of chromite in the sand.' The strange depression was to be named 'Ellendale A' (and subsequently 'Ellendale No. 4'). It was a volcanic pipe. The trail of indicators had led Hughes to the first pipe in what became known as the Ellendale field. This was a real turning point, but there was a problem. 'The chromite was the first thing I found,' Hughes remembered. 'The second was a peg belonging to Mount Isa Mines.'

During exploration, the only way to protect an explorer's rights was to stake out a mineral claim. Part of the Ellendale A pipe was covered by a Mount Isa Mines (MIM) claim. MIM had been prospecting for base metals such as lead and zinc. The Ashton JV now faced a dilemma. The outside world still didn't know Ashton was searching for diamonds. If Tanganyika, as manager, were to peg a claim at Ellendale, it might arouse suspicion. But if CRA pegged the claim, people might assume the company was there for lead or zinc. Accordingly, CRA pegged out some claims on the edge of the pipe, to provide a toehold. The MIM claims on the larger part of the pipe were due to expire during Easter 1977. Ashton had to wait till then before they could start pegging. It was a nerve-racking time for the JV. Absolute secrecy was necessary. Staff weren't even allowed to keep a diary, and the exploration groups maintained a carefully rehearsed veneer of indifference. As soon as the prior claim expired, CRA moved in to peg the whole of the Ellendale 4 pipe on behalf of the JV. The pegging was rapidly completed on Easter Sunday.

All in all, 1976 proved to be an unforgettable year for the Kimberley diamond search. It was a vintage year for finding pipes. February: Pteropus. May: Big Spring. September: Skerring. November: Ellendale. Tyler and CRA's shared commitment to finding pipes was rewarded. This was CRA's first year of funding the diamond search. With such a record of success, they could hardly believe their luck. In the space of twelve months, a venture that had been operating at a smallish scale and with sharp internal conflict was now moving ahead smoothly and at great speed. Mawby and Madigan were pleased and excited. They'd made a smart investment, and resolved to increase their rate of expenditure.

Now that London was largely absolved from finding money for the diamond search, all pressure on Tyler from 'head office' dissolved. It was, however, only a matter of time before his role as manager of the Ashton Joint Venture would come to an end. With the accelerated investment from CRA, the trigger point of $1.6 million in expenditure was soon reached, and this brought forward the changeover date for the JV's management. In January 1977, the role of JV manager moved to CRA, as did the forty-five people formerly on the Tanganyika payroll. Only Tyler and his secretary, Joan Preston, remained in Tanks' Australian branch. CRA asked Tyler to continue as chairman of the Ashton JV. Under the terms of the management handover, he was to remain a full-time employee of Tanganyika in 1977, and then in 1978 he was to be retained on half-salary by Tanganyika, and the rest of the time he would work as a consultant.

The quick wins from the exploration program had other implications, too, as Tyler remembered:

> CRA's instant success led to the belief that diamond exploration was a cinch. There was no understanding of the skill needed to collect a gravel sample. I remember overhearing a young CRA fieldie say, 'Just collect bags of sand in creeks.'

The exploration success, and the management handover, were catalysts for other changes within the JV. As exploration targets were identified and pipes were discovered, the various participants revised their perception of the value of their exploration asset. 'There was no doubt CRA had the bit between their teeth,' Tyler said, 'and their chairman told my chairman, Ronny Medlicott, that they were going to take a ten-year view, and they would ensure that "no possible source is neglected". I believe Medlicott and Morelli panicked as they considered CRA to be "willing and anxious to spend a lot more money than their partners are, and gradually to increase their interest".' This may have been a tactic on CRA's part to shake things up and flush out willing sellers inside the JV. If so, it worked.

Tanks' Medlicott and Sibeka's Morelli visited Australia in October 1976. 'Bruno Morelli still wasn't happy with the switch from alluvials,' Tyler said, 'nor was he keen on the proposal to spend half of the proposed $2.5 million budget for 1977 on regional work, and he must also have been under some other spending constraints.' Sibeka was unhappy about other factors too, including the federal government. When Sibeka looked to the future of its Ashton investment, all it could see was obstacles and, ultimately, failure. Medlicott, too, lacked long-term confidence in Ashton's prospects. And the timing was right for Tanks and Sibeka to realise a profit.

In January 1977, those two companies agreed to sell down their Ashton interests to the newest member of the JV. Specifically, Tanks and Sibeka each offered CRA an 8 per cent stake for $675,000. CRA would therefore spend $1.35 million for an additional 16 per cent of Ashton, in a transaction that would give the newcomer a controlling 51 per cent interest. According to the chairman of Tanks, the British group was 'fed up with Northern Mining', and the proposed deal would 'put control firmly into the hands of CRA'. Tanks and Sibeka didn't consult Tyler on the proposed deal, and nor did they inform Jennings and AO (Australia). The proposal immediately caused a storm within the JV.

Among other things, MENSA man Len Brown of Jennings was instantly aware of a critical defect in the notice of sale. Tyler would later explain the problem: 'Uncontrolled spending was not permitted under the Ashton Joint Venture Agreement, and the sale of an interest required that an offer be made to all parties. These facts seemed to escape Morelli and Medlicott.' Jennings and AO were incensed that

Tanganyika and Sibeka should seek to pass control to CRA without the courtesy of consultation. Both companies claimed their portion of the Tanks and Sibeka holdings. Tyler, too, was deeply disappointed by the Tanks move.

For Jennings, a further transaction would follow. Like the London-based groups, Jennings lacked long-term confidence in Ashton. Having seen Tanganyika and Sibeka reduce their interest, and now knowing CRA was an enthusiastic buyer, it sought to sell its enhanced interest to CRA—at an enhanced price. And waiting in the wings was another eager buyer of Ashton JV shares.

Malaysia Mining Corporation Sdn Bhd (MMC) was a newly created instrumentality of the Malaysian Government. The company had recently acquired the assets of London Tin, and as a result was also the new owner of AO. Initially, that business and the Kalumburu JV were probably not on the radar of what had become the world's largest tin producer, but the Malaysian executives quickly realised the potential value of what they'd acquired. In marked contrast to the prevailing London attitudes, MMC threw its support behind the diamond search project. The corporation would look to acquire any further interests in Ashton as they became available.

14
ELLENDALE

I N 1977, BULK testing of Big Spring 1 and four nearby pipes found diamonds, but only very small ones. The results from the Ellendale field were much more promising. Magnetic surveys, conducted mainly from the air, revealed that Ellendale 4 was an enormous volcanic pipe, around 76 hectares in area. The pipe wasn't outcropping but it stood out as a stark blob in the magnetic survey results. At the time, it was the third-largest known pipe anywhere in the world. And preliminary sampling showed Ellendale 4 was diamondiferous. It contained small diamonds—but it wasn't a kimberlite. The petrographers named it 'olivine lamproite'. This was definitive proof that kimberlites weren't the only source rocks for diamonds. The JV's explorers had done more than find diamonds in a new region: they'd found diamonds in a new type of rock. And things were about to get a whole lot more interesting.

'Hopes were raised even further', Tyler said, 'when Frank Hughes picked up a 1.76-carat diamond that was just lying on the surface.' That was on Ellendale 9, some 10 kilometres to the west of Ellendale 4. Hughes was mapping the pipe when he saw the gem lying on the ground in a sandy gutter. As he was walking by, the diamond gleamed in the moonlight. This was an extremely improbable find, given the rarity, even in diamondiferous areas, of stones that weren't bonded to the surrounding soils. 'Hughes was so surprised at how brightly it shone that he threw it several metres away and discovered it glittered enough to be easily sighted again.' CRA later gave Hughes this diamond as a memento.

The team set about gathering geophysical data. A total of 5500 square kilometres were surveyed from the air, and more than seventy volcanic vents were identified across the Ellendale field and nearby Calwynyardah. At Ellendale alone, more than forty lamproite pipes were identified, several of them measuring in the tens of hectares. In light of these finds, the JV turned its attention—and its money— towards intensively staking the pipes and assessing them, through bulk sampling, for diamond content.

'Once all the pipes were under mineral title,' Tyler said, 'we made a major investment in a 25-tonne-per-hour heavy media separation plant.' In August 1978, the plant was commissioned at a central location in the Ellendale field. All the major Ellendale pipes were trenched, and the most significant ones were sample drilled. When the plant processed the bulk samples, it soon became apparent that several of the pipes were significantly diamondiferous. Tyler followed closely the sampling results that came in on a weekly basis from the plant site. 'We would receive weekly telexes with all the figures,' he said. 'The tonnes of ore from each body treated. The number of stones, their carat weight and a listing of stones over 0.5 carats. It was very exciting. Some 92,000 diamonds were recovered from 230,000 tonnes of lamproite. Many pipes contained diamonds but Ellendale 4 and 9 were by far the richest. They yielded lustrous, well-shaped stones, often of good size.'

As the results came in via telex, they would be faxed to the JV partners using jokey code words taken from cricket, such as 'Bowler' and 'Silly mid-on'. Rees Towie was ecstatic. His office, around the corner from St Kilda Road in Melbourne, was in a round-windowed, multi-storey building that everyone at Ashton called 'the mouse house'. Late at night, Towie would respond with his own faxes that were laden with good-humoured obscenities.

Apart from being of great interest to the partners, the Ellendale results attracted the attention of specialist diamond thieves from

South Africa. West Australian police told CRA that known criminals were showing up in the Kimberleys under the pretence of looking for work with the JV as drillers and operators, but actually looking to steal diamonds. Some of them even secured work, albeit briefly, manning the drill rigs, and they scrutinised the drilled materials closely.

On 24 August 1978, almost five years to the day from when the JV's first diamond was discovered in sample M109, Tyler wrote to Bruno Morelli: 'I believe we can now say without fear of contradiction, that we have discovered a diamond field of international significance which could rival South Africa.' That same year, CRA's Russ Madigan visited the London office of the great diamond dealer Sir Philip Oppenheimer, brother of businessman and philanthropist Harry Oppenheimer. Most people in the diamond industry doubted Australia could ever be a source of high-quality stones to any significant extent. Oppenheimer was reluctant to meet Madigan, and when the meeting went ahead he was dismissive about Australia. That's when Madigan pulled out a calico bag and up-ended it. Magnificent Kimberley diamonds streamed out over the dealer's desk. 'Sir Philip nearly fell over,' Madigan later reported.

With encounters such as that one, and with all the activity in the field, secrecy was becoming impossible. Word began to spread and people began to get excited. 'Everyone knew', Tyler said, 'that the Ashton Joint Venture was evaluating Australia's first diamond field.' (Independent mineral hunter Graeme Hutton was one of the people who heard rumours that the JV had found something big. Hutton scouted Ellendale, saw the telltale signs of large-scale fieldwork, and at once start pegging nearby. 'We literally pegged sheep stations and cattle stations,' he said, 'throughout the west and into the east Kimberley.') On Australia's share market there was rising excitement about diamonds. In fact, in 1977 and 1978 the Ellendale discoveries fed a diamond mania.

The JV partners had been right to worry about publicity and the 'boom tendency' of Australia's mining sector. The stock-market excitement drove the share prices of diamond-exploration hopefuls to unrealistic levels. A swarm of exploration companies descended on the

Kimberleys. Across the region, dozens of speculators started pegging, even on country that had only meagre prospectivity. A hundred years after South Africa's first diamond rush, and more than 125 years after the Australian gold rush, the southern continent had its own diamond rush.

Alan Jones went to Malaysia to meet the new owners of AO (Australia). They were still resolute in their support for the venture, and continued to acquire equity in the Ashton JV whenever they could. By the end of 1978, they'd accumulated a 29 per cent interest. Northern Mining was still in the picture too, and it was the only participant in the JV that was listed on the Australian share market. Northern's share price had jumped thanks to Ellendale, and this provided a helpful indicator of the value of MMC's stake in Ashton.

With that value in mind, Jones convinced the Malaysians to offer a slice of Ashton to the Australian public. He told the MMC executives that while the exploration at Ellendale looked encouraging, it carried with it the prospect that the expenditure budgets were likely to increase dramatically. Under his proposal, MMC would carve out its interests into an ASX-listed company that, when floated, would realise enough cash to fund the Malaysians' share of the diamond exploration costs for the next three or four years, without ceding control.

Jones had discussed this idea with Laurie Cox of blue-ribbon stockbrokers Potter Partners. Cox believed Potters could underwrite a share issue that raised between $12 million and $14 million, and still allow the Malaysians to retain over 50 per cent of the new entity. Apart from raising money, such an offering would help meet the Australian Government's desire for increased Australian participation in mining projects. And should MMC wish to liquidate its Australian asset, it could readily dispose of its shares on the stock market. A positive for Jones was that if the Malaysians chose to sell out in such a way, there was a good chance the existing management team would be left in place, and he and his colleagues would therefore keep their jobs. The proposal also won the support of CRA. Listing the new entity on the stock market would give another market assessment (perhaps a more reliable one) of the Ashton JV's value, and hence CRA's share of it. The float proposal could be a win for all concerned.

With the assistance of Potter Partners, the Malaysians therefore created 'Ashton Mining' (the label was chosen to capitalise on the Ashton Joint Venture name) and prepared to place 40 per cent of the new entity on the Australian stock market. The entity owned most of MMC's share of the JV, along with some other assets. Diamond specialist Robin Baxter Brown was enthusiastic about Ellendale and Ashton. He wrote a 'Consulting Geologist's Report' for the Ashton Mining prospectus that set out his observations on the new entity, its prospects, and the geological and structural similarities between the diamond-producing areas of Africa, Australia and Siberia. Baxter Brown spoke glowingly of the 'technical skill and dedication' of the Ashton Mining team, and he assessed the size of Ellendale's pipes as 'comparable … to the best and largest pipes in South Africa'.

Jones set about building the new company. He revealed a talent for bringing together the right people and keeping them engaged and even inspired. For Ashton Mining, one of those people was Bill Leslie. A lawyer and accountant by training, and the inaugural chair and co-founder of the Australian Mining Petroleum Law Association (AMPLA), Leslie was an expert on corporate structures, and especially on joint ventures and partnerships. He'd advised some of the largest names in Australian mining and manufacturing, including BHP, Alcoa and Elders. As the principal mining industry partner at the law firm Blake Dawson (now Ashurst Australia), Leslie had been advising the diamond hunters. Now, he left Blake Dawson to become a member of the Ashton Mining board and of the company's executive committee. Tyler joined the Ashton Mining team, too, as technical consultant, and continued to chair the Ashton JV's policy committee, which was effectively the JV's board.

The Ashton Mining NL prospectus was issued on 26 September 1978 and the company was listed in December by issuing 28 million shares at 50 cents each, to raise $14 million. In this way, Australia's retail investors were invited to participate in the burgeoning Australian diamond industry. (A member of the FIRB was so impressed by the Ashton Mining story that he asked Jones to secure a parcel of shares for him in the IPO.) The Malaysians retained a 60 per cent interest in Ashton Mining, which in turn held 22.4 per cent of the Ashton JV.

Hence, based on the underwritten float price, the whole of the Ashton JV was valued at $156 million. The actual market value was substantially higher than that, because the shares were immediately trading at a spectacular 214 per cent premium to the issue price. The market's valuation of Ashton Mining implied a total value for the Ashton JV of $491 million, somewhat more than the initial investment of $100,000 in 1969.

(On the recommendation of Potter Partners, Ashton Mining was first incorporated as 'Ashton Mining NL', a 'no liability' company. The stockbrokers predicted a benefit of the 'no liability' status over an ordinary limited company: if Ashton Mining decided to issue new shares that were partly paid, then the shareholders would not be liable to pay a call on their shares but could simply forfeit them—a realistic option for speculative mining businesses whose market prices sometimes fell precipitously, such as when the venture turned out to be a dud, or when the principals ran away with the money. But Ashton Mining never had to resort to issuing partly paid shares, so it soon changed its status to a conventional limited company. That status was more appealing to conservative lenders and other project financiers. The scary-sounding, Poseidon-recalling 'NL' suffix was dropped and the company became 'Ashton Mining Limited'.)

For Tyler, there was a lot to be pleased about. In particular, the end of blanket confidentiality was a relief. 'At last we could talk about what we'd been doing for the previous ten years,' he said. Ashton Mining quickly became a stock-market darling. More than once, the market excitement reached fever pitch. This was not, however, a time for popping the champagne.

◈

In the economics of mining, yield makes all the difference. How many diamonds are in a given unit of ore? Rock is a terrible feedstock. It is uncooperative and unforgiving. Best to handle as little of it as possible. And at Ellendale there was a lot of rock—millions of tonnes of it. Would digging it up and breaking it apart be worth the effort?

Bulk sampling of ore (removed by trenching and by large-diameter drilling at Ellendale pipes 4, 7, 9 and 11) extended into the first half of 1979. The earlier discoveries had heightened expectations of the JV's activities, but from now on the Ellendale news would be bad. In the diamond field of more than forty pipes, only two of them (Ellendale 4 and 9) were shown to be significant sources of diamonds. And in those two pipes, the diamonds were handsome—Pipe 9 produced superb yellow fancy diamonds, much sought after by collectors—but the yield per tonne of rock wasn't. Despite what the explorers had hoped and wished, the prospects of profitable operation of a diamond mine on the Ellendale field were starting to look doubtful.

In the middle of 1979, the JV participants were confronted with a difficult truth. The results were in: there was insufficient value in a tonne of rock to justify the cost of recovering the precious gems. Despite the early optimism, mining at Ellendale would not be economic—at least not on the scale needed and anticipated by Ashton Mining and CRA. For the JV, Ellendale was an important milestone—it proved to the world that Australia could be a source of valuable diamonds—but it would never be a diamond bonanza. 'The diamonds were beautiful,' Tyler said, 'but there just weren't enough stones in any of the pipes to justify a major mining operation.'

To say this was a difficult time for Ashton Mining is an understatement. Following Jones's advice, the Malaysians had raised capital from the public on the basis of the Ellendale finds. But the field was turning out to be a bust, just like the Joris search for the elusive Copeton source three decades earlier. The diamond hunters had staked their reputations on the Kimberley search, and many other people had staked their money on it. 'By the middle of 1979,' Tyler said, 'things were starting to look gloomy.' Maybe the idea of finding a mineable pipe was a pipedream after all.

15

THE JEWEL BOX

AFTER THE DISAPPOINTMENT of Ellendale, the Ashton JV could easily have fallen apart. One or more partners could have changed course or pulled out. But they didn't. The partners continued on with their diamond search, including from an office and depot at Derby in the West Kimberley. In the regional exploration program, the JV had identified interesting targets at the other end of the Kimberleys, east of what is now the Great Northern Highway. (The 1978 Ashton Mining prospectus mentioned those targets.) In 1977, for example, kimberlite dykes had been discovered in the East Kimberley. But the JV hadn't yet gathered samples from there. Ewen Tyler later explained the thinking behind that strategy:

> For reasons of sample complexity, we had tried to do the easy part first, and we had avoided the eastern part of the Kimberleys adjacent to the Northern Territory border. We left what is called the Halls Creek Mobile Zone until almost last. We had known we had to move eastwards, because as early as 1974 we had identified the Wilson River as a kimberlite district.

In 1979, one of the JV's field crews would venture east of the Great Northern Highway.

Maureen Muggeridge had recently married another experienced geologist, John Towie, son of none other than Rees Towie. Soon after their marriage, husband and wife went back out into the field for the Ashton JV. Using helicopters to get into the valleys, they now sampled some of the watercourses in the East Kimberley between Halls Creek and Kununurra. At the time, Maureen was six months pregnant with their first child. It would later be claimed that the Ashton JV tricked rival prospectors by spreading the word that Maureen had gone on maternity leave, when in fact she was searching remote creeks with John.

Even by the standards of the Kimberleys as a whole, the East Kimberley is a mysterious, dreamlike place, rich with wonder and significance. It is a zone of extremes. Periods of little or no rainfall are broken by drenching falls. Time weighs heavily on the landscape. Some of the world's most ancient stone tools have been found near there, as well as some of the oldest rock art. The region's ubiquitous boab trees make the best of the climatic excesses by storing water in their swollen trunks. The oldest living Kimberley boabs date from the time of Christ. The Ragged Range and Purnululu National Park feature striking stone pillars that evoke the Moai of Easter Island or the columns of Luxor on the Nile. The oldest Kimberley rocks are more than a billion years old. The famous striped 'beehive' domes of the Bungle Bungle Ranges are comparative youngsters, dating from only 350 million years ago. Across the East Kimberley landscape, a spectacular menu of geological features has been laid out: ridges, tors, mesas, plateaus. For geologists, it's a playground and a lolly shop.

Smoke Creek is one of the many Kimberley waterways that drain into Lake Argyle. From sites at 5-kilometre intervals along the creek, Maureen and John collected samples and sent them back to Perth for processing. In August 1979, the lab reported two diamonds from a Smoke Creek sample that the geologists had collected near the junction with Dead Bullock Creek, on Lissadell Station, to the south of Lake Argyle. The sample also contained indicator minerals. Maureen and John were with Frank Hughes at the JV's Derby office when the telex clattered out the news from Perth.

The following day, the machine clattered again. Another sample had produced four stones. And on 30 August, further good news came. Five more diamonds had been found. At the Derby office, Hughes shouted, 'We've done it!' In more than one way, this was a poignant moment: six years earlier, Maureen had collected the legendary sample M109 at Pteropus Creek.

'One diamond was exciting enough,' Maureen later said. But to find this number in a single batch of samples was 'phenomenal'. 'Finding diamonds was no longer a novelty,' Tyler said, 'but the large number of stones meant Smoke Creek could be something very special.' Members of the JV descended on the creek to find out more about what was there. Russ Madigan would briefly become one of the excited diamond hunters. He later described the process:

> The system was that you had a sieve and you would fill it up and go down to the water and jig it up and down and tip a pile of sediment on to the ground, because any diamonds would have sunk to the bottom. The first time I did this the pile was covered in diamonds. And this happened wherever you dug a hole … It was like a jewel box.

The 'jewel box' of upper Smoke Creek featured concentrations of alluvial diamonds rarely found anywhere else on the planet: 10 carats per cubic metre. Some of the discoveries were incredible—ten or fifteen diamonds in each pan—but Warren Atkinson, CRA's head of diamond exploration, said the hunters shouldn't get too excited. The stones were down drainage from a thick Devonian conglomerate further up Smoke Creek, and in all likelihood were old alluvial diamonds being shed from that source. A similar type of conglomerate was well known in Brazil as a secondary source of diamonds.

To learn more about the Smoke Creek finds, the team began the methodical tracing of diamonds along the dry watercourse. A special field visit soon delivered welcome news: the source of the diamonds was above the Devonian outcrop. A continuous trail of diamonds led, high in a spur of the Ragged Range, to an ancient volcano.

On 2 October 1979, Atkinson and Hughes clambered up a steep hill, roughly halfway between Lake Argyle and the Bungle Bungles, to the top of the volcanic pipe. Skinks and dragons skittered across boulders. Kimberley kites circled high in the bright sky. Once at the summit, they knew what they'd found. They recognised outcrops of bedded volcanic breccia and tuff, Chris Smith later said. 'Frank raced down to Ellendale with a piece of the tuff to show me. You could see likely olivine pseudomorphs in it.'

The diamond hunters named the pipe 'AK1'—'Australian Kimberlite 1'—and it was soon being referred to as 'Argyle' after the nearby lake. (Technically, the pipe is olivine lamproite, not kimberlite. Inside the JV, the name 'AK1' was seen as a gentle dig at De Beers, whose own AK1 had recently been discovered, in Botswana. 'They had one,' Tyler explained, 'and now we had one.') There were positive signs that the Argyle pipe would be significantly diamondiferous. 'One of the first things we saw', Atkinson said, 'was a small diamond embedded in an anthill. We saw several of those.' With typical understatement, Hughes said the find was 'Very satisfying, very interesting'.

Volcanic pipes come in different shapes and sizes, and different ages. They didn't all break through the earth's crust at the same time. Some pipes are young in geological terms, some very old, and they look different at the surface depending on their vintage. (Ellendale 4 and 9, two of the world's youngest diamond-bearing pipes, are just 25 million years old.) Some pipes are more or less eroded by wind and water, others more or less obscured by soil and vegetation, and by rocks from other eras. The Argyle volcano is very, very old. Some 1.2 billion years old. And yet despite its age, the geologists could still see hints of the shape of the old crater.

Tyler was delighted. He was also amazed that the pipe hadn't been found before. 'It was outcropping', he said, 'and diamonds were everywhere.' From an exploration perspective it was a perfect location. The site was well drained in two directions, with ideal diamond-trapping media in both drainages: Smoke Creek to the north and Limestone Creek to the south-east. For the Ashton JV, the diamonds of AK1 and the nearby waterways promised to turn things around. But just as there had been at Ellendale, there was a competing title issue at Argyle. A German company, Uranerz, was exploring for uranium. It had a temporary reserve in the vicinity of the pipe and over part of Smoke Creek.

The Germans hadn't been exploring for some time and were unlikely to renew their tenement, which was due to lapse in September. 'It was like Ellendale all over again,' Tyler said. 'We were not able to secure under mineral title all the ground we wanted. Uranerz had a temporary reserve to the north and west of the pipe, and we had to wait until October of 1979, almost ten years to the day from Tanganyika's first diamond report, before they went away and we were able to apply for the ground we wanted.'

The JV's people waited under total secrecy until the German group's temporary reserve expired. In case radio transmissions were overheard, conversations between the ground crews and helicopters were restricted to only the most routine matters. To confuse anyone who might be watching, helicopters were sent off in random patterns and on phantom missions so the chopper traffic wouldn't point to Smoke Creek and AK1. To further confound the efforts of spies and rivals, the diamond searchers hired equipment and sent it off in bogus directions. Hughes booked every available helicopter and every four-wheel-drive vehicle in the region. All the rental vehicles from nearby Kununurra were driven to the CRA yard there. From local suppliers, Hughes bought up all the maps of the area. In Perth the JV's staff did the same, snapping up all the relevant maps at the state Lands Department.

Despite all these precautions, there was alarm when a semitrailer arrived on site full of pegs. Such a supply of pegs would be necessary if the JV was to secure an area the size of the Argyle prospects. But the truck posed a serious hazard. 'If this had been seen by a competing company,' Tyler said, 'the implications would have been obvious. A major discovery had been made.' (Explorers from De Beers had been in the area, and more than once they'd flown right over the Argyle pipe. They'd even camped at lower Smoke Creek.) Quickly the truck was driven under trees, and the field staff added more camouflage so any passing choppers and low-flying fixed-wing aircraft couldn't see the telltale load of pegs.

The final stage of Operation Argyle took place in the dead of night. On 2 October 1979, within minutes of the Uranerz tenure expiring, dozens of CRA fieldies carried out a carefully orchestrated operation to hammer in pegs with the appropriate notations, and claim the Argyle discovery for the Ashton Joint Venture. The JV applied for its own temporary reserves and covered the whole area with mineral claims. The future of the searchers was again looking bright.

16

JUMPED

IN JULY 1978, Ashton Mining's shares had been issued at 50 cents. With the discovery of Smoke Creek and AK1, the value of the shares skyrocketed. In October 1980, the company made a share placement to raise $10.5 million. At $3 each, the shares in the placement were valued at six times the original float price.

As a result of the recent finds and then the Ashton Mining float and placement, interest in diamonds continued to be intense among miners and explorers, too. Many searchers were in the field—not just those working for Ashton and De Beers—and they applied a variety of techniques and tactics, some of them underhanded or at least opportunistic. Afro-West Mining was a small company that saw a big opportunity at Argyle. Soon after CRA had staked out the pipe on behalf of the Ashton Joint Venture, an Afro-West crew entered the site and pegged over the JV's Argyle claims. In other words, they attempted to jump them.

There was no evidence Afro-West had ever actually explored at or near AK1. One reason why Frank Hughes had bought up all the maps in the area was to avoid 'address pegging'. And yet Afro-West, it seemed, was 'address pegging' with gusto. The overpegging said a lot about the Wild West culture that prevailed in parts of the Australian mining industry. It was old-fashioned cowboy mining at its worst.

The Afro-West tactic was more than a minor irritation. For the JV to do anything at Argyle, they had to have secure title to the deposit. It would be imprudent to go forward and spend real money testing the diamond yields without such title. The JV's participants were certain that natural justice would affirm their undisputed rights. 'In all equity we were the rightful owners,' Ewen Tyler said. 'The partners had worked for ten years to find this promising deposit.' But the claim jumpers were ready for a legal fight. 'Afro-West claimed the CRA miner's right was defective,' Tyler said, 'and they challenged our right and title.'

This may have been merely a stratagem, but, disastrously for the Ashton JV, there was some validity to the Afro-West gambit. Tyler summed up the predicament: 'Partly as a result of an omission by CRA, and partly as a result of a government error in the gazetting of mining regulations, it appeared the miner's right used by CRA at Argyle was in fact defective.' In 1979, the Western Australian Government had made a minor amendment to the *Mining Act*. The Ashton JV had overriding temporary reserves, but sections of the Act concerning such reserves were ambiguous. The upshot was that Ashton's title was suspect. Mining journalist John McIlwraith explained the problem in these terms:

> Appearing in the Warden's Court, CRA's counsel said that after the company first pegged the five claims, it was found that two of them did not satisfy regulations on width and breadth ratios. CRA then pegged them again and lodged written applications for the new claims. The company had a miner's right at all stages and would claim that Afro-West was not a bonafide prospector.

Though the legal position was murky, the leaders of the JV were optimistic of winning if the matter ever went to court. 'It would be utterly unjust', Tyler said, 'if, through some quirk of the law, the original claims were invalid.'

To the Ashton JV members, it soon became clear that there was another way to resolve the pegging dispute. Specifically, it could be resolved by paying $4.7 million. In an especially shadowy episode,

Tyler heard from Russ Madigan who heard from a bloke in a Perth pub that that amount of money 'in an envelope' would settle the issue. Darkening matters still further, Afro-West found an ally in the corrupt West Australian politician Ray O'Connor, who was formerly police minister and would later serve as premier. O'Connor had recently come under suspicion following the execution-style murder of a brothel keeper, Shirley Finn, with whom O'Connor was said to have been in a relationship. He would later be jailed for an unrelated fraud.

Tyler, Madigan and all the other JV partners refused to take the 'money in an envelope' route, as did the premier, Sir Charles Court, who saw through O'Connor and the Afro-West claim. In his political memoir, Court recorded his reaction to the overpegging and the request for money. He also recorded his belief that the Ashton partners were in the right:

> [The JV's mineral claims] were being challenged by a company that hadn't got a chance in hell of developing a project calling for all this expertise and capital, and literally holding the whole project to ransom.
>
> Eventually, when I got to know more intimately the detail of it, I started to find out who these people were and what it was all about. I got a message, amongst many, that there was nothing that $4.7 million wouldn't fix! That didn't amuse me. It was blackmail of the first order. As I said to Cabinet, I was always taught about blackmailers that their first demand is their lowest. They gambled on the fact that CRA would be prepared to pay a large sum to get them out of their hair so there wouldn't be a court case …
>
> When I saw the representatives of these people, I just had to tell them, 'You understand that if anyone was stupid enough to meet your demands, as soon as you were out of the way, your mates would come along with a similar demand, only bigger. So the answer is no.'

To defend their rights, the Ashton JV partners decided to go to court.

◈

In September 1980, the Ashton JV received from the Western Australian Government permission to undertake further evaluation work at Argyle. In parallel with that work, Ashton spent almost two years litigating its rights at Argyle, but there was no legal end in sight. 'The title issue was dragging on,' Tyler said, 'and it seemed its passage through the West Australian courts might end up with an appeal to the Privy Council in London.' None of the JV participants liked the idea of fighting the case all the way to that distant forum. Such a legal battle would be expensive in money and, perhaps more importantly, time. 'It could've deferred development for years,' Tyler said. For some members of the JV, such a delay posed an existential threat. The peril was greatest for the newly listed entity, Ashton Mining Limited. Properly testing the Argyle deposit was proving to be costly. Money was already rushing out the door, and there was a very real prospect that Ashton Mining would go broke if it had to wait for the legal process to play itself out.

Tyler and Len Brown were friends with Ian Warner, a senior partner with law firm Jackson McDonald. Politically connected and prominent in the West Australian Liberal Party, Warner had done pioneering work in mining law. In a conversation with Tyler and Brown, he suggested a legal circuit-breaker. The Western Australian Government might be prepared to pass legislation that would affirm once and for all the validity of the JV's claim at Argyle. Tyler agreed this was worth a try: he viewed Premier Court as a valuable friend and ally. Court had been the first political figure to learn of the contents of M109, and since that time he'd followed the JV's progress with interest. As Tyler said, 'Sir Charles had known from the outset the validity of our claim at Argyle, and we had temporary reserves over the whole area. I had taken Sir Charles into my confidence when he was leader of the Opposition in 1973, about the discovery of our first diamond on my birthday.' Since that time, Kalumburu and then Ashton had had a special arrangement with the Court Government with regard to access to land for diamond exploration, as evidenced by the secret map in the safe of the chief geologist.

Warner lived near the premier in a neighbourhood by the Swan River. He and Court were associates through the state Liberal Party, of which Warner was president. Warner was also close friends with Court's sons, with whom he'd grown up. To convince Court to legislate, Warner went to the premier's home. 'We've got this problem,' he explained. 'We might not win at the Supreme Court, but the real Supreme Court is the WA Parliament.'

It would be common sense, he argued, to settle the mining title issue in legislation: specific laws would have to be developed anyway, as a routine matter for any major mineral development. In principle, the Argyle legislation could serve multiple purposes. It could correct any defects in CRA's miner's right. It could establish the basis for fees and taxes such as mineral royalties. And it could create a legal framework for mine security and other practicalities associated with the ultimate construction and operation of a diamond mine. 'We were going to need a state agreement and we were going to require special diamond security legislation,' Tyler said. 'The question was, could the government get it all in a package of legislation that the state parliament would pass?'

Sir Charles Court was a complex and cultured man. In World War II he'd served with distinction, rising to the rank of lieutenant colonel. Before the war, he'd been a champion cornet player. (This musical background helps explain his 'Vamp in G' comment.) In government he applied a practical, no-nonsense approach. 'He had a can-do reputation,' Tyler said. 'He knew about making decisions.' After considering Warner's proposal, Court's government agreed to enact special legislation and to negotiate a complementary state agreement. The decision to legislate to establish secure mining title was a first in Australia.

The JV partners had reason to feel grateful. But the agreement needed to be thrashed out, and the government's negotiating team— including Court himself and the minister for mines, Peter Jones—took an aggressive line. 'The pressing need for secure title was a strong bargaining chip for Sir Charles,' Tyler said. The Ashton JV, moreover, went into the negotiation from a position of weakness. In statements to the media, Rees Towie had created high expectations about the buried treasure at Argyle, and therefore the extent to which the state might share in the bounty. For Tyler, this caused no end of trouble:

Rees continued his great performances at Ashton JV meetings. He discovered that De Beers' Harry Oppenheimer and I had both been directors of Kansanshi Copper Mining Company in Zambia. After that he was obsessed with De Beers. He became convinced that I was a De Beers plant! This did the Ashton Joint Venture, including Northern, a great disservice when he talked up, using Albert Joris [son of Jules Joris], the value of the Argyle product. This put information into the political arena that meant Argyle had a perceived value far greater than reality.

Towie's tactics eroded Ashton's position in the government negotiations. 'Because of the expectation of diamond values built up by Northern,' Tyler said, 'the Western Australian Government thought the joint venture was sitting on a bonanza. Northern found an Australian diamond valuer [Albert Joris] who could produce values well in excess of what we believed to be the appropriate prices. This led to more tension, more cost and a higher expectation of the worth of the deposit in the minds of the public and governments. What had been our secret affairs were now becoming major public issues.'

When the negotiations came to an end—they were completed in record time—the results were far from satisfactory for the JV, as Tyler explained:

> The media had taken up the issue of the value of Argyle diamonds, and it was widely believed that the diamonds were of much greater value than the official reports of the Joint Venture indicated. When the government came to set the base royalty, an FOB royalty rate of 7½ per cent was established on the basis that the project could well support such a rate. It was said that the rate could not be less than that charged to the iron ore industry, an industry well established.

The new and hypothetical diamond industry was being treated like the tried and true iron ore industry, only worse. In addition to the base royalty, the Ashton JV had to agree to share future profits with the state. Tyler described that requirement as 'the sequestration of a major part of the Joint Venture's assets'. Effectively, Tyler reflected, the state of Western Australia would now have a significant share in the proposed diamond mine:

> The profit-related royalty was set at the extremely high rate of 22½ per cent, for an industry which had yet to produce one carat of diamonds from a commercial operation. The government was giving itself a 22½ per cent interest in the deposit.

Apart from the high royalty, the state agreement established the obligation to create a diamond cutting and polishing operation in Western Australia. The government didn't want the diamonds to be simply dug up and sent out of the state. They wanted to build a local diamond processing industry, just as they'd previously done with the iron ore industry. This would later prove to be a major headache for the JV participants, as would the 'transitional arrangements' that included the construction of a mine town at Argyle. 'We paid dearly', Tyler said, 'for the lack of secure title, in the form of a very high royalty and also a township requirement.' Most galling for the partners, this high price had been caused by a defect in the government's own legislation—and it had been exacerbated by the efforts of one of the JV's own participants.

Rhetorically, the Western Australian Government welcomed private investment, but Tyler saw Court's hard line in the negotiations as counterproductive, a perverse response to what the JV was trying to build in the Kimberleys. The government, Tyler said, was 'milking the cow before it was born'. But the JV was prepared to live with the legislation and the agreement. Securing title was paramount. 'We were smarting about some of the burdens imposed upon us,' Tyler said, 'but we had title to our deposits, and the expectation that our venture would make a profit for the Joint Venturers and the government alike.' The negotiations left the Ashton participants feeling bruised but relieved.

In November 1981, the West Australian parliament passed the *Diamond (Ashton Joint Venture) Agreement Act 1981*. (The parts of the state agreement requiring legislative force were reflected in the

Act, which also amended the West Australian *Crimes Act*.) As a consequence of the Act's passing, mineral title was finally awarded to the Ashton JV. 'We brought in a special bill', Court said, 'which had special conditions in it so far as the title and the responsibilities and the role of Argyle Diamonds were concerned.' Parliament's deliberations on the legislation took about three hours. During this time, Tyler sat alone in a position of honour in the Speaker's gallery, as the guest of Minister Peter Jones—and as the son-in-law of Arthur Watts. He felt a sense of history, and not a small amount of trepidation.

Largely crafted by Eric Freeman of the West Australian Crown Law Department, the legislation was an extraordinary piece of legal drafting. It extinguished utterly, emphatically and repetitively the opportunistic claims of Afro-West, and contained several features that were unprecedented in Australia. Managing a diamond mine requires special security provisions. The new legislation established exceptional quasi-police powers for Argyle, including powers to stop and search people and vehicles. (Nineteenth-century diamond miners had had even stronger powers. Under a royal charter from Queen Victoria, Cecil Rhodes' British South Africa Company was permitted to create a police force, launch military expeditions, occupy territory and establish diplomatic relations with other states.)

As the architect of the legislative solution, Warner was accused of 'usurping' the power of the Supreme Court. 'That's exactly what we did,' he later said, 'and it was appropriate.' Once the legal work was done, Warner confided in Len Brown about the lawyer's fee. What, Warner asked, should he charge? 'You can charge anything for this,' Brown said. Thus reassured, Warner settled on what he thought was an outrageous figure. Outrageous or not, it was paid right away. He'd given the JV something that was invaluable. Now that the mineral title issue was resolved, the Ashton Joint Venture could set about determining exactly what the Argyle deposit contained, and what the partners might actually do with the diamonds there.

17

A MAJOR FORCE

Throughout the exploration program, the Kalumburu and Ashton crews had seen De Beers choppers in the air and on the ground, and had suspected the global syndicate of following the local diamond searchers around. In the early stages of field testing of gravel samples, the Australians had parked a 5-tonne-per-hour dense media separator (DMS) at Wyndham while preparing to embark on a 1700-kilometre trip to the King George River area. The DMS was a distinctive piece of equipment and, for a geologist, a readily identifiable one. According to diamond exploration consultant Nick Norman, the equipment was indeed noticed:

> It is probably no coincidence that there happened to be a De Beers geologist in Wyndham at the same time. He trailed the DMS for two weeks; this took him to Kalumburu. Chris Smith, camped nearby, got a message that the De Beers man wanted to come and talk to him. Not surprisingly he made it abundantly clear over the radio that visitors were not welcome, and the geologist left. The Kalumburu JV's cover had been blown.

Soon after the Argyle discovery was announced, De Beers geologists wanted to visit AK1. As a matter of industry courtesy, the Ashton

people let them come and have a look. There was no airstrip at the
site, so the visitors had to fly in by helicopter from Kununurra. Once
there, the De Beers people crawled all over the pipe they'd narrowly
missed discovering. One of the visiting geologists picked up a large
lump of lamproite. He rolled it around in his hands and examined
it with fascination. For the rest of the day he carried the heavy rock
around the site. Then, just as he was about to board the helicopter
and depart, an Ashton JV representative told him he had to leave
the rock behind.

To establish the actual diamond content at Argyle and the real
value of the diamonds there, the Ashton JV embarked on a major
evaluation of AK1. Were the first discoveries indicative of the deposit
as a whole? Did the pipe contain diamonds all the way down?
At what grade? And at what quality? Would it be worthwhile digging
the diamonds up? And what revenues could the miners expect if
they did so?

To answer these questions, CRA cut long surface trenches and sank
large-diameter (200-millimetre) drill-holes at 50-metre intervals in
a grid pattern across the pipe. Unlike the sampling of creeks, which
could take place only during the dry season, the drill-testing of the
Argyle pipe went on throughout the year. That meant drilling in
high heat and high humidity, and sometimes between downpours
of heavy rain. The 20-centimetre-diameter holes, producing cores
that were 20 metres long, were giant compared to what was normal
practice elsewhere. Every length of drilled core produced 1.5 tonnes
of potentially diamondiferous material. The drilling was carried out
to a depth of 80 metres, which corresponded to four lengths of core.
Overall, the pipe was thoroughly probed and scraped and gouged. In
the entire history of mining, few large deposits had been scrutinised
so extensively.

The Ashton geologists carefully studied the sparkling cores and
associated geological data. The first news from the drilling was
reassuring: the diamond yield was more or less consistent from top
to bottom. The geologists engaged mathematicians from UWA, who
used the field data to prepare extrapolations and predictions about
the diamond yields. The academic statisticians confirmed with a high

degree of confidence that the whole extent of the pipe structure, as sampled in the drilling, would yield a consistent grade of diamonds. The shape and geology of the Argyle pipe were unusual, there were few precedents for assessing and modelling the sampling figures, and much innovation was involved in arriving at the predicted yield. A lot was riding on the sampling and the analysis. After the disappointment of Ellendale, Argyle would be mined only if there was incontrovertible evidence of commercial yields. The JV participants needed compelling evidence to convince their owners and bankers to stake the project.

To further reassure the participants and their backers, CRA sank half-a-dozen shafts that were much bigger again: 2.5 metres square. These shafts, reaching depths of between 60 and 80 metres, produced 9 to 10 tonnes of material per metre of shaft extracted. And they continued to yield a very satisfactory grade and size-distribution of diamonds. To get a second opinion on the sample analysis, the Ashton JV engaged a group of geo-statistical experts. They and others agreed that Ashton's statistical modelling was the only way to properly attack the problem of understanding the pipe's value—and they agreed that the statistical results were highly accurate.

A clear picture of the Argyle deposit began to emerge. A 3D image of the pipe looked like a giant tooth, or the figure of a ghostly man. The large, deep-reaching pipe contained more than 100 million tonnes of ore, at an exceptionally high grade. 'Proven and probable' reserves were estimated to be 60 million tonnes with a grade of 6.8 carats of diamonds per tonne, plus 14 million tonnes at 6.1 carats a tonne. Based on these figures, it seemed that the project would be able to support an operation mining 3 million tonnes of material a year, giving the mine a life of twenty years or more. These were extraordinary numbers. At most diamond mines, grades were measured in carats per hundred tonnes. At Argyle, the measurements were in carats per tonne. The richness of the deposit was unprecedented.

After still further testing, the grade of around 6 carats to the tonne was confirmed down to a depth of 150 metres. This was encouraging, but there was a catch. Though the yields were high, the average values were low. 'It was obvious at the outset that we had an extremely rich deposit,' Ewen Tyler said, 'but it was equally obvious that the diamonds were not of top quality.' The profile of diamond types was 55 per cent industrial quality, 40 per cent cheap gem, and only 5 per cent gem-quality diamonds. Based on the high proportion of industrial diamonds, the average estimated value of the Argyle stones was around US$6.50 per carat, compared to a typical international value of US$60 per carat.

The potential output at Argyle was up to 25 million carats per year. That was three times the amount of diamonds coming out of South Africa, and more than double the amount from the Soviet Union, which was then easily the world's largest producer. The total value of the diamonds at Argyle was estimated to be more than US$3 billion. In 1981, the *New York Times* announced that Australia was about to become a major force in the world diamond business.

For that prediction to come true, however, there were still important steps to be taken and significant challenges to be overcome. The Ashton JV partners needed to raise the money to fund the necessary investment at Argyle. They had to maintain good relations with their Indigenous hosts and neighbours at Glen Hill, Doon Doon and Turkey Creek. They had to select and train a local workforce with expertise in diamond mining and classification. They had to make arrangements to sell the recovered and sorted gems. They had to keep the state and federal governments onside. They had to keep their own sometimes fractious and precarious partnership together. And they had to convince the diamond world, and ultimately consumers, of the quality and reality of Australian diamonds.

18

DISTRIBUTION IS EVERYTHING

M INING THE DIAMONDS at Argyle was going to be expensive. The estimated total cost was somewhere north of $300 million, a high figure for a mining development that was deeply speculative. Each of the JV partners resolved to borrow money to fund the mine. But before they could start talking to banks, the participants needed to answer a big question. They had confidence about the diamond yield: the pipe was certainly rich with stones. But would they be able to sell them once the stones were extracted? International banks, the partners knew, would be prepared to finance the mine only if there was some assurance that the goods were marketable, and that they would in fact find markets.

In the words of Russ Madigan, 'Selling the product is always the key to a successful mine, however excited the miners might get about finding it'. Selling bulk minerals is straightforward, as is selling gold. For bulk commodities and precious metals, there are well-established markets and well-known prices. But diamonds are different. Ashton Mining director Bill Leslie described the problem:

Neither CRA nor Ashton Mining had any experience in selling diamonds. They did, however, have a lot of experience in selling minerals where prices, demand and forecasts were readily available, whether it was on the London Metal Exchange, Chicago or elsewhere, and there were Japanese, Chinese and other coal and iron ore buyers only too keen to offer prices and contracts. But with diamonds, there was none of that, only a black box called the CSO and its buying arm the DTC that bought at least 80 per cent of all diamonds mined.

The 'CSO' was the Central Selling Organization, the 'DTC' the Diamond Trading Company. Both entities were part of the De Beers–Anglo American empire. Together, they controlled the great majority of the worldwide diamond industry. (The De Beers–Anglo American group also had substantial interests in coal, copper and gold production.) These pillars of the diamond market dated back to the great discoveries of nineteenth-century South Africa, and they served a very specific purpose. The first big discoveries had posed a real danger that the worldwide value of diamonds would crash. When Cecil Rhodes gained control of the diamond fields at and around Kimberley, he quickly moved to stabilise the prices paid for stones by managing supply and demand.

Under Rhodes' leadership, the producers and sellers agreed to cooperate to maintain the price of gem-quality diamonds at luxury levels. From 1893, the Diamond Syndicate he founded became an established feature of the trade. Thereafter, De Beers and its offshoots exerted tight control over the diamond market. Control of the market succeeded in keeping prices as stable as possible. That stability suited all concerned: governments, producers, merchants, retailers— even, it was claimed, customers. As De Beers chairman Harry Oppenheimer later said to Leslie 'over a drink in the long room at the Australian Club':

Who loses? The producer is happy because he knows he has stable prices, the dealers because they know the value of their stocks will not diminish, governments because they can rely on the taxes they collect, and the fiancé because he has the confidence that the value of the ring he has just purchased will not go down the minute he walks out of the shop.

Though diamond prices were generally stable, there were slumps from time to time, such as when new deposits of diamonds were found or when global economic growth slowed. During the Great Depression, demand for diamonds plummeted and De Beers struggled to sell enough gems to cover its operating costs. Production was halted and Kimberley became, for a time, a ghost town. De Beers reportedly hoarded 10 million carats of unsaleable diamonds—in milk cans.

The CSO set London prices for more than 1000 qualities of rough diamond. It operated through a network of tied agents. Affiliates of the CSO sorted diamonds into gem-quality and industrial grades, and then the gem-quality stones were offered on an unforgiving 'take it or leave it' basis in special showings that were called 'sights'. Diamond historian Eric Burton described how this worked:

> The buyer states the quantities, shapes and sizes he requires. He is given the full range of goods but cannot make his own selections … If a buyer does not want the full range of goods, he still has to buy the whole parcel. He will then have to sell subsequently, if he can, the stones he does not want.

One De Beers man referred to this process as 'feeding the ducks': 'The ducks come paddling over and you throw them the bread and they eat what you throw.'

In 1981, the great majority of the world's gem-quality diamonds passed through this system. During slumps in demand, the CSO defended prices, such as by stockpiling gems, applying sales quotas and even standing in the market as a buyer. When diamonds were sold, the CSO retained a share of the revenue, ostensibly to cover handling and marketing. These facts were widely known, but the finer details of the diamond market, and how the CSO operated, were mysterious. The CSO was beholden to no-one except De Beers. It wasn't required to report its diamond sales or stocks, and it guarded its secrets closely.

From talking to the Sibeka people, Ewen Tyler had a general idea of the workings of the diamond market and how rough diamonds were valued. Since that time, the Ellendale diamonds had provided the

Ashton Joint Venture with further precious insights into the valuation process, and into aspects of how De Beers handled the buying and selling of diamonds. Tyler knew that in the diamond market, distribution was everything. Decades before, at Copeton in New South Wales, there had been intense difficulties in finding a market for the 'Can-ni-faire' stones. Now, the Ashton JV only had a business if it could sell the diamonds, and if it could sell them well.

All diamond miners faced that challenge, but at Argyle the hurdles were especially high. If the Australian diamonds were to be mined, the JV would need to sell them on such a scale that there could be a major impact on the world price. The *New York Times* reported that 'with its anticipated production, Australia could dominate the market. The world production in 1980 was about 40 million carats, or 10 tons of diamonds, valued at $4 billion. If the Ashton mines are as rich as some think, the site could produce 40 million carats a year.' The fear at Ashton, as well as at De Beers, was that introducing tens of millions of carats into the delicate diamond market could cause a long slump. Australian diamonds could be victims of their own success.

To better understand the market, the Ashton JV engaged top-tier strategy firm the Boston Consulting Group. BCG would analyse the market and its submarkets for industrial diamonds, cheap gems and high-quality gems, including high-value fancy gems such as pink, purple, blue and canary-yellow ones. The consultants would then prepare a report that the JV could use for planning and to support discussions with potential financiers.

In principle, there were several potential ways to sell the Argyle diamonds. The JV partners could sell the gems through the CSO, just as most other producers did. Or they could market their diamonds via the less developed and possibly more volatile Indian industry, perhaps under a semi-formal and multilateral arrangement. Or they could 'go it alone' and market all of Argyle's production directly. BCG would study each of these options in detail, and the JV partners would read the consultants' report with great interest.

Within and around the JV, there was much deliberation on the sale options. Mumbai merchants strongly supported and petitioned for the Indian route. India's cutting and polishing industry went so far as to send a delegation, with Indian Government representatives, to Australia to try to persuade the federal government to insist that Argyle's diamonds be sold directly to the Mumbai industry. Perhaps an Indian Government trading organisation could buy most or all of Argyle's production for resale to Mumbai and Surat cutters and polishers.

The case for India was certainly credible. That country had a long tradition in diamonds: alluvial diamonds had been gathered in Hyderabad as early as the fourth century BCE. Some people argued that the Ashton team would reap higher returns under the Indian option compared to dealing with the CSO. Overall, the feeling in the team was that the Indians had the best intentions and their option might work, but that market realities could easily swamp the good intentions. One fear, for example, was that the Indian buyers could establish a new cartel that stripped market power from the miners. Also, the subcontinental option had a crucial defect: the Indian Government refused to guarantee a floor price for the Argyle diamonds. Without that, the JV partners decided the risk was too high. And moreover, there were tactical reasons for not pursuing this option too far. The JV members were wary of passing a 'point of no return': if they went a long way down the Indian route as an alternative to dealing with De Beers, could the Australians then turn around and decide to go with the CSO, or would De Beers say it was too late? For all these reasons, the discussions with the Indians were brought to an end.

There was also little support for the 'no deal' solution of selling all the mine's diamonds directly. That path threatened to bring enormous practical problems for the JV partners. The partners had no in-house valuers, for example, and nor did they have staff who could classify stones and prepare parcels of them for valuation. Overall, the partners' knowledge of the market was decisively limited, and outside the De Beers cartel there were few people upon whom they could call for expertise. All these considerations coalesced into an unavoidable conclusion.

Bill Leslie had learnt something crucial when advising lenders on past projects: he'd seen the importance of counterparty strength in cash-flow financing. 'With a stable cash flow from a blue-chip counterparty,' he said, 'the balance sheet of the borrower was almost irrelevant. In De Beers we had one of the best blue-chip companies in the world.' The whole board of Ashton Mining recognised that their company would be best placed if it chose the CSO route. Otherwise, the diamonds couldn't safely be turned into money, and the banks couldn't be convinced to play along and finance a mine at Argyle. The executives at CRA reached the same conclusion.

In more than one way, the interests of Ashton Mining, CRA and the CSO were aligned. The owners of the Argyle deposit didn't want to undermine the international market for diamonds. They wanted to sell their diamonds as well as they could. Other newcomers had arrived at the same judgement. Even the Russians, in the Soviet era, had contracted for a time with the CSO. In 1959, the Russians had agreed to market their diamonds via De Beers. In the 1960s, the Soviets boycotted apartheid South Africa and the agreement wasn't renewed. That was the public line, but the Russians continued to adopt CSO prices and sell quantities of diamonds via De Beers. Even when they sold diamonds outside the CSO system, there was a degree of coordination, as Leslie explained:

Occasionally [the Russians] would sell a large quantity direct into the market in Europe, probably to meet some urgent foreign exchange requirement, which at times deflated the prices of those classes of goods. If that became a concern, and it had on occasions, representatives from De Beers would visit Moscow and, after one or two nights at the opera and good wine, the Russians would agree to toe the line. The time from that meeting to when the discount selling ceased was usually six months, and the CSO reckoned that that was how long it took for the price maintenance recommendation to go up the bureaucratic line, get approval and come back down again.

The value of diamonds is precarious, as is the overall diamond market. The De Beers business model was all about control—of production, pricing, distribution and marketing. (The De Beers language for this is 'single channel marketing'; economists use words like 'vertical integration', 'monopsony' and 'monopoly'.) The control was sometimes hard, such as through direct ownership; and sometimes soft, such as through the legendary Oppenheimer charm and persuasion. But it was always about control. Miners around the world accepted the business model and the De Beers approach. They saw value in De Beers' efforts to maintain the perception of value and the smooth functioning of the global market. 'Our research,' Leslie said, 'indicated that De Beers, since the days of Rhodes, had been very good at developing the market and marketing diamonds. Better to be with them than against them.'

19

AN ASTONISHING SIGHT

T<small>HE MODERN STORY</small> of diamonds is in large part the story of five Oppenheimers: Bernard, Louis, Ernest, Harry and Nicky. Bernard Oppenheimer was the eldest son of a German cigar merchant. (The family name comes from the German winemaking region of Oppenheim.) Late in the nineteenth century, Bernard went to Kimberley in South Africa for the London-based diamond dealing firm of Dunkelsbuhler (the Oppenheimers and Dunkelsbuhlers were related by marriage). There, he learnt the business and prospered, becoming the firm's chief representative. He witnessed the major turning points in the creation of Cecil Rhodes' diamond empire, including his triumph over his early rival, Barney Barnato; the amalgamation of De Beers and Kimberley Central; and the establishment of the Diamond Syndicate. Bernard was a signatory to the first contract between De Beers and the syndicate.

Bernard's younger brother Louis was also in South Africa, having arrived there in 1886 at the age of sixteen. He studied under Bernard before moving to London to manage Dunkelsbuhlers' head office. According to Oppenheimer biographer Anthony Hocking,

> There he arranged a job for his favourite brother, ten years his junior and fourth in the family hierarchy. Ernest Oppenheimer reached London on May 22 1896. It was his sixteenth birthday.

Ernest soon progressed in the Dunkelsbuhlers hierarchy, and displayed a natural talent for sorting stones. To him, each had a personality of its own: there was a glow in his eyes as he explored it.

In 1902, Dunkelsbuhler sent Ernest to manage the Kimberley office. Journalist and author Emily Hahn records in *Diamond* a story about Ernest's first days in Kimberley:

I recall the day I first saw Ernest. It was in the sorting room where he was working in Kimberley. He had just got to town, and I noticed him immediately; it was a little place and you always did look twice at strangers in those days. It was 1902, and a warm summer day. His sleeves were rolled up and I noticed his arms immediately. I thought I'd never seen such muscular arms on any man ... Well, I asked the man in charge of the office, 'Who's that fellow with the big arms?' and he said it was a new man, Ernest Oppenheimer, who'd just been sent out from London. He said, 'I don't think very much of him from what I've seen so far. He's terribly shy, and he doesn't seem to be very bright.'

On Ernest's advice, the firm soon made a beneficial investment in the newly discovered and extremely rich Premier Mine. His stocks rose quickly, and he became the leading figure in the world diamond market. He founded the Anglo American Corporation of South Africa and engaged the legendary New York financier and bibliophile JP Morgan as his banker. Always courteous and frank, he was respected for his approach to business—and to politics. He represented Kimberley in the South African parliament. Opposition figure John Cope said Ernest seemed to be possessed by a 'strange and impelling form of humility':

It was not an abasing form of humility. Without uttering a word Sir Ernest appeared to say to you: 'Look here, we are just two people interested in a problem. I am only too pleased to help you and I am sure you'd be the last person to let me down.'

His manner conveyed he was not the least concerned whether anybody thought him important or not; that there was no such thing as privilege between equals, and that he was really glad you'd bothered to come along and discuss what you had considered a most important subject with him. He could turn down a request or suggestion as firmly as anyone else. But somehow that refusal was merely a conclusion that flowed inevitably from the logic of his responses.

Ernest was knighted in 1921. In 1958, his son Harry took over as global head of Anglo-American and De Beers. Through subsequent decades, in an industry that regarded itself as exclusive and exceptional, Harry steered the company exceptionally well. As chairman of De Beers Consolidated Mines Ltd and De Beers Centenary AG, he succeeded his father as the pre-eminent figure in the world diamond industry.

Under Harry's leadership, De Beers continued to search for diamonds—including in Australia, where the cartel's search was mostly a failure. When news first came of the scale of the Argyle discoveries, the De Beers camp was sceptical. In 1981 or thereabouts, journalist John McIlwraith was on a plane flying between Ireland and Heathrow. Seated next to a senior De Beers executive, McIlwraith suggested Argyle might produce as many as 24 million carats per year, more than the combined output of all De Beers' mines at that time. The De Beers man smiled indulgently. 'I hardly think so,' he said.

Even when the scale of the deposit sank in, the De Beers camp was dismissive. In conversation with the American *National Jeweler* magazine, a spokesperson for De Beers would later opine, with carefully chosen words, that while the scale of the Australian deposit was indeed impressive, it was important to keep in mind that most of the Argyle diamonds were industrial-grade. General Electric and De Beers, the spokesperson said, were the two leading producers of synthetic diamonds for industrial uses, so space could easily be made for Argyle's stones by adjusting the synthetic output.

Attitudes like that were in the foreground when De Beers entered negotiations with the Argyle partners. Now in his seventies, Harry

Oppenheimer came out of semi-retirement to lead the efforts to broker a deal with the Australians. Day-to-day, the main negotiators for the CSO were Harry's son Nicky, Harry's nephew Anthony, and De Beers executive Tim Capon. Russ Madigan of CRA led the Ashton JV team, which included Alan Jones and Bill Leslie from Ashton Mining, and Mick O'Leary representing the Argyle venture's new corporate entity, Argyle Diamond Sales. Leslie had a dual role in the team, representing Ashton Mining's interests in his capacity as both legal adviser and board member.

In 1981, the Australian negotiators arrived in London. The first meeting was at 2 Charterhouse Street, the fabled British headquarters of the CSO and global hub of the diamond distribution system. Upon their arrival the visitors were taken straight to the enormous sorting hall, the 'holy of holies' as Leslie described it. In the vast space, scores of sorters worked at bench after bench with sparkling diamonds. 'An astonishing sight,' Leslie said. He suspected this initial tour was intended to serve multiple purposes. It was a way to dazzle the Australians, he thought, and to impress upon them the power of De Beers in the market. 'As well as being a gesture of welcome, it was also no doubt intended as a way of showing the strength of their hand,' he said.

Leslie described Harry Oppenheimer as 'a slight and dapper man, well-tailored', the consummate City of London gentleman: 'He had a firm but warm handshake and a friendly, welcoming smile. His charm and tact were legendary, as was his ability to maintain control of his empire.' Oppenheimer's warm hand controlled 80 per cent of the world's diamond production, 40 per cent of South Africa's gold, 50 per cent of its coal and more than 10 per cent of the world's copper. Over the following months, the Argyle negotiations continued in London, Kimberley (South Africa) and Perth. At some stages in the negotiations, Oppenheimer was present in person, at other times not, but in all cases he called the shots for the De Beers side.

The parties brought very different styles and very different knowledge to the negotiations. Madigan was up-front, even brash, whereas the CSO men were far more subtle and reserved. The slightest lift of an eyebrow could mean 'No' or 'Definitely no'. Like Madigan,

Leslie was accustomed to the Japanese style of negotiating on minerals contracts. The Japanese were 'extremely polite and courteous but hard to read':

> One knew with the Japanese that the deal or proposal they put on the table was not what they expected to get, or indeed even wanted. The Japanese negotiators had the need, even at the highest level, to be able to take something away from the negotiations so as to be able to report to their superiors or board, that they, as negotiators, had gained some benefit or advantage from the negotiations. And the way they ensured this was to offer some concession with the quid pro quo that you gave them something.

With the Japanese it was all very uncertain, whereas with De Beers, 'you were left in no doubt what they wanted: control of the marketing of the Argyle goods at the best possible price. They were quite straightforward, despite their reticence to divulge details of the workings of the CSO.' Crucially, Alan Jones was deft at bridging the different styles of the two negotiating teams. Throughout much of the discussions he acted as a kind of corporate translator and mediator, seeing sense and merit in both sides' perspectives. 'He brought people together,' Leslie said. 'That was his special strength.'

Diamond geology is very different from diamond marketing and distribution. The Ashton Mining–CRA team went into the negotiations with many unknowns. What would De Beers be like to deal with day-to-day? And what price trends could the Australians expect? As Leslie said,

> It was extremely difficult for Ashton and CRA to run figures on future price trends because of the lack of figures on overall sales or supply or stocks of goods, let alone individual market segments. We had no way of ascertaining with any degree of certainty whether the market was homogenous or segmented, and if segmented, how the segments interacted.

The negotiations began with a shortage of trust on both sides. There were fears among the Australians that De Beers was playing a double game: that the cartel was more interested in getting useful information about the Argyle mine than in reaching a deal to sell its output. During one episode in London when the CSO was sorting samples of Argyle stones, the CSO people were very cagey, refusing to explain to Ashton's accountant, Laurie Fitzgerald, 'what the immediate purpose of this exercise was'. McIlwraith captured the Australian team's recollection of this episode:

> Fitzgerald retrieved the worksheets from this exercise in London, and would not return them. There were some protests from the highest levels in the CSO, at Fitzgerald's apparently impulsive act, but it was privately regarded with approval by his superiors, for the suspicion was that De Beers was anxious to examine the diamonds for matters related to geology and location as much as marketing.

There were other potential hazards, too, apart from the risk of being double-crossed. Russian scientists were rumoured to have produced small synthetic diamonds that were virtually indistinguishable from natural ones. In the US, there was talk that General Electric had made a big investment in research on synthetics. 'These were further uncertainties in the supply-demand equation,' Leslie said.

In the preceding fifty years, the Oppenheimers had accumulated a fortune that was reckoned in billions of dollars. They were possibly the wealthiest family in the mineral world. De Beers had a strong arsenal and deep pockets with which to defend its monopoly. The Oppenheimers went into the negotiations from a position of strength. But, notwithstanding a lack of experience with diamond selling, the Australians were also confident. 'Argyle contained more diamonds than all other reserves in the world,' Leslie said. 'We weren't just price takers. We had a significant position in the world of diamonds.' For the established trade, there was something deeply frightening about that. In London and Johannesburg, there were fearful discussions about the scale of the Australian discovery and how the world market might accommodate Argyle's output. The diamond market already faced political and legal pressures. Now, De Beers had to prepare for a

Prospecting for diamonds, Kimberley, 1985 (State Library of Western Australia/Stevenson, Kinder & Scott Corporate Photography)

Robert Williams, a prawn boat, bringing supplies from Darwin (Ewen Tyler)

It was a challenge to get equipment and supplies delivered to remote exploration sites for the Kalumburu Joint Venture (Ewen Tyler)

Work in the field at the Skerring kimberlite: Maureen Muggeridge in the foreground, and (*left to right*) Robin Baxter Brown, Eddie van Cutsen and Chris Smith (Ewen Tyler)

Early jig plant on the King George River: (*left to right*) Alan Jones, Eddie van Cutsen, Mick Paltridge, Len Brown, Iain Macdonald and plant operator (Ewen Tyler)

Testing at the Argyle site, showing trenching to determine diamond content of alluvial deposit (Ewen Tyler)

Location plan of the then proposed Argyle Diamond Mine, 1983; AK1 is the diamond pipe
(Ashton Mining Limited)

Eight-inch diamond drill core taken to determine diamond content (carats per tonne) at the Argyle Diamond Mine (Ewen Tyler)

A 34.5 km buried pipeline was constructed to supply water for processing the surface deposits and the AK1 plant (Ashton Mining Limited)

Site of one of six small shafts on AK1—using suction, the plant removed broken kimberlite from up to a depth of 65 metres, c. 1983 (Ashton Mining Limited)

The Argyle plant during construction, c. 1984 (Ashton Mining Limited)

Alluvial plant operators worked night and day producing the first diamonds for valuation (Ewen Tyler)

Argyle plant operator Su Short atop the alluvial plant, 1994 (Ashton Mining Limited)

Picking diamonds from alluvial plant concentrate (Ewen Tyler)

Twenty million tonnes of waste rock were removed to prepare the pit for mining, c. 1985
(Ashton Mining Limited)

The Argyle processing plant near completion—the conveyer from the primary crusher is obvious on the hillside (Ewen Tyler)

Diamond ore operations at Argyle, c. 1990 (State Library of Western Australia/Richard Woldendorp)

The Argyle diamond mine and adjacent processing site, 1985 (State Library of Western Australia/Stevenson, Kinder & Scott Corporate Photography)

The Argyle Diamond Mine screening plant, 2001 (State Library of Western Australia/Stevenson, Kinder & Scott Corporate Photography)

The newly constructed accommodation village at the Argyle Diamond Mine, c.1986 (Ashton Mining Limited)

The Argyle diamond mine, 2001 (State Library of Western Australia/Stevenson, Kinder & Scott Corporate Photography)

Australian trainees sorting Argyle diamonds in Perth, c. 1984 (Ashton Mining Limited)

A selection of rough Argyle diamonds of different colours (Bill Leslie)

Pink diamonds are Argyle's signature stones; this is a 7.48 carat rough pink (Ashton Mining Limited)

Surat, near Bombay, was the major polishing centre in India for Argyle diamonds, c. 1987 (Ashton Mining Limited)

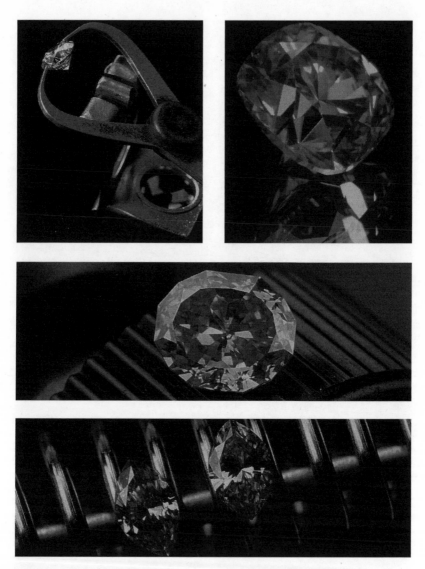

The ADS cutting and polishing facility in Perth processed the best of Argyle's gems: the oval shape, purplish pink diamond (*centre*) is 1.00 carat in size; and the marquises (*below*) are both 0.51 carats in size. (Ashton Mining Limited)

Stuart Devlin's 18-carat-gold automated Carousel Egg, set with 3039 champagne and cognac diamonds (Ewen Tyler)

The Argyle Library Egg by Kutchinsky (Rio Tinto)

Artwork for Argyle Diamond jewellery advertisement, 1981 (State Library of Western Australia/ Stevenson, Kinder & Scott Corporate Photography)

deluge of diamonds from a new region and a new player. Who could say what effects the enormous increase in output would have?

Apart from the scale of the deposit, Ashton and CRA had other arrows in their quiver. The new Fraser Government had retained some Whitlam-era restrictions on foreign investment. It continued to vet foreign takeovers and to require at least 51 per cent Australian ownership in new resource developments. The mining industry lobbied hard against that second rule, which the miners saw as a dead hand on investment. In 1978, the government announced a common-sense compromise, a type of phased 'corporate immigration' that relaxed the majority ownership requirement. Under the new rules, majority foreign-owned companies that were on the way to becoming majority Australian-owned could still invest in Australian mining businesses and Australian mineral development if they met certain 'naturalisation' criteria.

To be regarded as 'naturalising', a company had to have at least 25 per cent Australian ownership; a majority of Australians on its board; and a public commitment, approved by the government, to move to 51 per cent Australian ownership. For the purposes of applying laws about foreign investment and takeovers, companies that met these requirements were treated as if they were Australian-owned. Tanks Australia, MMC and AO (Australia) were all entirely foreign-owned and hence would not have been able to develop a mine in Australia. But by putting their interests into the Ashton JV, and then by making a public offer to Australians via the Ashton Mining float, they were able to meet the 25 per cent local ownership threshold and enter a 'naturalising agreement' with the FIRB.

Ashton Mining attained naturalising status on 5 February 1981. CRA had already gained that status under the new rules. The two entities were therefore allowed to develop the Argyle deposit. In the CSO contract negotiations, the naturalising status of CRA and Ashton Mining was especially important, as De Beers would not have been able to develop such a mine directly; and it had no intention of becoming majority Australian-owned. (The rules about naturalisation had some curious consequences. Naturalising companies were permitted to acquire other Australian companies, but at the same time their special legal status meant they themselves were shielded from foreign takeover. In the words of Bill Leslie, when it came to foreign takeovers, naturalising companies 'could be predator but not prey'.)

There were other reasons, too, for De Beers to play nice in the negotiations. The CSO had to maintain its monopoly image with other producers and sightholders. It had to be seen as a powerful player in the market, and an attractive option for future producers looking to do deals. CRA and Ashton Mining, moreover, always had the option of walking away from the De Beers discussions. Other parties were interested in the Argyle stones, and those parties would happily bypass De Beers and deal directly with the JV parties. Though they didn't particularly want to, the partners could ultimately choose to go it alone by reviving the Indian discussions, or by leveraging their British and European relationships, including those of RTZ.

◈

Questions of price and volume were uppermost in the Australians' minds. They were concerned to ensure the Argyle goods would be promoted, and that other De Beers goods would not be favoured to the detriment of Argyle's. Leslie described it this way: 'We had to be sure that goods of the Argyle qualities received a fair share of the marketing budget. And we sought comfort that De Beers' diamond promotion activities would not adversely affect our range of goods.'

Most fundamental were the questions of supply and demand. Just how many gems could the market absorb? And at what price level? Would 20 million carats at an average of US$10 a carat be acceptable? No, that was out of the question, the De Beers people said. How about 10 million carats at US$10 a carat, or 15 million carats at US$6.50? Yes, they said, diamonds at that price and quantity could 'probably be absorbed'. Russ Madigan suggested to Harry Oppenheimer that the contract might include a floor price for the average production from the mine, as a safety net or downside hedge for the new venture. Perhaps, Madigan said, the CSO could offer Argyle a minimum price of US$5 per carat? Oppenheimer's reply put an end to such talk.

'Well,' he said, 'if we had a mine that required that sort of guarantee, I do not think we would regard it as worth developing.'

Another thing to worry about during the negotiations was the outside chance that another diamond deposit of a similar size might be discovered somewhere else in the world while Ashton Mining, CRA and De Beers were still talking. Against this complex backdrop, the negotiations quickly became bogged down. What proportion of the Argyle output should the agreement cover? And what diamond qualities? And where should they be processed? These questions became major sticking points. The Australians were determined to retain the right to sell some of the mine's output independently. This would provide a benchmark set of prices so that the diamond industry newcomers could know if they were being treated well by the old hands at De Beers. 'If we were being screwed,' Leslie said, 'at least we would know about it.'

The Australians argued that if they lacked the right to conduct independent sales, the Australian Government was unlikely to grant a diamond export licence and the contract could well be in breach of Australian trade practices laws, not to mention American antitrust ones. Also, the Australians set out another critical requirement: some of the Argyle stones had to be processed in Western Australia.

The Oppenheimers for their part counter-pushed for all the diamonds to be cut and polished overseas. But, the Australians replied, clause 30 of the state agreement required that there be a diamond processing industry in Western Australia. The CSO comeback was that the agreement should be changed. The Australians responded that that would be impossible: they couldn't and wouldn't be changing the state agreement. And moreover, even if they could change the state's requirements, in all probability there would be federal ones to deal with. Establishing a cutting and polishing business in Western Australia was likely, for example, to be an Australian Government requirement when it came to Argyle obtaining export licences.

At a meeting in Johannesburg, the negotiations reached a critical juncture. Oppenheimer was present, as were Madigan and O'Leary, along with Argyle's Geoff Billard and Ken Perry, who'd done the 'legwork' on the Australians' negotiation strategy. The meeting didn't go well, according to Billard: 'There was a general feeling that the discussions had failed and, at least in the foreseeable future, there would be no agreement.' He continued:

> De Beers had expected Argyle would capitulate to an exclusive sales agreement and had even booked a private celebratory dinner at the Johannesburg Club that evening. Argyle held firm during a very tense meeting. (Mr Oppenheimer was chewing Minties and folding the wrapping papers into the tiniest parcels!) In the end, the meeting broke up. The dinner was cancelled and Ken Perry and I went directly to the airport to fly to Bombay that evening. Meanwhile, Russel [Madigan] met one-on-one with Harry Oppenheimer and he agreed in principle to what Argyle had requested. This was a breakthrough and a significant event for both De Beers and Argyle—and for the world diamond industry. It changed the way a producer would participate in the industry.

The breakthrough came after Oppenheimer and Madigan agreed the stalemate in the talks was 'bloody ridiculous'. Together, they'd broken the impasse. 'Harry was always tough but fair, and of course the ultimate gentleman,' Madigan recalled. Harry had learnt a lot from his father. This last-minute resolution led to a compromise, but some of the De Beers people were unhappy with the process and the substance of the agreement. According to McIlwraith, 'There was dismay on the part of many De Beers and CSO executives over what they regarded [as] the generous terms agreed to by their chairman.'

As finally drafted, the contract acknowledged the JV's obligation to process some diamonds in Australia. The quantity retained for local processing was to be not more than 60,000 carats per year, from a range of qualities. These gems would supply an Argyle processing facility that could employ up to twenty full-time diamond cutters. Building and supplying such a cutting and polishing factory in Perth would make the agreement more acceptable politically.

The contract further stated that in the event that there were insufficient high-quality gem diamonds coming from Argyle, the buyer would turn seller and supply the West Australian diamond cutters, 'so far as reasonably practicable', with further quantities of gem diamonds in the range of qualities required by the sellers. De Beers was naturally happy to make this commitment. Such sales would be on the normal commercial terms that applied to sales by the CSO to other sight-holders. In effect, this part of the contract turned the Ashton JV into another De Beers sightholder, and therefore another route for the CSO to sell its gems and to influence the diamond market.

On the matter of sales by the Argyle owners outside the CSO agreement, De Beers gave ground there, too, and agreed that the Australians could hold back a quarter of the 'cheap gem' diamonds and a quarter of the industrial-grade stones, plus a quantity of the larger and more colourful gem-quality ones (these were described, colourfully, as 'Special Goods and Fancies'). Tim Capon showed sound foresight in his support for this provision, which again helped make the agreement more acceptable politically and gave the deal a degree of protection from US antitrust regulators. If the CSO had agreed to buy all of Argyle's output, Capon told McIlwraith, then there could be legal challenges under American monopoly laws: 'As the US represented a very big market for diamonds, this was a risk that could not be entertained.'

Other points of negotiation included the level of the CSO sales margin, how diamonds would be classified (as many as 2800 categories of diamonds would ultimately be used), and how the JV would be assured of no funny business in the CSO's handling of the diamond sales, such as by 'bumping' or 'pushing' diamond qualities to obtain a price advantage or an additional margin. (This was just one of the many ways in which a novice diamond producer could be ripped off.)

There were dozens of practical issues to be worked through, such as the mechanics of excising 5 per cent of the mine's production and allocating it to Northern Mining so that Rees Towie's company could sell it via its own channels. (One idiosyncrasy of the project's unincorporated joint venture structure was that the participants owned their respective shares of the diamonds individually and directly, rather than as a share of a pool.) These and other issues were written up in a draft contract that gave both parties comfort. On this basis, Ashton Mining and CRA were able to reach a deal with the global diamond behemoth.

On 17 December 1982, the parties concluded the 'Diamond Export Sales Agreement'. With the conspicuous exception of Northern Mining, the Argyle miners agreed to sell their diamonds to De Beers. Formally, the contract was to be made with a Lucerne-based De Beers–owned entity, the Diamond Corporation (Switzerland) Limited, referred to in the contract as 'DiCorp'. The contract would give the miners valuable flexibility and, hoped the miners, it would give their bankers valuable certainty.

De Beers agreed to buy, via Argyle Diamond Sales, 100 per cent of CRA and Ashton Mining's share of the mine's gem-quality diamonds, 75 per cent (by weight) of their share of the cheap gem ('Indian goods') diamonds, and 75 per cent of their share of the industrial-grade stones. The contract encompassed diamonds mined from AK1 as well as alluvial diamonds from Smoke Creek and Limestone Creek. The reference prices for the stones would be the London selling price based on the CSO London selling sample. The initial production was to be 25 million carats per year—more than half the total world production at the time.

The contract confirmed that the Australians would retain up to 60,000 carats per year for local processing and direct sale. The fine print also included an unusual provision, one that all suppliers had to sign as a condition of selling diamonds through the CSO: a 'reduced purchases' clause that De Beers could invoke in the event of a diamond market downturn. In those circumstances (analogous to a 'force majeure' contractual event), DiCorp could reduce its purchases consistently across its suppliers. By this means, all the suppliers would shoulder some of the burden by either reducing production or stockpiling stones until the market improved.

The Australians understood the basis for this clause and why it was so important to the CSO. But the clause presented major problems for the JV members. For Ashton Mining in particular, it was a threat to the certainty of cash flow that would be crucial for obtaining bank finance. The negotiations went back and forth on this issue—Leslie said there was 'a good deal of handwringing and various suggestions'—until a creative concept was devised. The makeshift solution was this: 'Have a reduction in purchases, without actually reducing purchases'. Leslie explained it in these terms:

> When the CSO declared 'reduced purchases' and cut purchases to less than 85 per cent of the contract level, then in the case of Ashton Mining and CRA, DiCorp would continue purchases at 85 per cent, and the amount of the excess over the level of reduced purchases would notionally reduce the amount of a fictitious reserve, 'the advance purchases reserve' [APR]. When the market picked up, the APR would be restored to its initially agreed level by Ashton and CRA delivering diamonds to DiCorp, which would be credited against the APR.

In this way, the Argyle miners achieved the downside protection they'd originally sought in the form of a price guarantee. Under the final agreement, DiCorp (aka De Beers) was committed to providing a cash flow of at least 85 per cent of Ashton Mining and CRA's projected sale proceeds during a market downturn. (According to the contract, the sellers would be required to stockpile the amount the buyer was not required to take—or reduce the mine production—and the buyer was obliged to buy those diamonds in subsequent years.) The JV parties hoped this bandaid provision would be enough to satisfy future lenders that there would be sufficient cash flow for the parties to meet their debt-servicing obligations. From De Beers' point of view, the artifice of the APR would allow the CSO to tell other sellers that the reduced purchases were being applied to everyone equally.

Based on these terms, the CSO and the Australians were ready to implement a historic agreement for the marketing of Kimberley diamonds to the world. But before they could finally sign and execute their agreement, the parties still had to climb over a very big obstacle.

20

A SOUTH AFRICAN MONOPOLY

CHARACTERISTICALLY, NORTHERN MINING had elected to take an independent line. Its leaders continued to dispute the diamond prices that were to be available under the CSO contract. Rees Towie described the arrangement as a plot, and accused his JV colleagues of being in the pocket of De Beers. Ewen Tyler was again a focus of Towie's conspiracy theories. Towie had already decided Tyler was a De Beers plant, perhaps even the personal agent of Harry Oppenheimer himself! And Towie knew that Tanks had originated as a member company within the De Beers mining empire. Now, he claimed, De Beers was pulling the Ashton JV's strings through a complex and shadowy web of shareholdings that involved Rio Tinto, Tanks, sundry foreign governments and sundry international banks.

Diamond-producing Zaire had recently left the De Beers–CSO universe, and the break-up had been ugly. Towie and others accused De Beers of artificially depressing the diamond market as payback for Zaire, which reportedly had to cut its annual production from 10.2 million carats to 6 million as a result. 'We have got to be careful,' Towie confided to the *New York Times*. His overarching fear was that De Beers would dominate and bully the Argyle owners, just as he felt it had done in Africa. In pursuit of other ways to finance the venture and sell his share of the diamonds, he spoke to CSR, Rothschild's banking group, General Electric, and investors in Hong Kong and Japan. Towie even discussed the project with Kerry Packer. The Australian media magnate said he would rather not take on De Beers in a corporate brawl, but he did offer to buy Northern Mining. Towie also reached out to politicians such as Paul Keating in Canberra and Steele Hall in South Australia. His indiscreet, scattergun approach would again prove costly for the JV.

The most practical consequence of Towie's misgivings about the CSO, and his decision to stay outside the Argyle diamonds export contract, was that he would have to find an alternative way to sell Northern Mining's diamonds. Under the terms of the Ashton JV agreement, Northern owned 5 per cent of the diamond output out-right, and it could sell them whichever way it chose. Towie quickly made plans to set up a sales channel via an Antwerp diamantaire.

Under the proposed CSO contract, the remaining Argyle stones would be allocated 56.76 per cent to CRA and 38.24 per cent to Ashton Mining. Having quarantined some of their future output from the CSO, CRA and Ashton Mining would now have to make arrangements to market those stones directly. They would do so by setting up an organisation to sort the diamonds and, outside De Beers, to sell 2,965,750 carats of industrial diamonds, 2,672,000 carats of Indian goods, and a small amount of special grade and fancies (diamonds of 10.8 carats or more in size, and 'fancy' coloured goods). Over and above the De Beers contract, therefore, the Ashton JV partners would need to become substantial diamond marketers in their own right.

Commercially, geologically and topographically, the Australian and African diamond industries were strongly connected. A South African visitor to Lissadell Station once remarked, 'This is very like South Africa or Tanzania and the Serengeti plain. The topography is the same, and I half expect to see an elephant walking into view.'

The Asian and African cattle breeds that roamed the East Kimberley savannah added to the exotic picture, as did the boab trees, the termite mounds and the lean Kimberley wallaby, whose dark-brown cheek-marks brought to mind those of Thompson's gazelle.

The Ashton–CRA deal with the CSO had one major caveat: it was subject to final approval from Australia's federal government. The government had the power to require export licences for any production sold overseas. In other words, Canberra had the power to ban the export of diamonds. Obtaining approval to sell the diamonds was far from straightforward. Diamonds are political. Australia's politicians and officials would scrutinise the proposed marketing arrangements carefully, and the Ashton JV partners would have to navigate an international clash of perceptions and ethics.

In 1982 Malcolm Fraser was prime minister, and he opposed the idea of selling diamonds to an organisation that was based in South Africa and therefore implicated in apartheid. 'In the mind of the prime minister,' Tyler said, 'South Africa was a dirty word.' For several reasons, those concerns were unfair. Members of Harry Oppenheimer's family had been persecuted at the hands of the Nazis. Now Oppenheimer was very much an internationalist and, as a member of the South African parliament, he'd long been on the right side of the debate about apartheid. Oppenheimer's company may have originated in colonial South Africa, but by this time it was modernising as a 'producer cooperative' whose participants represented all parts of the world and all points of the political spectrum.

In Australia, attitudes towards South Africa and the De Beers empire were diverse and somewhat conflicted. Opposition to apartheid was almost universal, but few people felt awkward about receiving a Rhodes Scholarship or employing a Rhodes scholar—or voting for one.

Naturally, conveying the complex realities of South Africa and De Beers to politicians and journalists was difficult. At various points on the journey to Argyle, representatives of the Ashton JV had met with politicians as part of their efforts to build relationships that would hopefully help smooth the way for the diamond searchers' plans. Now, with the need for export approval pressing, CRA and Ashton Mining lobbied hard.

Jones and Tyler met with the deputy prime minister, Doug Anthony. The leader of the Country Party, Anthony had a pragmatic, not-very-ideological outlook. He lacked in particular the prime minister's qualms about dealing with De Beers and South Africa. He understood that without a credible sales contract, the Argyle mine wouldn't fly. And he knew that the most credible, bankable contract would be with De Beers. 'Doug was on our side,' Tyler later said. 'He understood that without a sales contract with the CSO, the mine was unfinanceable, and therefore no mine would eventuate. He promised to get Fraser onside.'

Executives from CRA also spoke to Anthony and others in the Fraser Government, as did the Oppenheimers and the principals of the De Beers subsidiary Stockdale Prospecting. But, at the same time that CRA and Ashton Mining and their new allies were convincing people that contracting with De Beers was the only viable way to go forward and bring Argyle into production, Towie and his associates were running a counter campaign to criticise the CSO agreement and the parties to it. Fed by Towie, sections of the media portrayed the CSO as a racist organisation through which Australian diamonds should not be marketed. The proposed CSO contract was a murky document, Towie argued, one that would undervalue the Argyle diamonds and cede control of the mine to an odious foreign power.

Politicians began to voice the same lines. Bill Hayden was leader of the federal Opposition. In August 1981, he called for the Commonwealth Government to control exports of Australian diamonds. Speaking at Perth Airport, Hayden said export controls would stop the Argyle deposit from being sold out to foreign interests, and particularly South African ones via De Beers and the Oppenheimer group. He was concerned, he said, that CRA 'is selling out Australia's interests by offering De Beers a long-term low-price contract … It appears the diamonds will be marketed by De Beers at rates well below market value—40 per cent below.' If that happened, Australia stood to lose $150 million to $200 million every year. 'This is against the national interest and so far the federal and WA governments have done nothing to intervene.' These and subsequent words from Hayden echoed Towie's.

Just days before, Paul Keating, as Labor's spokesman on minerals and energy, had used similarly Towie-esque language, and he repeated it in the national parliament. The Ashton Joint Venture had no choice but to respond. Publicly they stated that while talks had indeed begun with the CSO, discussions had also been held with other sales channels, and no decision had been made. The claims of underpricing were also wrong, they said: Towie and others were misleadingly applying the value of the Smoke Creek 'jewel box' stones to those of AK1.

Tyler and Jones arranged to meet Keating for lunch. On the appointed day, the MP was called away but sent a representative from his office, along with his parliamentary colleague Kim Beazley, who hosted the lunch in Keating's stead. As a West Australian MP in the national parliament, Beazley understood the importance of Argyle. According to Tyler and Jones, he 'was very supportive'.

Beazley subsequently wrote to Jones, striking a conciliatory tone.

> Parliament of Australia
> House of Representatives
> 9th September
>
> Dear Mr Jones,
> Thank you very much for your letter and helpful enclosure. I would very much like to meet your representative. I understand from Mr Campbell that a meeting might be arranged next week when Mr Keating returns to parliament.
>
> I think if you read the debate of the week before last you will see that neither Mr Keating nor myself suggested that the Ashton Joint Ventures were controlled or owned by De Beers or that selling through the CSO was necessarily the wrong course. We did point out that De Beers was [*indecipherable*] influential in the CSO and that Australia should be concerned about the terms on which it sold to the CSO.
>
> Yours sincerely,
> Kim C Beazley
> P.S. Please excuse the handwriting. My secretary is in Perth.

Several of the JV's leaders, including Jones and Sir Leslie Froggatt (chair of Ashton Mining), had considerable respect for Keating. Jones and Froggatt had met him previously over lunch, and had discussed with him the value of the CSO potentially training local workers for the Australian diamond cutting and polishing industry. They saw him as intelligent and potentially sympathetic. 'He understood our plans,' Jones said, 'and he supported them. He had a brilliant brain.'

Now, though, a well-briefed Keating again expressed in the national parliament his concerns about the proposed export agreement, which he saw as 'a matter of national importance'.

Debate in House of Representatives, 15 October 1981:

The Hon Paul Keating:
I direct a question to the Prime Minister about South Africa and diamond policy. In view of the fact that the Ashton diamond mine will provide an increment equivalent to half the present total world production of diamonds, does the Government see this development as a remarkable opportunity for the establishment of a totally new and massive industry for Australia not only in mining but also in processing? Is the Government continuing to ignore this huge potential benefit, as the Deputy Prime Minister indicated to the House a few weeks ago, by its failure to set in place a diamond marketing policy, or is the Prime Minister now in a position to apprise the House of the Government's policy towards this new and exciting prospect?

Is the Prime Minister aware that with Zaire and the Soviet Union having left the De Beers Central Selling Organization, the CSO is now particularly vulnerable to a large low-cost potential producer such as Ashton? Finally, in the light of the Prime Minister's firm view on South African policy, what does the Government intend to do to guarantee that Australia's huge diamond output will not be swallowed up by the South African diamond syndicate, serving only to make the De Beers monopoly stronger and more resilient at a time when its old high-cost diamond mines are rendering it less and less competitive?

'It is imperative,' Keating said, 'that we do not let Ashton fall into the hands of De Beers.'

The equally well briefed Doug Anthony had been primed to respond to such a question, should it ever be asked in the parliament. But he was holidaying at the time and Malcolm Fraser was caught off guard without his deputy. Fraser rose and, playing for time, said he saw no advantage in a policy stance that merely served the interests of De Beers.

> The Hon Malcolm Fraser:
> The honourable gentleman has asked a detailed question. I will have the matter examined and see what information can be provided to him. I would like to comment in particular on the last part of the honourable gentleman's question. I can see no advantage to Australia or to Australian industry in having arrangements in which Australian diamond discoveries only serve to strengthen a South African monopoly in these areas. I believe that that would be contrary not only to the interests of Australia but to the interests of Australian corporations. Any examination that we would undertake would be against that background.

For CRA and Ashton Mining, this was nothing short of an emergency. The political differences about dealing with De Beers placed the whole project in significant peril. Without the CSO deal, obtaining bank finance would be all but impossible. And without a lot of money borrowed from willing banks, the mine couldn't go ahead. True to form, Keating didn't let the prime minister off the hook. On 20 October 1981, he rose again in the national parliament.

> Mr Keating:
> I refer the Prime Minister to his answer last week on diamond marketing policy. I ask: Does he stand by that answer? If so, does he deny statements in the Press and on radio by Sir Charles Court that he had conveyed to Sir Charles that he regarded diamond marketing as being the exclusive responsibility of the Western Australian Government? If Sir Charles's claims are true, how does

the Prime Minister square this with his answer last week and his earlier pronouncements on South African policy as well as the Commonwealth's legitimate constitutional control over exports as it is practised with other significant mineral commodities?

Mr Fraser:
A sentence which I did use last week was accurate but a number of the conclusions drawn from it—including, I think, by the honourable gentleman—are drawing a very long bow indeed. The sentence which I used last week indicated that there would be no point for Australia in an arrangement that merely served to strengthen an overseas monopoly or corporation at the expense of Australia or an Australian corporation. Without using the exact words, that is the substance of what I said. I am sure that the honourable gentleman would confirm that. That is so no matter what the arrangement is and no matter what the commodity is because we are concerned with the Australian interest, the Western Australian interest and the interests of corporations which operate in Australia. Therefore whatever is done obviously needs to have these considerations in mind.

Quite plainly, the Western Australian Government and the corporation involved are working to achieve resolution of a number of matters. Precisely how the diamonds might be sold has not yet, as I understand it, come on their agenda in any firm way. But when arrangements are made they need to be ones that will be in the interests of Australia, in the interests of Western Australia and in the interests of the corporation. That is not in conflict in any way with what I said last week. If there is any honourable gentleman who believes that it would ever be in the interests of Australia or a corporation which operates in Australia to make arrangements that would serve only to strengthen some overseas monopoly, he has a very strange view of it indeed. But it is worth noting, I think, that these matters need to be worked out ... There is a great attempt by somebody—I am not sure whether it is the honourable gentleman; maybe I am attributing too much to his initiative—to build a difference where I do not believe there is any.

After a debate on sales tax, Keating rose again.

Mr Keating:
I desire to put another question to the Prime Minister to indicate
to the Parliament that the Commonwealth, particularly the Prime
Minister, has not buckled to parochial coalition interests in respect
of diamonds. I ask the Prime Minister whether he agrees that the
foreign investment aspects to which he has just referred have already
been cleared by the Government, with CRA being a naturalising
company and Ashton Mining having been approved as a national
mining company? Could the Prime Minister then tell the House,
if he says that there is no proposal to establish export controls,
what instruments of the Commonwealth he envisages being used
to guarantee that the marketing of Australian diamonds proceeds
in the national interest?

Luckily for Fraser, Anthony was back from holidays, and he gave a
convincing answer on Fraser's behalf.

Mr Anthony:
Concerning the naturalisation of the firms involved with the
Argyle diamond project, I point out that authority has been
given for them to become Australianised companies and therefore
the majority interest, we hope, within a period of years will be
Australian and will be Australian controlled. As regards the style
of marketing of the diamonds that might take place, that is still
unknown as the company is carrying out an investigation as to
what are the best means it might use to market its diamonds. That
might take some considerable time.

    If the question is whether the Commonwealth has authority
to exercise controls over exports, of course it has; and there is no
dispute about that. That is the authority of the Commonwealth
government. Whether this government or any other government
would want to get into the area of exercising export controls on
precious stones is another question completely. Four years ago
we lifted controls on precious stones, covering such things as

sapphires and opals, because it was shown that administratively it was an impossible operation. I certainly would not like to think that officials of my Department or other government officials were to be given the job of assessing the value of individual diamonds, a most difficult and complex question. What action might be taken cannot be considered until the question of how the diamonds are to be marketed is put before the Government.

The Argyle partners pulled out all stops. They turned to their political networks on the right and the left. Beazley, Anthony, Court, Ian Warner, Keating, Fraser. Ashton's bridge-builder, Jones, again arranged to meet with Keating. This time Keating attended, and he agreed not to push the matter further. 'He saved the day for us,' Jones said. Beazley also helped pave the way for a political solution, as did Anthony. With the help of these and other well-placed supporters, the diamond men had succeeded in making enough noise and applying enough pressure to force Fraser to seek a quick way out of the whole affair.

The prime minister agreed to let the Western Australian Government make the call on whether or not the sales arrangement was acceptable. And he committed his government to sticking by that decision, whatever it was. After this, things moved quickly. The Western Australian Government supported the CSO deal. (Perversely, the high Argyle royalty proved to be useful, as it gave the Western Australian Government a direct stake in the Argyle venture, and therefore a strong interest in seeing it go ahead.) With the blessings of the federal and state governments, the parties to the marketing agreement could finally sign the deal. The Argyle JV members now had a basis upon which to seek financing for their diamond mine.

Once the CSO agreement was finalised, Harry Oppenheimer sent his new associates a message. 'We are family now,' he said. 'Whenever you travel to South Africa, you must visit me and we will have a meal together.'

21
FINDING THE MONEY

A T THIS CRITICAL stage, there were further changes to the Ashton JV's membership. The Belgian diamond outfit Sibeka had first joined in as an explorer, but the exploration phase for Argyle was over. Sibeka sold out completely to the other parties. Ashton Mining bought Tanganyika's Australian subsidiary, Tanaust, and Ewen Tyler joined Ashton Mining as a full-time executive director. The JV agreement gave the partners the right to buy stakes in the venture *pro rata* when they became available. On advice from law firm Mallesons, Ashton Mining skirted around that requirement by buying Tanaust outright (that is, they bought the whole company, not just its interest in the JV). Several of CRA's leaders were infuriated that Ashton had gone outside the JV agreement in this way. 'CRA was left owning less of the project than it would have liked,' Alan Jones said. Many years later, Rod Carnegie was still giving Jones the cold shoulder on account of this.

Northern Mining, too, saw changes. Ownership of that company passed to the notorious Australian entrepreneur Alan Bond. Northern had come under attack in the share market, and Rees Towie offered to sell its Argyle interest to Ashton Mining and CRA. His price was $45 million, but the other JV members valued the stake at around half that amount. Towie then turned to Bond, whom he saw as a white knight. He was wrong. When the sale to Bond was finally executed, Towie felt dissatisfied with the terms, and especially the price. 'What I thought was a light at the end of the tunnel', he later said, 'turned out to be a train coming the other way.' Run over or not, this would not be the end of Northern's part in the Argyle story.

Gradually, the picture at Argyle became clearer. The scale of the deposit. The likely value of the product. The investment required to bring the deposit into production as an open-pit mine. All these were established by 1982. Two years earlier, the US Bureau of Mines had estimated total world reserves of diamonds at 1.259 billion carats. Now, total reserves at Argyle alone were estimated to be 1.2 billion, making the deposit by far the largest diamond resource in the world. To further put the scale of Argyle into perspective, one estimate of the total number of diamonds ever produced in the history of the world, since 700 BCE, was 2 billion carats.

The expected cost of the investment at Argyle was rising. Estimates ranged from $310 million to $450 million. Each party in the joint venture would be responsible for securing its own share of funding. As a result of the ownership shake-up, Ashton Mining now owned 38.24 per cent of the Ashton JV, and that meant it had to find 38.24 per cent of the cost of building the Argyle mine.

CRA, Ashton Mining and Northern Mining all decided to finance their share of the mine cost by arranging bank borrowings secured by their respective individual interests in the deposit and its development. All three parties would seek to fund their share of the development separately, secured against their separate but undivided interests in the project's mineral rights and future cash flows. This was another first for the modern diamond industry. No-one in living memory had sought to fully fund a diamond mine largely with external debt. (De Beers, the only private group in recent times to bring major deposits to production, could always do so from its internal resources. The Soviets could rely on state funds.) The directors of CRA, Ashton and Northern would be educating bankers and introducing them to a whole new world.

Ashton Mining appointed the firm Kleinwort Benson to advise on the financing process, including the appointment of a lead banker and the assembly of a syndicate of funders. Patrick de Pelet was Kleinwort Benson's principal adviser on the deal. Brittany English by background, he was 'more English than the English'. Two KB staffers worked full-time from Ashton Mining's offices: Richard Watkins, who insisted on using an abacus instead of a calculator, and Jonathan Sanders.

Thanks to de Pelet's advice and Watkins' abacus, Ashton Mining was ready in 1982 to engage bankers for its share of the Argyle debt raising. From offices on St Kilda Road in Melbourne, the company approached several banks and encouraged them to participate in a tender for the lead banker role. The banks were curious but sceptical. They'd never seen this kind of thing before, and most of them didn't want to take the risk. New York–based Chase Manhattan Bank was one institution that gave serious thought to putting in a proposal. Because the opportunity was unusual and highly uncertain, it decided to enter the tender jointly with a major local bank, ANZ.

Andrew Jefferson Berry III was a Chase vice president and head of a team pursuing project-financing opportunities in Australia, New Zealand and New Guinea, mostly with a natural resources focus. He reported to Chris Malton, another Chase vice president who was managing director for Australasia. Though Berry was now a banker, he'd trained as a geological engineer (at the University of Arizona) and had started his career with the CIA at Langley. Highly astute, he liked to make up his own mind about things. On the question of Shakespearean authorship, for example, he believed Christopher Marlowe was the true author of the plays. Thanks to his work in the resources sector, he knew a little about the diamond market: how De Beers operated as a cartel, not unlike OPEC, and how it maintained what he called a 'surge bin' and a 'slush fund' that helped it manage the diamond market by buying low and selling high.

Now, Berry tried to get his head around the economics of the opportunity at Argyle, asking:

What was the mine, at the most basic level? Seven carats per tonne, ranging in reality from 2 to 50 carats a tonne. Each carat two-tenths of a gram. The diamonds were worth on average maybe

US$7 per carat, which meant around US$50 per tonne. In theory.
But what value was actually there? And could it be realised?

'There was the threshold question,' Berry said. 'Did you believe in the
mine or not? How did you know if there was value there?'

To better evaluate the Argyle prospects, Berry looked for relevant
benchmarks and comparators. Chase knew CRA and had previously
funded several CRA-led bulk-mineral ventures. There were relevant
benchmarks, too, from other fields of mining and mineralogy. In
Queensland, the bank would soon assemble US$115,000,000 for
Canadian company Placer's Kidston goldmine. That mine had on
average around 1.4 grams of gold per tonne (plus some silver), an
amount not dissimilar to the estimated value per tonne at Argyle.
But compared to the proposition of financing Argyle, the Kidston
gold loan was child's play. A single company, Placer, had 100 per cent
of the mine; and even more important, the economics of goldmines
are straightforward. As a product, gold is well understood and easily
marketed. It can be sold anywhere, and the value is regularly and
transparently set on trustworthy exchanges such as the London Metal
Exchange. The economics of goldmines boil down to how efficiently
the metal can be extracted from the ore. For Berry, the Placer deal
would be all about whether the borrower could control its costs.
Argyle, however, was much more complex. There was much more to
the diamond venture than just cost management.

What was the ultimate value of the mine's output? No-one really
knew. 'Gold is gold,' Berry said. 'An international commodity.
Diamonds are different.' (For one thing, you can melt gold into bars,
but you can't make a big diamond by sticking small ones together.)
Unlike gold, diamonds were sold across a wide range of market
categories, some expensive and many very cheap (despite their
glamorous aura, diamonds are mainly an industrial product).
Diamonds, moreover, were mostly sold through a single wholesale
channel—one in which De Beers' CSO was dominant, and in which
the selling was far from transparent. Berry had had the tour of the
CSO's Charterhouse Street operation. He'd seen the cartel's personnel

sorting diamonds into the thousands of categories whose values ranged from thousands of dollars to a few cents per carat.

At the last minute, ANZ got cold feet and pulled out of the pitch for the joint lead manager role on the Ashton Mining financing deal. It could see no viable pathway towards the necessary internal credit approvals. For the higher-ups at ANZ, there were just too many reasons to steer clear of the project. The choice now for Chase was whether to back away too, or go ahead with a solo bid. When the tender closed, there was nothing in the box at Ashton Mining's offices. Then, half an hour after the closing time, Chase dropped off its indicative and heavily caveated proposal. 'It was an awkward half-hour before then,' Jones remembered. In this way, Chase won the lead banker role with no competition.

Once Chase's involvement became public, it attracted a wave of scepticism. How, people wondered, could the deal be done with such uncertainty and without a powerful guarantor? First Boston was a 'Bulge Bracket' bank based in New York. In Australia it was advising CRA on the raising of debt to fund its 56.76 per cent interest in the Argyle project. Australian-born and Harvard-educated Chris Beale of First Boston was leading this work. When Berry went to lunch at Lazar restaurant in Melbourne, Beale walked over to his table and delivered a blunt message. 'You're mad,' Beale said. 'You will never get this done without CRA's support. When you're ready, come and speak to us.' The inference for Berry was clear: Ashton Mining would need explicit CRA backing, perhaps in the form of a project completion guarantee, to buttress its Argyle debt. Only then would it have any hope of raising the money. But what price, Berry wondered privately, would Ashton Mining have to pay for that backing?

Chase's proposal was still conditional on the bank's own internal sign-offs. Berry now had to navigate a gruelling process of credit approvals. His Australian office reported to the bank's Asia Pacific headquarters in Hong Kong, which in turn reported to New York. The necessary sign-offs included endorsement by the bank's US-based Global Mining and Metals Group, led by Tony Coe. Berry flew to New York, where he stayed at Hilton's Vista International Hotel in the World Trade Center.

Bill Mulligan was an energetic, outspoken and highly trained geologist. Inside Chase's Mining Department, he was the senior technical director. That role made him responsible for technical reviews and sign-offs on all Chase financings in the mining sector, worldwide. It was a powerful position, as Berry explained: 'If Bill didn't like a financing opportunity for technical or industry reasons, then the deal would not be done.' Though short in stature (he was 167 centimetres), Mulligan was super-fit and had wrestled competitively at university. During a trip to Perth, he visited the Swanbourne nudist beach. Shedding his clothes, he ran back and forth along the beach until, disappointed that no-one paid him any attention, he eventually gave it up.

His colourful and sometimes controversial style was also on display in the following episode. One evening at Chase Manhattan in New York, Mulligan was working late in his office, which was decorated with a large Melanesian penis sheath. He had to finish an urgent deliverable for a cement industry study. The secretaries had all gone home and Mulligan needed to make a copy of the study for the bank's president and senior management, who occupied the 'holy' seventeenth floor at the David Rockefeller–inspired One Chase Manhattan Plaza on Wall Street. Mulligan went into the copy room but the copier wasn't working so he called for a repairman. Some hours later the Xerox guy arrived. Mulligan pointed at the machine and said, 'This is a piece of shit.' At that moment the much larger repairman pushed the former wrestler against the copy-room wall. Reflexively Mulligan lashed out and landed a punch.

Later, Mulligan telephoned Berry. 'I'm in real shit,' he said. 'I beat up the Xerox repairman.' In the wash-up, the global chairman of Xerox and the global chairman of Chase both became involved. An apology from the top man at Chase placated the Xerox people, and miraculously Mulligan kept his job.

◈

In 1982, Andrew Berry had introduced Bill Mulligan to the opportunity at Ashton Mining. After that, the pair worked on the opportunity together, and Mulligan was now on board and fully across Ashton's plans. The next step in the credit approval process was to present a financing proposal to Dominique Clavel, a Frenchman and vice president at Chase Manhattan. Berry knew Clavel well. Among other things, they and their families had been next-door neighbours on Ridout Road in Singapore when Chase posted them there in the early 1970s. Now, Berry was hopeful of a positive hearing.

In the world of banking and finance, deals seldom turn out exactly as predicted. When thinking about a potential loan, the credit approvers need to know what it looks like in 'downside' scenarios. If the projected cash flows are not achieved, will the borrower still be able to service the loan? Clavel applied this filter to Ashton Mining's Argyle financing proposal. Carefully he studied every aspect of it, and how the cash flows would look in different situations. He reached a critical conclusion: he couldn't see the project working in a low-performance scenario, or perhaps in *any* scenario. The value was too uncertain. The venture had too many variables, including the geology, the government, the Indigenous owners, the JV partners, the CSO and the diamond market. 'There is no way', he said, 'that I'm going to approve this.' He turned the proposal down.

22

ARE THERE DIAMONDS?

I T WAS ENTIRELY within Dominique Clavel's power to block the financing deal. But he said his decision wasn't final. Instead, he would bounce the request up the line to John Philpot, senior vice president and chief credit officer in Chase's International Department. 'Dominique could've made it "all over" for us,' Andrew Berry said. 'But he didn't.' Berry and Bill Mulligan presented to Philpot the same proposal document that Clavel had rejected. Philpot knew Mulligan and Berry well. He respected them, but he was baffled by the Argyle financing proposal. 'I have no idea what this is,' he said. 'I have no understanding of what I'm looking at.'

To cut to the chase, Philpot asked the first of two questions: 'Are there diamonds there?'

'You bet there are!' Mulligan said. (Another account of this conversation has Mulligan answering: 'A shitload!')

Philpot then asked whether the diamonds could be extracted and marketed economically. Berry and Mulligan answered in the affirmative. 'OK,' Philpot said. 'We're in for 175, but I only want to be left with 25.' In other words, he would approve underwriting the whole US$175 million but only if Berry and Mulligan could syndicate the facility so Chase's final exposure was no larger than US$25 million.

Philpot looked at Berry and asked pointedly, 'Can this selldown of exposure be done?'

'It will be done,' Berry replied.

In this way, after a lot of work and a long lead-up, Chase Manhattan's approval came very quickly. 'It took six months', Berry said, 'to get to three minutes.'

The ensuing episode at Ashton Mining's head office in Melbourne has entered company legend. It is referred to as 'Custer's Last Stand'.

The board of Ashton Mining had become increasingly nervous about whether the bank financing could ever be completed. Sir Leslie Froggatt was the board's high-profile chairman. (Formerly chair and CEO of Shell Australia, he'd also been vice chairman of Trans Australian Airlines, and would become chairman of the major wine producer BRL Hardy.) Froggatt was putting intense pressure on Alan Jones, as Ashton Mining's managing director, to square the financing away. From New York, Berry now telephoned Jones at St Kilda Road to give him the news of Chase's internal credit approval. 'I'll be back in Melbourne in a few days,' Berry said. For Jones, that was way too long. 'I need to show Sir Leslie something *now*,' he said. 'And I need something in writing.'

Berry quickly scribbled down the details of the approval. Then he searched around inside the World Trade Center for a fax machine. Soon, at the other end of the phone line, a document rolled off the fax. The document wasn't quite official—it was composed in Berry's scrabbly handwriting—but it was something, and it would be enough for now. Three days later, Berry was back in Australia, and he delivered by hand a proper approval letter to Jones and Froggatt.

Froggatt, always astute, grabbed Berry as soon as he could. 'Before we have tea,' he said, 'we need to pose for *The Age*.' A journalist and a photographer were there, ready to capture the moment that the funding offer became official. For Froggatt, this was entirely strategic. A write-up and photo in the newspaper would make it more difficult for Chase to flee. When the article appeared, the headline read: 'Chase commits to $175 million'. 'It was a colossal sum at that time,' Jones said.

◈

At the very same moment, CRA was raising debt for its part of the project. CRA was a large, diversified miner with a strong balance sheet and deep existing relationships with financiers. Ashton Mining was a smallish company, majority-owned by a Malaysian Government business enterprise, and without any other operations or cash flow. The processes of seeking funding were very different for the major Argyle partners.

In planning its debt raising, CRA had held off approaching funders, perhaps in the hope or the expectation that Ashton Mining would struggle to raise funds and then, at the eleventh hour, CRA might ride in and guarantee the smaller partner's financing in exchange for a good slice of that partner's share of the project. On a personal level, CRA liked the leaders of Ashton Mining (though some at CRA were still cross about how Ashton had snaffled up Tanaust). But it liked their assets, too. In an ideal world—or ideal for CRA—it might have owned the mine outright. A smart play for Rod Carnegie was to take control of much of Ashton Mining's Argyle stake—say, a further 10 per cent interest in the mine—in exchange for guaranteeing its financing. With something like that perhaps in mind, CRA readied to borrow more than it needed for its share of the project.

But Chase Manhattan had now cut off that scenario. In the search for finance, there was an immediate shift in the partners' relationship. Once it became clear that Ashton Mining might be able to obtain independent financing after all, CRA and Ashton were competitors as much as collaborators. CRA moved quickly and with energy to lock up most of the obvious funders: the bigger banks and the bigger names in mine finance. Through a syndicate of banks led by Australia's Westpac, CRA would raise US$235 million. (The European Banking Corporation would lead Northern Mining's debt raising.)

After 'Custer's Last Stand', Chase moved quickly too, in the hope of offloading the US$150 million within its US$175 million commitment. Berry and Mulligan embarked on a series of meetings with international banks and other funders, to seek their support for the project. Froggatt helped with many of the introductions, particularly in Australia and Europe. Notwithstanding the introductions, though, the pickings were slim. As a result of CRA's debt raising, there were few prospective banks left for Chase and Ashton Mining to approach. They had to make do with the leftovers, and the financing was therefore even more difficult, over and above the novelty of using external debt to fund a diamond mine. Mulligan said to Froggatt, 'If we get this deal done, can you get me a knighthood?' 'Yes,' Froggatt replied. 'If you do this deal, you will be a knight.'

Chase thought Malaysian and South African financiers might be good prospects. Banks in those countries hadn't financed a diamond project before, but they were interested and implicated in the diamond world, and they were especially keen to read the CSO contract and see its dark and obscure provisions, such as those for 'reduced purchases'. Other financiers, too, saw the Argyle debt raising as a learning opportunity, and a rare means to peek inside the Oppenheimers' black box.

The five-month financing roadshow took Mulligan and Berry to Singapore, Kuala Lumpur, Hong Kong, Melbourne, Canberra, Sydney, Perth, Paris, Frankfurt, Johannesburg, Toronto, New York and Boston. At meeting after meeting there were many questions. The diamond project's bankers were greeted as figures of wonder and curiosity, but also of pity. What was this strange opportunity they were trying to sell?

In addition to bankers, Berry and Mulligan saw diamond dealers and sundry diamond-industry 'hangers-on'. At one meeting in London, the pair met a Czech diamond valuer who was a former tennis champion. During the meeting, the valuer pulled casually from his pocket a neatly folded tissue that, when opened, revealed more than a million dollars' worth of fancy cut diamonds. Early in the roadshow, encounters such as that were astounding. By the end, they were routine.

The Argyle mine was far from being built, but the JV partners were by now gathering diamonds from four sources: Smoke Creek, Limestone Creek, the shafts sunk for sampling, and the test trenches cut into the lamproite pipe. The rock from the sample drilling and trenching was run through the old Tanks plant. The output was a milestone: the first batch of mined diamonds from Argyle. On the global roadshow, Berry carried glossy images—he called them 'glamour photos'—of the first rough diamonds to be mined at the site. Ewen Tyler had given him the photos in the hope he could use them to convince potential funders. Berry also distributed the BCG analysis and the CSIRO modelling. These were more baffling than helpful: several of the international bankers thought the BCG and CSIRO documents were incomprehensible to all but physics PhDs.

Some of the more sceptical bankers wanted to tour the Argyle site, to confirm it really existed. Getting there was difficult: flying into Perth or Darwin and then by a smaller plane to Kununurra, and an even smaller one to the newly scraped gravel airstrip at Argyle. Tyler led one visit in which bankers toured the site. In tracksuits and business suits they clambered over the ranges, just as Frank Hughes and Warren Atkinson had done in 1979. Then they were led to a makeshift building set up with tables and, in petri dishes, diamond samples from Smoke Creek, Limestone Creek and the test holes and trenches. When the time came to leave, the bankers started walking out but the new head of Argyle security told them to stop. One of the diamonds was missing.

At the start of the tour, the visitors had been briefed about site security and the stringent procedures that were in place. More than one of them had immediately pictured being probed with rubber gloves. Before that drastic stage, the floor and furnishings were searched, as were pockets and trouser cuffs. The missing diamond was soon found. Someone had moved it from the table to a shelf. Was this an attempt—perhaps interrupted in the execution—to steal it? Was it a prank by someone in the visiting party? Or was it a test, a way to see if the Argyle people were as serious as they said about security? Tyler took the latter view, suspecting that one of the financiers had moved the stone as an informal challenge to the security arrangements. (If that is true, no-one has ever owned up.)

At every turn in their mine-finance world tour, Mulligan and Berry faced scepticism. There was much interest and curiosity, but no actual offers of financing. Berry was staying at the Carlton Hotel in Johannesburg when he reflected glumly that after twenty-five pitch meetings, not a single bank had taken up the opportunity to participate. He was worn out and empty-handed. There were many reasons for the banks to be cautious. Apart from the novelty of Australian diamonds, the unincorporated joint venture structure was a barrier. Formally, it meant that a bank lender would rank second to cross-charges between the JV partners. (The banks could improve their position with complex side-contracts, but it was still an unusual form of security, and a weaker one than most bankers would accept.)

The main problem was that most of the banks, like ANZ in Australia, simply weren't equipped to properly evaluate the Argyle opportunity. Berry was reflecting on this gloomily in his South African hotel room when a cryptic message arrived, via the hotel reception, from his secretary in Melbourne: 'Somebody is in for 25.' An Australian Government economic development agency, the Australian Industry Development Corporation (AIDC), had decided to participate, to the extent of US$25 million, on the grounds of promoting economic development in the Kimberleys. Maybe, Berry thought, the financing might not be a blowout after all.

From this point on, Chase had a stronger and more credible story to tell and other funders felt more confident about coming on board, given someone else had already taken the leap. Berry and Mulligan soon offloaded the rest of the US$150 million of Chase's US$175 million underwriting. The funding package, as finally assembled, was provided by a grab bag of fourteen institutions. Apart from the AIDC, there was the Bank of Boston, a conservative New England bank; Berry was surprised when it committed US$25 million. The Continental Bank of Canada also came to the party, as did an obscure German institution (Deutsche Genossenschaftsbank, or DZ), a French one (Banque Paribas, which had a Sibeka connection) and, proving Berry's intuition had been right, three banks from Malaysia and one from South Africa.

As a condition of the deal with Chase, Ashton Mining had to raise some more equity. It did so via a further offering of shares on the ASX. There was also an equity requirement in CRA's funding deal; CRA was able to fund its own equity requirement using internal cash flows.

Mulligan's Xerox-guy story had a surprising coda. Once the financing was completed, Xerox featured Ashton Mining and the financing deal in press advertisements for its fax machines. According to Xerox, its revolutionary machine allowed people to 'mail letters over the phone'. The Ashton Mining financing deal was special because it was the first financing to have been completed entirely via fax. The advertisement quoted Ashton executive Doug Bailey's words to that effect.

In December 1983, the participating financiers gathered at the Regent Hotel on the Kowloon side of Hong Kong harbour to formally sign the Ashton Mining financing agreement. The mood was jovial and there was a lot to celebrate. In the sphere of mining finance, CRA and Ashton had broken new ground. Argyle would be the first diamond mine to be financed outside the De Beers universe. Jones said he saw the successful financing as his biggest achievement as Ashton Mining CEO. He now had a basis on which to go forward with CRA and Northern to construct the mine. The deal was especially complex. Three parties had sought finance simultaneously for the same project, and to some extent they had tripped over each other on their respective roadshows. Adding further to the complexity, the Ashton Mining share of the funding was itself subdivided into tranches. 'Intellectually,' Berry said, 'the financing was the most challenging project of my career.'

In the history of Australia, the secessionist 'Hutt River Province' is a political and geographical oddity. In a region on the West Australian coast, the eccentric founder of the 'Province' set up an unrecognised alternative government and styled himself prince. In Perth, some months after the Hong Kong signing event, Ashton Mining hosted a dinner for the bankers. At the Parmelia Hilton hotel, Sir Leslie Froggatt took the podium. 'Will Bill Mulligan please come up?' he said. Mulligan came up. 'Kneel before me,' Froggatt said. Then he brought out a sword and touched Mulligan's shoulders with it. Remembering his promise to Mulligan, he'd bought a knighthood, along with a sash and a crest and other regalia, from the breakaway region. 'Arise,' he said. 'Sir William of the Hutt River Province.'

23

MANDANGALA

I N MORE THAN one way, John Toby was a man between worlds. He had kinship connections with two East Kimberley tribes: his mother was Miriwung, his father Kija. He was born in town, at Wyndham, and lived for a time at Kununurra, but he grew up in the bush, on cattle stations at Spring Creek and Rosewood. And he lived most of his life at the frontier between Indigenous and European cultures.

Born in the 1930s, Toby would later relish childhood memories of epic fishing trips: 'We used to go down the river fishing and things like that, a long way on the Ord River, fourteen mile [22 kilometres]. Did that in a day and went back the next day.' The Ord formed part of the eastern boundary of Toby's ancestral country at Glen Hill, on Lissadell Station, to the west and south-west of Lake Argyle: 'from round Mandangala up to Wesley Spring, Devil Devil, round to Flying Fox, up Billy-goat, round McCarthy Spring [and] up to a place called Cattle Creek Yard'.

At Rosewood, Toby was seven or eight years old when he started riding horses. Around this time, he encountered other Indigenous people living in a variety of new and traditional ways. Some were permanently settled on stations or in town. Some would periodically go on long treks into the wilderness. And a small number maintained a fully nomadic life. For the young Toby, those people were figures of wonder and even of fear:

> They'd say, 'Why should we mix it with these fellers that work for the white feller? Think we should let 'im go back to the station or just destroy 'im?' The bush people thought like that about us and that was why we used to be frightened of them, but luckily we'd just manage to get through somehow back to the station, sneak away.

At the age of about twelve, Toby began working for the meagre wage of 50 cents per week, 'and keep, too, like tucker and tobacco'. He worked at a series of different stations in the Kimberleys and the Northern Territory, trying them out and being tried out by the white station hands and managers. On a visit to Wyndham, he discovered there was better money to be made in town and that the public works and main roads departments offered equal pay, '[no] matter what colour you were'. So he moved to Kununurra, a newish town that had been established around 70 kilometres west of Wyndham to service the Ord River irrigation scheme.

The Kimberleys' Indigenous leaders inducted Toby into the ancient traditions such as Jaru, Kija and Miriwung law and Dreaming stories. He also learnt the law of the colonisers:

> Well we have the whitefella's law too as well. But the white feller hasn't got our Law much. It's only just coming up isn't it? I mean people have to give people time to think about it, other than just going in blind. It makes a shock to the people who are not given enough time to wake up. They're waking up now … The white man makes new laws, well we never make new. We still have our own Law, our own way.

Even when he was living in town, Toby kept a watchful eye on his grandfather's country. When he discovered Glen Hill was vacant and the government had bought it as part of a larger purchase for the Doon Doon Aboriginal community in conjunction with their

Dunham River pastoral lease, he went and had a word with the people at Doon Doon: 'I said to them, "It's the grandfather's station. I'd like to move back into it, an' if you people agree." And the Dunham River people knew it was my grandfather's country and so they said you can go back any time you want to.'

As Robert Roberts had done at Oombulgurri, Toby led around twenty-five people back to his ancestral land. Early in 1980, they took possession of the Mandangala outstation on the small Glen Hill pastoral lease. ('Mandangala', Toby explained, 'is the waterhole right alongside … where the station Glen Hill was.') For Toby, this was a case of 'going back to where I started from'. Apart from participating in the wider reclamation movement, on a practical level the return was a way to ensure the future of his family and community. Raised and trained as a stockman, Toby planned to revive and restock the station.

The returning people brought a truck and a tractor. They lived in tents and traditional humpies, with the hope of constructing more substantial housing and station buildings later. Toby also made plans to collect an existing building from Wyndham. By February 1980, the community had graded a road (to Lissadell Station) and erected some sheds. Toby set about preparing the paddock and yard for cattle: 'I've got no money for it, but I'll just have to stick it out. I might be able to get a few bulls into the meatworks if I can make the booking at the same time as Dunham or Turkey Creek. That's the only way I can get money to run the place.'

For Aboriginal people in the north-east Kimberley, the term *ngarrangkani* ('the Dreaming' or 'Dreamtime') refers to two bodies of law and tradition: the beliefs, standards and sanctions that guide behaviour today; and the events of a distant past in which totemic, anthropomorphic ancestors travelled across the country, modifying the landscape and establishing the social order. As Rod Dixon, Cath Elderton, Steve Irvine and Ian Kirkby wrote for the book *Aborigines and Diamond Mining,*

These anthropomorphic ancestor beings left behind them, within the landscape, part of their spirituality, which Aboriginal people believe endures as a potent and vital force, and may be 'called up' through ritual and song. These places or sites represent the tangible evidence of Aboriginal cosmology. Their destruction is of concern to Aboriginal people, who believe that interference with such places releases the forces inherent there to the detriment of all life forms in immediate and adjacent areas. The continual destruction of sites has and will continue to undermine the Aboriginal moral and social order prescribed by Aboriginal Law.

In the country around Glen Hill, there are sites specifically sacred to men and to women. A network of Dreaming tracks—the pathways of the primeval beings—crisscrosses the land. Having repopulated Glen Hill, Toby was now the principal custodian of the sacred sites and Dreaming tracks around AK1. Within the diamond searchers' claim area, there were three sites of high cultural significance, including the 'Barramundi Dreaming' site, which was sacred in particular to Kija and Miriwung women. Also, just outside the claim area, there was the culturally significant 'Debil Debil Spring', also known as 'Devil Devil'.

According to the Miriwung Dreaming story, a Dreamtime barramundi lived in the river at Bandicoot Bar. A crane saw the barramundi and speared it, but the fish got away. Travelling up the Dunham River and on to Glen Hill, the fish scraped off some scales as she passed through the gap in the hills. The scales are visible as white rock on the hillside. Women tried to catch the barramundi in nets, but she jumped over the trap and escaped between the two hills of the Ragged Range, heading down to Bow River, where she came to rest as a white rock.

The Kija version of the story adds several details to the picture. A group of women chased the barramundi into a cave near the Barramundi Gap. The women prepared to catch her with nets, but she jumped over them, shedding her scales and leaving them behind as sparkling diamonds in the shallow water. The barramundi then leapt through a gap in the rocks. Landing in the deep water of Cattle

Creek, she turned into the white rock. Three of the pursuing women also turned to stone.

◈

Apart from raising cattle, the people of Glen Hill fished in the nearby rivers and creeks (when they were in flow). On one such fishing expedition, John Toby took a few people across the stock camp road that led to the old Smoke Creek bore and the new Glen Hill road. Along the way they noticed earth piled up in a line. This was the first the Glen Hill residents knew of the possibility of mining activity on their land.

Rammel Peters, a Kija man of the Warmun Community of Turkey Creek, described what happened:

> They went over to make sure what it was. They found it was [a trench] 8 or 10 feet [2.4 or 3 metres] deep. Then they … came back and reported it to the community that afternoon. Next morning we had a meeting about the trench. Well, our advisor Mike Dillon and a few people from the community went out and saw a drain and … a track going up to Devil Devil Springs. They found a little dam filled in where the spring runs down the creek at Devil Devil Springs. They came back up here [Turkey Creek] and Mike rang the Museum up and we waited for three days until two Museum *kartiya* came up. We had a meeting with them. They said we can't do anything. They [the miners] have already gone through and we can't stop them.

The community contacted two anthropologists, Kim Akerman from the Kimberley Land Council and Peter Randolph of the Western Australian Museum, who travelled to the area and surveyed the sacred sites as the basis for a report. While this work was underway, the miners kept working. As Rammel Peters told Rod Dixon from Northern Territory University, 'It was getting worse and worse … We asked them to stop the mining. They didn't really take notice. They stopped for a while—about six weeks. But they started again.' Kingsley Palmer and Nancy Williams of the Australian Institute for Aboriginal Studies prepared a new report on the area's sacred sites. According to Peters,

> When Kingsley and Nancy took the traditional mob out there they took a lot of women and kids with them and they showed them all the sites and *ngarrangkani*. Women went separately with Nancy. They found a road going up through that hill, through the Barramundi sites.

The site works that disturbed the land were part of the initial sample testing of the alluvial deposits and the volcanic pipe. To the Indigenous people, these preliminary works looked like a lot of activity. The disruption caused was far from trivial, and in some places it was very significant, but it was tiny in comparison to what might be coming. Few people in Australia had any experience of what an open-cut diamond mine might entail. If the mine development got fully underway, CRA and Ashton Mining would move millions of tonnes of ore. They would blow it up, dig it out, break it apart and spread it out as vast piles of tailings. An enormous mechanical processing plant would rise like an alien megastructure in the East Kimberley savannah.

In February 1980, John Toby hardened his opposition to the diamond finders' plans:

> I think that place where they are now, they shouldn't dig there because that's where the Dreamings are. But there is another place we can show them where they can dig a hole. There's plenty of other places outside that area. If the mining people want to know where that Dreaming Place is, maybe we should get solicitors to talk to CRA and show them where it is. Bring Charlie Court up to show him. He's been up with the CRA people. But he should go there with Aboriginal people. I know what a big mess they're going to make there. I'm worried. I think we'll have to stop it.

24
WINAN

'THAT MINE'S MAKING too many roads,' John Toby told Bob Nyalcas, chairman of the Warmun Community. 'They've started to mine the [Barramundi] Gap. What're we going to do about it. What can we do, what can we do.' One thing they could do was to use the white man's law. Just as the Oombulgurri experience was a model to be emulated, so too the people of Glen Hill could emulate the Indigenous leaders in the Northern Territory, who had taken up the legal fight for land rights and justice.

The JV's works at the Barramundi site were potentially in breach of the *Aboriginal Heritage Act*. In June 1980, Toby initiated a formal complaint, alleging CRA had committed such a breach. But the legal fight was over almost as soon as it had begun. Paul Seaman QC advised that there was insufficient evidence for a successful prosecution. Other factors, too, influenced Toby's thinking. Earlier in 1980, there'd been a major dispute over whether an oil exploration well could be drilled at Noonkanbah in the south-west Kimberleys. There, the traditional owners had argued the proposed drill site was sacred land, but Charles Court's government insisted the well go ahead. It did, and there was no oil. When Toby saw the dispute at Noonkanbah, he started to change his mind about opposing mining on his land. The legal and political obstacles to asserting Aboriginal rights and protecting Aboriginal heritage looked insurmountable:

> With the Liberal Government what could we do, at that time? At Noonkanbah they got a bloody convoy to come out and arrest the people. They [the Noonkanbah community] had all their people fighting but here, y'know, it was only me ... I didn't get any help from ADC [the Aboriginal Development Commission] or DAA. I wanted Glen Hill to grow a bit ... but I had nobody supporting me. I don't mean European helpers—but my *own* people.

Toby had previously sought money from the Turkey Creek community to invest at Glen Hill. The request had been turned down, and this reinforced Toby's view that he was unlikely to get local help. So he decided to talk to *kartiya*, and commenced discussions with the Ashton JV on the possibility of compensation for the damage done near AK1. The discussions grappled with wicked questions: not just about the scale of compensation, but the extent of future mining activity, and how the significant sites would best be protected. The discussions did not start well. When historian Bruce Shaw visited Toby in June 1980, he 'appeared depressed':

> When I left him he was debating the moves he might make. Disturbance to one of the sacred sites near Glen Hill was a *fait accompli*. [He] was considering some sort of agreement with the companies whereby compensation for the loss of the land might be made and adjoining sites left undisturbed.

Alongside difficult discussions with the miners, Toby held difficult discussions with his community—about what activity could be accepted, and which sites were not negotiable:

> [Barramundi Gap] was a woman's site. But the women came and told me, 'Go ahead because that barramundi is only beef, we eat it. It's food we eat ... We eat that fish, it's all right. They can dig' ... But Devil Devil Springs—that's the most important place

and Wesley Springs. I want them [looked after]. I don't want [the miners] to go near there.

For the Ashton JV, there was a strong imperative to engage with the traditional owners properly. Following a path first established by the Kalumburu JV at Oombulgurri, the current JV sought to establish a suitable, long-term arrangement with the Indigenous people of the East Kimberley. They approached the discussions eager to reach an agreement with John Toby and his community. Toby, too, was now determined to reach an agreement, in order to lead his family and his community to a different future.

Bob Nyalcas later spoke of how Toby led his people to the agreement:

'What do you reckon *kangkayi*,' he asked me, 'should we let the mine go ahead? We might get something from the mine'. I told him, 'No way!—but you can go ahead. If that's what you decide, well, we'll have to go along with what you say.'

Later on old Neil [Butcher] came along with Milton [Newman] and George Gauci [of CRA] to have a yarn. I told them, 'You can go ahead. We don't know what we've got here. There might be uranium, diamonds, gold. You can go ahead. We can't stop you. There might be something there that can help people.' Well they thought that was very good of me—but we couldn't stop them from doing it. In [Aboriginal] Law, we go along with what John says. He had made his mind up and we had no choice except to go along with him.

The Western Australian Museum commissioned reports that detailed fifty-eight sites of social and religious significance to people in the region. Three were within the JV's claim area, one of them coinciding with AK1. The museum also identified the families of Kija and Miriwung people who had the strongest claim to AK1 and the surrounding country. Now, the joint venture sought the museum's help to identify the traditional owners of the area that included the pipe. Toby, his brother George Dickson, his sister Evelyn Hall, his father-in-law Tim Timms, and Timms' half-sister, the artist Peggy Patrick, were all identified as principal custodians of the area. These leaders, along with around forty other traditional owners, were now living at Glen Hill Station.

The representatives of the joint venture did not dispute the identification of sacred sites at Argyle. They were hopeful that the mine development could be conducted in a way that protected and accommodated them.

In July 1980, Toby withdrew his complaint under the *Aboriginal Heritage Act*. Around that time, CRA flew Patrick, Toby and his wife, Mona Ramsey, to Perth where they met with Mick O'Leary, George Gauci and Neil Butcher, CRA's youthful-looking manager of Aboriginal affairs. Patrick described the meeting:

> The first time when I and John, and Mona I think, went to Perth we just went down to see that *kartiya* who showed us the diamonds, what diamonds were, what diamonds looked like … We went to see a small bloke who owned the mine. He was small like a kid. He owned a lot of mines in different countries.

Later that month, there was a major gathering at Glen Hill. Thirty-four people from the Mandangala community—including nineteen officially identified as traditional owners—met with representatives of the Ashton JV to negotiate an access agreement. 'We took people out to Glen Hill with planes, motor cars and everything,' Toby said. 'The old people. The people that we got up there were the right people.' Toby, Dickson, and Evelyn and Patsy Hall led the negotiations for the Mandangala community, with advice from respected lawyer Michael Hunt. O'Leary, Frank Hughes and Gauci led the Ashton JV's side of the talks. According to O'Leary:

> John Toby opened the discussion with a wish to leave something for the younger generation, and we soon came to an agreement that we would support them in the development of Glen Hill. Toby listed their immediate needs at the station, which we recorded, and it was also agreed that we would provide ongoing support for some

years into the future. In return, they would raise no opposition to the development of the Argyle project.

Patrick remembered it this way:

> John [Toby] said, 'What do you mob want to do? This is our place' ... He told us in the meeting, 'If you let this mine go ahead, we'll get money. We'll get money and we'll share things around. We'll share it with those people who own this country, who own that place from their father, from their grandfather, from their mother.'

Soon after the Glen Hill meeting, there was another flight to Perth. Six members of the Mandangala community flew in a light plane chartered by CRA: Toby, Dickson, Evelyn Hall, Ramsey, Timms and Patrick. In a letter to Senator Susan Ryan, shadow minister for Aboriginal affairs, Russel Madigan defended the miners' approach. He claimed the lawyer advising the Indigenous people 'spent two days being briefed by the Aboriginals and negotiating on their behalf, before the final signing of the Agreement'.

As a result of this, the JV established a 'Good Neighbour Policy' that included commitments on the scope and impact of mining activity, ongoing Indigenous consultation, local employment, and a program of capital works. Under the policy, the JV partners agreed to provide funding for vehicles and education, along with houses, a primary school and other buildings at Glen Hill.

The school was especially important to Toby. He shared with Robert Roberts a pragmatic view of development, and of cultural blending. He was happy to take the best from modern and traditional technologies and ways of life. Having had no opportunity to go to school beyond Grade 2, he saw the value of education for the next generations: 'That's why I was keen that none of my kids never missed school ... I wanted to give them the chance I missed out on.'

In addition to capital works, the agreement and policy encompassed grants and projects in the fields of culture and medical research. As much as $500,000 was reportedly spent on projects in the first year of the agreement, and up to $3 million per year later on. The miners delivered ute-loads of goods to the local communities in order to sweeten the deal. According to Nyalcas, there was 'tinned meat, blankets, all kinds of tucker'.

The Aboriginal Cultural Material Committee recommended that the site coinciding with AK1 be declared a protected area. But in September 1980, ministerial approval was granted under Section 18 of the *Aboriginal Heritage Act 1972* for the JV to utilise all three sites located within its Argyle claim.

Some local people welcomed aspects of the Argyle agreement and the Good Neighbour Policy. Some even saw the prospect of a mine itself as a positive development. The Glen Hill Agreement and the Good Neighbour Policy were direct sources of income and investment and, more importantly, explicit acknowledgements of Aboriginal rights— to the Argyle land and, as compensation for the exploitation of that land, to a share in the fruits of the mine. 'From this perspective,' Rod Dixon wrote, 'it is possible to see the Toby family's decision to sign the Agreement, not as a betrayal or reversal of their previous objectives (viz. to achieve recognition as traditional owners of the site and therefore their entitlement to compensation for its disturbance) but as, in fact, the very achievement of these objectives.'

But the agreement sparked a major controversy in the East Kimberley. John Toby was criticised for having been too ready to strike a deal, and for being too familiar with *kartiya* ways. There were disputes, too, about who should have signed the agreement, and who should benefit from it. Had Toby adequately discharged his obligations to people entitled, via the Indigenous concept of *winan*, to share in the material benefits of the mine's development?

Kija man Joe Thomas described *winan* this way:

> That money *kartiya* call royalties, we call *winan* … Say that you came to my place at Bow River. You come up and sit down and talk to us … and you ask for something valuable from us—it might be

good soil, it might be valuable stones or something like that ...
We'll *winan* that to you ... We'll give you *winan* and you give us
back something for using our land, using our station. *Winan* is
part of Aboriginal Law ... We've roamed this place for a long time
now. We'll agree with you, as long as you give something back.

The concept of *winan* extended deep into the past. As Nyalcas and
Dixon noted, people's expectations of *winan* from diamonds were
analogous to how traditional goods—such as pearlshell from Derby,
and wooden spear shafts from the East Kimberley—had long been
distributed incrementally, from community to community, 'along
winan routes for the benefit of "all"'. The concept also extended far
into the future. According to *Kija* man and acclaimed Kimberley artist
Jack Britain, '*Winan* is forever. When a man dies, the young people
will take it over.'

Had Toby discharged his obligations? The answer was no: he was
not perceived to have fulfilled his duty to the wider community.
Most funding under the agreement was tied to capital works at Glen
Hill. There was little room or flexibility for other payments, or for
an explicit Indigenous voice in decisions about how the money was
to be spent. This made it impossible for Toby to fulfil his obligations to other people who had interests in the region. He couldn't
use the Argyle money to fulfil his commitments to people who had a
traditional right to share in the rewards from the mine.

Too narrow in their funding and governance, the agreement and
policy failed to match expectations of what was equitable. They
aligned neither with Indigenous law nor with *winan*. Despite the
material benefits they brought, and the recognition of Indigenous land
ownership, they became the focus of much debate and considerable
ill feeling.

Among other criticisms, the proffered compensation was said to
be incommensurate to the millions or even billions the miners could
make if the venture proved to be viable. The controversy over the
agreement and policy again exposed a regrettable truth: the political
and riven nature of Indigenous affairs. There were gulfs between
families and tribal groups, and between different representative bodies

and government agencies that sought to orchestrate Indigenous matters. The agreement had been reached against the wishes of the Kimberley Land Council and without the imprimatur of the Warmun Community Council at Turkey Creek. It drew criticism also from the Western Australian Government, the Western Australian Museum and other organisations.

Toby thought the reactions to the agreement and policy were unfair. 'I don't know why [people] were angry,' he said. 'After telling me to go ahead, they got angry at me.' He was placed in 'considerable strife'. Violence was threatened. 'I nearly got my throat cut,' he said. 'I nearly got a spear right through my guts.' Something had to give.

Late in 1980 and early in 1981, Toby met with people from the surrounding communities with a view to remaking the agreement and the policy so they better reflected *winan* practices. According to Dixon,

> These meetings called on John Toby to take action to ensure a widening of the terms of the Good Neighbour Policy in recognition of the claims of people other than those resident at Glen Hill. At the same time, East Kimberley Aboriginal resource agencies, the Aboriginal Legal Aid Service and the Kimberley Land Council undertook extensive lobbying of the Government and media to achieve an extension of the Agreement to other communities.

In July 1981, the Argyle partners agreed to extend the scope and financial terms of the Good Neighbour Policy to the Turkey Creek and Doon Doon communities. Dixon documented how this helped Toby repair his standing in his community. By securing the extension of the mine's *winan* sharing, he was perceived as 'coming on good again' by 'recognising the demands of Aboriginal custom'.

Under the extended funding arrangement, known as the 'Good Neighbour Program', projects and services would also be delivered at Turkey Creek and Doon Doon. Despite this resolution, some people felt they'd been misled about the level and use of funds available under the program, not to mention the protection of sacred and traditional sites. The feeling of having been tricked just added to the sense of loss inflicted by the disruption of *ngarrangkani*.

25

WESTERN AUSTRALIA INCORPORATED

B Y 1983, THE Ashton JV was inching closer to having an actual diamond mine. The evaluation of the Argyle deposit had been completed, the Good Neighbour Program had been established, and the miners had clear title and permission to go ahead. Thanks to the thorough evaluation of AK1, the prospects and costs of mining diamonds at Argyle were much clearer. The average expected value of the rough gems was between US$6 and US$7 per carat, and the expected cost of mine development had been revised upward, by $160 million, to the daunting figure of $470 million.

That same year, the state Liberal government was defeated and a Labor government came to power, led by Brian Burke. Thus began the infamous era of 'WA Inc.' Burke had started his career as a journalist, initially at the *West Australian* newspaper and later in television and radio, but he came from a political family. His father, Tom, had been a federal MP from 1943 to 1955. Brian was determined that his government be seen as entrepreneurial and 'open for business'. The tagline on West Australian numberplates was changed to 'State of Excitement'. The new government was avowedly pro-business and pro-mining. But, in more than one way, the interaction between the Argyle parties and the Burke Government was less a partnership than a collision.

Two years earlier, the West Australian parliament had endorsed the state agreement that secured the Ashton JV's title over the Argyle deposit. Several routine provisions of the agreement had been carried over from previous ones that had been reached with large natural resources businesses such as Alcoa and BHP. The 'standard' version of a state agreement anticipated that the resource developer would carry out a feasibility study, then submit it to the state government for approval in a form that incorporated provisions for a mining lease, townships, roads, railways and so on. In the case of Argyle, the agreement referred to the construction of a mine town near the deposit, to support the mine's development and production phases. The wording was broad enough to encompass the possibility of a workers' village adjacent to the mine or, alternatively, the expansion of an existing town, in this case Kununurra.

A fully serviced mine town would typically include housing, shops, schools and other services and amenities. Such towns had been built at several major mineral development sites in remote Australia—and many of them were disasters. Ewen Tyler and his colleagues knew well the hazards the new towns could bring. They'd seen the bleak townships in the nearby Pilbara, which had brought acute social problems; the JV's leaders feared that the unique features of a diamond mine would make the problems of a mine town even worse. 'Mine towns are difficult enough places in which to live,' Tyler said, 'but a mine town with the everyday suspicions and stringent security requirements of a diamond mining operation could be intolerable.'

The Argyle team would need to build a large workforce, and the JV's principals knew that most of their current and future employees would rather live outside the East Kimberley—perhaps in Perth, Broome or even Bali—and work the mine in long shifts, on a 'fly-in fly-out' (FIFO) basis. (One commute option, briefly considered and quickly rejected, involved a 100-kilometre monorail between the mine and Kununurra.) The JV's principals also gauged the wishes of the Indigenous communities in the area. They, too, were fearful of a mine town and what it could bring. For the people of Glen Hill, there was the danger that such a town could undermine the whole rationale for their return to the area.

Alan Jones was among several principals in the Ashton JV who saw that FIFO commuting would be the way of the future for remote mine development. For the period up to 1987, that type of commuting was explicitly permitted under the 'Transitional Arrangements' in the state agreement for Argyle. Tyler had always expected that the Court Government would, if it came to the crunch, permit an extension of those arrangements if the diamond miners could show they were the best way to support the mine and accommodate its workforce. The Ashton JV's legal advisers believed, moreover, that the state agreement gave the JV the right—but not the obligation—to establish a mine town and associated infrastructure. They believed, likewise, that the idea of expanding Kununurra was also an option they could take up or reject.

The Argyle partners were establishing a new industry that had unique challenges. 'All things considered,' Tyler said, 'one might have thought that the expectation to build a mine town—a feature of other state agreements—would be waived.' But this wasn't to be. With the change of government, any nuances in the state agreement, and any concept of a tacit understanding, were entirely lost. CRA, Ashton Mining and Northern Mining were told that their project couldn't go ahead unless the parties built the town. 'The obligation to build a mine town was enshrined in the legislation,' Tyler said. 'A town that no-one wanted.' The Argyle partners were already well down the road of financing the mine when this bombshell fell. The town obligation would change the costs and economics of the project.

Mick O'Leary of CRA and Argyle Diamond Sales went to see Burke. O'Leary told the new premier about the understanding, with the previous government, that the mine town provision in the state agreement would not be enforced, and that Argyle could have a FIFO workforce if that was what best suited the workers and the project. Burke promised to look into the matter. Using questionable economic modelling of the proposed mine's 'multiplier effect' on statewide jobs and economic growth, Western Australia's Treasury tried to work out the potential economic benefits of building the town, based on the investment required. The officials estimated that the state would lose around $60 million in revenue if the town wasn't built. They used this as the basis for advice to the government.

Burke and O'Leary met again, and the premier sought a payment to the government of $60 million as compensation for not building the town. O'Leary couldn't believe what he was hearing. The idea of compensating the state hadn't been raised before and hadn't occurred to him or his colleagues. He left the premier's office furious and upset. Others in the JV reacted in a similar way when they heard the news. They saw the government's claim as daylight robbery. 'We were stunned and angry,' Tyler said. 'We all screamed loudly, but we would have to pay what in my view was blackmail.' This was the third time that the project's principals felt they were being extorted. 'We were already contributing $160 million more than anticipated,' Tyler said, 'in development in the state [due to the rising expected cost of building the mine], but that wasn't enough.' Nor, it seemed, was the exceptionally high profit-sharing royalty.

Premier Burke engaged the services of Laurie Connell, a controversial figure and self-styled merchant banker, to extract the money from the Ashton Joint Venture and to change the terms of the state agreement. Bill Leslie and others from the JV went to Perth to discuss the payment with Connell and other representatives of the state government. 'I will never forget being picked up at the airport by a chauffeur wearing white shoes and driving a Rolls,' Leslie said. 'It felt like Las Vegas.' Connell said he understood the JV's view that the mine town was optional and the wrong way to support the mine, but the JV partners had to find the $60 million anyway. Only then would they be released from the obligation. 'Connell said we had to pay,' Leslie said, 'whether the state was entitled to the money or not, and that was that.' Connell said the $60 million was what the state had calculated as a saving for the JV from using the commute option rather than establishing a town. 'This would be a windfall gain and should go to the state and not Argyle.'

From here, the bargaining began. CRA produced figures that showed the 'saving' would be much smaller, only around $25 million. The JV's representatives offered to pay that amount. This was rejected, Leslie said, 'and there was much back and forth about the level of the payment and how it would be structured'. Alan Jones liked Burke. He found him genial and personable. But during the deliberations on the level of the mine town payment, Burke was offended by a casual remark that O'Leary made. CRA's Rod Carnegie hosted a dinner at the exclusive Weld Club in Perth. The whole West Australian cabinet was invited. Burke tells the story in his 2017 autobiography: 'This night, the ministers sat at different tables and two heard Carnegie ask O'Leary, "What's this new premier like?" O'Leary replied, "Well, he's just a television journalist really."' In a breakthrough for the diamond miners, the government agreed to structure the compensation amount as an advance payment of royalties, which meant it would be tax deductible. The government also dropped the level of its demand to $50 million, but refused to go any lower than that. The JV had to agree: the delay and hence the lost revenue would have been too great. (Connell at one point threatened the Argyle team that he would see them in court, 'next year'.) When finally the payment was settled on, O'Leary met with the premier and shook his hand, speaking positively of the miners' future relationship with the government. 'That's good, Mick,' Burke said dryly. 'I'm just a television journalist doing my best.'

The drama of the $50 million had an unexpected second act. Burke used the money to buy from Alan Bond—ostensibly for the people of Western Australia—the 5 per cent Northern Mining stake in the Ashton Joint Venture. 'The fact that the state already had a 22 per cent interest, through the royalty agreement, did not seem to matter,' Tyler said. Reportedly more than $40 million, the price paid was equivalent to the asking price Rees Towie had put to Ashton and CRA a year earlier. So now, in effect, the JV was being forced to pay for someone else to own the Northern stake at a price much higher than it was worth. 'This was a bitter pill to swallow,' Leslie said.

In 1983, Burke's government created a freewheeling corporate entity, the Western Australian Development Corporation, 'to promote the development of economic activity in Western Australia'. The WADC became trustee of another new entity, the Western Australian Diamond Trust, which would hold the Northern stake in Argyle. In

Burke's words, this convoluted manoeuvre was a way 'to minimise any political fallout' from the payment to Bond: 'the whole transaction could rightly be presented as swapping a town for a significant share in the mine, and that cast things in a very different political light'. To make the deal look even better, in 1984 units in the diamond trust were sold to the public in an issue underwritten by AMP and guaranteed by the Western Australian Government, which promised to maintain an annual distribution of at least 8 cents per unit until the end of 1991. The issue attracted great interest in the media and among investors, and was oversubscribed by a factor of two. Burke was delighted:

> The price the Government had paid for the 5 per cent share was recouped with a $3 million profit; it retained 5 million units in the trust, which gave it a seat on the [WADT] board, and the purchase price had been paid by the joint venture for a concession that would previously have been granted for no charge whatsoever.

Connell was close to Bond. For what was meant to be a modest fee, paid by the government, Connell acted for the state in the purchase of the Northern stake. A subsequent royal commission inquired into the matter of the transaction and the fee. It found that the modest reward wasn't the only payment: Connell had also received a fee from Bond, one that was significantly more generous. (At the royal commission, former attorney-general Joe Berinson testified that when the state cabinet had discussed the Argyle project, diamonds were passed around the cabinet table.) Burke later wrote: 'The fact that Connell had arrangements with the Government and with Bond was a serious error and it may be a proper criticism to say it is something I should have known about.'

Burke's leadership, and that of his associates, is remembered for the unhappy mixing of business and government, and periodic forgetting of the principles of sound public administration. For the Argyle partners, the mine town episode left a bitter aftertaste. Apart from the windfall gain won by Bond, and the fat fee earned by Connell, and the expropriation of yet another slice of Argyle by the state, Tyler saw much to dislike in the episode. In the big picture of the mine and the region, it was a backwards step:

> The manoeuvre by Brian Burke [to extract the $50 million and spend it on Northern's stake] always irritated me greatly, because that extra funding could have been used wisely to supply the Argyle mine with hydro-electric power from the dam site, built years before, on Lake Argyle. Instead, we would have to import diesel fuel from overseas to meet the mine's power needs.

Tyler believed Ord River hydro-electric power—coupled with major mineral investment—could underwrite economic development in Australia's remote north.

26

THE DECISION TO MINE

IN TOTAL, THE Ashton JV had spent $125 million searching for diamonds and evaluating the Ellendale and Argyle deposits. The main result from that big lump of expenditure was the clear conclusion that diamonds could be mined profitably at Argyle. The AK1 deposit was assessed as having the highest grade of any diamond mine in the world. It was expected to have a mine life well in excess of twenty years. 'Forty to fifty years was not an unreasonable expectation,' Ewen Tyler said.

But for the Ashton JV partners, the decision to mine was far from easy. There were major obstacles at Argyle. The rugged site posed many challenges: the climate, the topography, the remoteness, the lack of infrastructure. The deposit had been found by helicopter and by following wild creeks, not roads. Then there was the scale of the deposit. The mine would only work if the processing plant could handle immense quantities of rock, which would have to pass through the plant on a scale never before attempted in a diamond mine. For these and other reasons, even though the yields were available in theory, the mine's viability was still far from obvious. Mick O'Leary remarked that, at one point, only he and Tyler were really pushing to make the project a reality.

Perhaps the biggest obstacles were mental. Among politicians, bankers, investors and the general public, there was little awareness of the economic potential of diamonds in Australia. At every stage of engagement with governments and bankers and the community, the proponents of the Argyle mine had had to overcome deep prejudices and a lack of understanding. But by the end of 1983, things were finally falling into place for the diamond venturers. In September, the financing packages were finally locked away. Then, in October and November, the last outstanding government approvals were given. Based on these, and what had been learnt about the deposit, in November 1983 the Ashton Joint Venture committee formally made the 'Decision to Mine'.

The total budgeted mine-site cost would soon be revised to $430 million. This would cover construction of the processing facilities, the office and accommodation buildings, and the commencement of mining at AK1. The JV parties would spend this money at a greenfield site, on unproven technology, and in an industry of which they had little experience.

At this point there were further changes on the corporate side and in the project's leadership. The Ashton JV split into two joint ventures: a mining business, the 'Argyle Diamond Mines Joint Venture', and an exploring entity, the 'Ashton Exploration Joint Venture'. Up until the Decision to Mine, Tyler had been chair of the Ashton JV. Now, he stepped down as chair of the main JV entity—'I felt', he said, 'that I had completed my task, the parties had made their decision to mine, and my dream had almost become a reality'—and became head of the new Ashton Exploration JV. He also retained his role as executive director on the Ashton Mining board.

The actual construction of the mine was always going to be a large undertaking, and with CRA now leading the mine development phase, it was going to be done in a big way. That was how CRA was used to doing things. 'They didn't want to go underground at Argyle,' Ashton's Doug Bailey said. 'They only built things that could be seen from space.'

CRA assembled a team that was commensurate with the scale and difficulty of the undertaking. 'They brought the A Team,' Bailey said.

'People who'd done it all before and knew what could happen. They knew where the risks were. They brought a lot of their own ways of doing things. Their own exploration procedures. Their own insurance arm. Their own procurement arrangements. Because of their depth of experience in mining, they could call on a wide range of expertise in mine development.'

That depth of capability was crucial. Hundreds of workers poured into the area. They built an all-weather airstrip—one of the largest private airstrips in the Southern Hemisphere; a 737 could land there comfortably—that was connected to the mine site by a sealed road. A water supply was secured and construction commenced on the processing plant and the mine site itself. At its peak, the construction workforce would reach 1200 people, housed in a camp near the deposit.

George Gauci, an experienced metallurgist, was engaged to plan and manage the mine's operation. Bernie Bent was Argyle's construction head. Engineering, design, procurement and construction for the main AK1 mine were to be completed by a joint venture between CRA's engineering arm, Minenco, and Van Eck and Lurie (VEL), a South African company that specialised in diamond processing plant design.

Most of the construction took place in 1984 and 1985. In those years, Tyler went to the site every quarter as Ashton Mining's representative to observe the rate of progress and to help solve practical problems. 'I believe I assisted in the resolution of some conflicts during that time,' he said. 'Because it was, in so many ways, my child, I felt a real sense of responsibility in its growing up.' The practical problems were many. Trouble with construction planning. Trouble with a stranded convoy bringing equipment and supplies from Perth. Trouble with unions.

Before construction began, there were rumblings from the Transport Workers' Union about which unions should represent which workers on the site. The TWU sought to gain representation over the heavy mobile mining equipment that was to be used on the Argyle site—a move that the Australian Workers' Union opposed.

In 1984, the dispute culminated in a TWU attempt to blockade the Argyle construction site. The circumstances for the picketing workers were less than ideal. For some weeks, they were 'housed in tents and uncomfortably situated in an inhospitable landscape'. According to John McIlwraith, a compromise broke the blockade:

> The TWU's members would be recognised in trucking companies who might occasionally be required to perform work at the process plant site. However, this proposal became somewhat obscured in later hearings, and another round of litigation began.

Not just more litigation but also another set of picket lines, which were set up in March 1985: 'This was intended to stop all construction materials arriving at the project, still with the claim that the union's members should have access to work in both the construction and production phases.'

The Australian Workers' Union had widespread coverage of workforces throughout the West Australian mining industry. That union argued strongly and frequently that, on the basis of precedent alone, most of the jobs at the mine should go to AWU workers. Argyle's leaders tended to agree with this position, but the TWU very much did not. For two years the demarcation dispute dragged on through various courts and arbitration bodies, including the full bench of the Arbitration Commission, until the TWU finally abandoned its campaign.

Though the strike and blockade received wide publicity, and though the litigation was costly in executive time and company money, the dispute had little effect on progress in the mine's construction program. According to CRA and Rio Tinto's official record of this episode,

> More serious, but not in the public eye, were problems with contractors. About halfway through the construction phase, it was apparent the project was behind schedule. One contractor, in particular, had cashflow problems and complaints about the structure of its contract.

There were also engineering problems, and construction was running off-track. These early issues in the mine development were solved through negotiation, and by a change in personnel at VEL/Minenco, and with the help of a new adviser. Nick Crossley, an American, was a highly regarded engineer and mining consultant. He'd worked with Newmont in Africa and knew the chair of RTZ. (Newmont and RTZ co-owned a mine in Africa.) At Argyle, he was brought in as Tyler's adviser on the mine development. With assistance from Crossley, Tyler gave practical guidance to construction manager Bernie Bent, and to Leon Davis, the new project manager from CRA.

◈

In the meantime, and in parallel with the mine development, the JV commenced production of diamonds by mining the alluvial deposits in and around Smoke Creek and Limestone Creek.

Gauci, Bent and their teams built the alluvial mine and plant and brought them into operation. The mining of alluvials began in November 1983. The engineers upgraded the bulk sample testing plant, initially to a capacity of 2000 tonnes per day and then to 4000 tonnes a day, to process the alluvial gravel. The flow sheet for the improved plant was sketched on a table napkin at lunch. Though the miners referred to the improved machine as a 'pilot plant', it was, according to Tyler, very much 'a commercial-scale plant by most standards'.

For more than a billion years, AK1 had been shedding diamonds through erosion. Unlike diamonds mined from kimberlite and lamproite ore, the alluvial diamonds were discrete, individual stones, already freed from their host rock by weathering. Unlike at the much bigger project upstream, therefore, the alluvial gravels would require no crushing. Starting with alluvials offered a low-cost entree into mining, at an early date. The alluvial mining process was much simpler, and spectacularly rewarding. The high-grade gravels yielded bigger, better-quality stones. According to the official record of the mine development, 'The whole of the 4000 tonnes per day upgrade cost about $17 million and it paid for itself in six weeks due to the fortuitous discovery of a natural gravity trap in upper Smoke Creek, which yielded 60 carats of diamonds to the tonne.'

The alluvial mining operation gave the JV a welcome flow of cash at a time of major spending on the mine project. As McIlwraith wrote, 'The higher proportion of gem quality diamonds retrieved [from the alluvial operation] meant that at its peak the venture was earning at least $50 million a year, of which about $20 million was profit.'

There were other dividends, too, from alluvials, as CRA and Rio Tinto noted:

The operation of the alluvial plant through to 1985 provided valuable experience in operating a diamond mine in the Kimberley and in sorting and selling diamonds. It was a valuable proving ground for equipment as well as an excellent training ground for operations staff.

Boab trees grew in the alluvial plains, but the miners worked around these ancient organisms so they would not be disturbed. Bailey had vivid dreams of large, beautiful alluvial diamonds trapped in the trees' roots.

◆

Despite the wonderful alluvial deposits, the main game was always the volcanic pipe. One way to manage the risks of mining AK1 and the miners' exposure to the diamond market was to run the mine very hard, in order to produce as many diamonds as possible. A rich store of diamonds, so the logic went, would help insulate the project from the many market hazards. The Argyle mine would have to produce more carats per year than any other mine in the world. It was designed to handle at least 3 million tonnes of material per annum, with scope to expand and exceed that amount. And a unique processing method would be adopted, to make sure every individual diamond was identified and extracted.

To do that, and to accommodate the immense quantity of ore for processing, the project's engineers designed new sorting machines on a much bigger scale than had been used at any previous diamond mine. Of a bespoke design, the machines would be the key to ensuring

Argyle could manage the huge volumes of throughput that would be necessary to make the project profitable.

There were other practical challenges apart from the scale. The average size of the Argyle diamonds was small, so the number of individual stones to be handled was enormous. In Melbourne, a CRA development team grappled with the question of how the miners could recover more than 400 million diamonds a year—or over a million stones per day—and sort them into thousands of classifications. There was much experimentation in Perth and onsite to test different ways to recover diamonds. Most of the experiments failed, but a viable process was eventually arrived at.

With the VEL team from South Africa, CRA's Minenco devised a multi-stage, high-precision method to treat 3 million tonnes of ore per year. The Argyle treatment plant would consist of crushing, scrubbing, screening and heavy media separation stages, followed by a final diamond recovery phase. As ultimately conceived, the process echoed some of the innovations made at Tanks and Kalumburu's Perth lab— including the use of X-rays, heavy media and magnetic separation.

The process was supposed to work like this. First, the volcanic ore would be blown up, gathered up and crushed up. The crushing would consist of primary, secondary and tertiary stages in which the precious ore would be rolled, ground and smashed. Then, to separate out heavy minerals such as diamonds, the pulverised gravel would be run through heavy media, just like in the old days of using malodorous TBE for sample preparation in Perth. Also as in Perth, magnets would be used to remove magnetic material during the heavy media phase. After drying, the resulting fine-grained heavy media concentrate would be dropped through custom-built sorting machines.

Those machines would make use of a helpful property of diamonds: when exposed to X-rays, they emit flashes of light. After being dropped into vertical tubes crisscrossed with X-ray beams, diamonds in the fine-grained concentrate would (hopefully) fluoresce, and a light meter would detect the flashes of light, then trigger a blast of air from a valve. If the computerised calculations of velocity and weight were correct, the air would blow the diamonds out of the falling concentrate and into a separate channel, from which they could be recovered. Sophisticated software would synchronise the light meter and the air valve. Much of how that was actually meant to work was crucial intellectual property and a closely guarded secret.

The collected diamonds would then be cleaned in acid to remove the dull coatings that natural diamonds wear. Finally, the washed stones would be sent to Perth for sorting into sales categories based on their carat weight, colour and clarity. AK1 wasn't an undifferentiated lump of rock. It would yield different types of ore, including softer, more weathered rock from the top of the pipe, and harder, unweathered rock from further down. The processing plant had to be able to treat every type of Argyle ore, in massive quantities and a single process. The plant was designed and built in modules and to a high engineering standard so it could be expanded at minimal cost, and so it would remain in use throughout what was hoped to be a long mine-life.

◈

A big mine would need a big workforce. The novelty of the mine was matched by a novel approach to recruitment of workers. Mick O'Leary recalled the crucial early decisions about staff: 'Right from the beginning it was decided that we would employ CRA people, the company being the managing partner of the venture, to launch this project even though we were not, as they would say in the industry, "diamond people".'

To assemble the project's leadership team, CRA plucked executives from mine sites at Bougainville in Papua New Guinea, and at Cobar, Broken Hill and Woodlawn in New South Wales. To guide the recruitment of mine workers, CRA's general manager at Argyle, George Gauci, conceived of the 'hypothetical ideal' FIFO employee:

> From the beginning, it was emphasised that nobody from the mining industry would be recruited, for they would bring with them pre-conceived attitudes and Argyle was keen to train people to have a more flexible and self-motivated approach.

As many as 16,000 people applied for the initial 400 operational positions on offer. 'At one stage,' Ewen Tyler recalled, 'there was a queue several hundred metres long snaking its way along Adelaide Terrace in Perth, as prospective employees lined up to lodge their applications.'

Gauci recalled that the task of screening applicants was immense. He and his team spent a lot of time shaping the Argyle workforce. Which applicants would thrive in the remote conditions and on a fly-in fly-out basis? 'The last 600 on the "shortlist" … were interviewed with their spouses, to ensure that there was at least some indication of the challenges involved in two weeks of separation out of every four.'

Gauci prioritised the recruitment of women, an emphasis that was seen as novel, even bold, in 1980. His goal was that women would secure at least 15 to 20 per cent of the jobs. He was also determined to have a high proportion of Indigenous people working at the mine.

Much practical effort was put into planning the commuting arrangements and into the design of the mine-site accommodation. Commuting had been shown to work on the offshore oilfield at Barrow Island, to which oil workers flew from home bases in Perth and elsewhere. But the onshore use of commuting was largely unknown in Australia, though it was widespread overseas. To better understand the logistics, Argyle representatives visited oil and gas fields in Central Australia, and sought advice on mining and oil commuting schemes in the remote north of Canada.

For the accommodation, Argyle engaged town planner Bruce Tomlinson to design the miners' village. Tomlinson had worked as an architect on mining towns elsewhere in Western Australia. At Argyle he faced familiar challenges. The site had to be on high ground to avoid possible flooding in the wet. It had to be some distance from the ore bodies, on non-diamondiferous ground. And it had to be away from the sacred sites of the Kija and Miriwung people. The completed Argyle village cost $20 million. As finally conceived, the design of the motel-style rooms emphasised home comforts, personal space, and 'the individuality of the worker'. Each room had its own view, a 'generous-sized bed', an ensuite bathroom and lockable storage.

The accommodation village was oriented away from the mine so that between shifts, the workers could feel they were leaving the mine behind. If the village turned its back on the mine site, it also shunned the remoteness and harshness of the Kimberleys. The finished complex featured a cinema, a swimming pool, and an office/cafeteria/ services building half surrounded by a pleasant rockery, garden and moat. The mine's Australian directors faced pressure and criticism from the London-based shareholders, who thought the village was too extravagant. Unhelpfully, local people began referring to the mine accommodation as 'Club Argyle'. Shops in East Kimberley towns sold T-shirts with Club Argyle branding. The site came to be known in the industry as one of the best FIFO set-ups around.

27
DIGGING FOR DIAMONDS

Preparing the argyle diamond mine began with the removal of 20 million tonnes of overburden and waste material. In 1985, development of the mine was completed on time and within the revised $430 million budget. On 1 December, open-cut mining began at AK1. Mining of the pipe started at the southern end, which was about 140 metres higher than the lowest part of the northern end. By mining the southern part first, the deposit was given a more level profile, making further excavation easier. Also, at the southern end the diamond grades were better. 'It was literally a mountain of diamond ore,' Alan Jones said. 'There wasn't much overburden.'

After blasting, giant hydraulic excavators scooped up the diamondiferous rock from AK1. The miners loaded the ore into 150-tonne trucks for delivery to the crushers. From there, it moved on conveyor belts through the scrubbing and screening phases to the gravity system and the air and X-ray sorters. This milestone, the full commencement of processing, was sixteen years from the start of the Kimberley diamond search, and six years after the pipe's discovery. The mine development was respectably fast: the world average time to bring a new diamond ore body into production from discovery was fourteen years.

George Gauci became general manager of operations at the mine. Ewen Tyler continued to visit the site every quarter. A typical project of this scale would have taken perhaps a year to achieve its design capacity. But Argyle was in full production within three months. Old hands from the mining industry remarked on the dedication of the whole workforce, from the most senior people to the most junior. The completion of construction and the commencement of mine operations was certainly a time for champagne. As soon as the crusher began to crush (on 17 July), Tyler brought out a crate of Veuve Clicquot. 'No-one could have been more thrilled than me,' he said.

The pieces of ore were crushed to a cut-off size of 18 millimetres, roughly 25 carats. The same process also smashed the larger diamonds. That fact seems shocking: we are used to thinking of big diamonds as especially valuable, and the thought of smashing a big, clear diamond, or perhaps a big fancy coloured one like the Hope Diamond, feels like a small tragedy. But the smashing was deliberate. Designing the process to identify and capture larger diamonds would have been too expensive: it would have required extra stages of ore processing, so that smaller diamonds could not hide in bigger blocks of quartz and other rock. Ultimately the design of the process rested on a trade-off: the loss of bigger diamonds versus the expense of more thorough processing. It was a matter of the ratio of processing costs (measured in millions of dollars) to the likely increase in revenue (measured in hundreds of thousands).

A few larger diamonds did get through the crusher, but these were flukes. One of the biggest gem-quality diamonds from AK1, a 41.7-carat white diamond about the size of a peanut shell, survived the crushing process due to its unusual elongated shape. Another big Argyle diamond, weighing 42.8 carats, was found by chance in a truck tyre before it could be broken in the crusher. The average size of Argyle diamonds (0.058 carats) was smaller than at Ellendale (0.141 carats). Unlike the practice at mines in Siberia, the Argyle team screened out the smallest diamonds and sent them to the tailings dump. 'We had no interest in such things in production,' Tyler said.

Argyle's ore had the highest diamond concentration of any mine in the world, but there was still a lot of ore for every diamond:

around 1000 pieces of rock for every diamond that travelled down the conveyor belts. One of the plant operators at the mine was struck by how such an unpromising stream of rubble could contain great riches. The rock flowing along the belts looked like road metal, he said. That analogy was surprisingly appropriate. At Argyle, the road and airstrip were built out of tailings from the early sampling and trenching, from which many diamonds were not extracted. Locally, the road is referred to as the 'diamond-studded highway'. From Africa there are similar stories of diamond-rich gravel and earth being used to make city paths and bricks, and of people using knives to dig rough from diamondiferous pavements and buildings.

The Western Australian Diamond Trust owned 5 per cent of the Argyle JV, and it took its cut in the form of diamonds. To make that feasible, the miners devised a clever solution. A mechanical sorter took a random selection of 5 per cent of the diamonds, across all categories that went through the processing line. Like balls on a roulette wheel, the selected diamonds rolled off the main line and into the WADT diversion. The diamonds separated in this way were then delivered to the trust and marketed separately from the other Argyle output. The method of selecting diamonds needed to be rock solid. The trust's share had to be statistically unbiased: a fair selection from the overall output. Working that out required complex modelling and Bayesian mathematics. The JV engaged the CSIRO to crunch the figures.

There had been challenges in the mine development phase, and now there were just as many in the early stages of mine operation. The JV spent around $25 million on an audit plant that never worked on any of Tyler's visits. (This plant was supposed to be a way to check for leftover diamonds in the tailings coming out of the main processing plant.) Every time Tyler visited, the only traffic lights on the haul road from the alluvial mining operations were on the blink. Working conditions were difficult. Personnel struggled in the early years, and so did the equipment. Argyle's kimberlite rock was much harder than the ore at diamond mines overseas and at CRA's other mines in Australia. The shadowy man that was AK1 wouldn't give up his diamonds without a fight. Thanks to the extra-tough rock, the mine equipment had an unusually short life. As Ashton Mining's

Doug Bailey remembered, 'The kimberlite ore wore everything out, including the trucks. We had to develop rubber-based truck-trays. South African mining techniques didn't work at Argyle.' The miners established an intensive maintenance schedule, with major overhauls every six weeks and regular replacement of key parts, such as the concrete and steel rollers and crushers.

Other teething problems were more surprising. A running track was built between the accommodation village and the airstrip. Initially the track had no lighting, and on dark Kimberley nights, determined joggers tripped over and injured themselves. Permanent track-lighting was installed, but the lights confused pilots, who were in danger of landing on the running track instead of the airstrip. A beacon on a hill near the mine also created problems for pilots, as did the hot Kimberley air, which provided less lift for aircraft wings.

The airstrip was long and well built, but only certain kinds of aircraft could make the long flight from Perth. Some landings were hazardous: wandering cattle and unpredictable wallabies grazed alongside the airstrip. They also strayed into the accommodation village. Crocodiles, too, were an unexpected presence there. Nearby Lake Argyle is home to as many as 35,000 freshwater crocs. According to a story repeated at the site, a mine worker caught a young freshie and let it go in the moat next to the village cafeteria. More than one person started feeding the reptile. It grew. The miner in question was identified and let go. The croc, too, was found and exiled. Then another worker brought another young croc, and the cycle of reptilian life continued.

Other problems were not animal but mineral. The ingenious X-ray sorting was capable of recovering stones down to a size of 1 millimetre. The use of a machine for diamond recovery proved to be an essential feature of the mining process. As Bailey later said, 'We had to use X-rays and air blowers because of the volume of concentrate we were processing. It was unprecedented. No mine had ever processed this many diamonds.' Diamonds were so numerous they flowed through the sorting machine at an incredible rate, constrained only by the speed of the compressed-air blower, which had a maximum work-rate of 180 blasts per second. The sound of the blast valves firing was like a machine gun.

This mechanical process was essential, but it was also fallible. The process separated the diamonds from the HMS concentrate. Once the diamonds were extracted, the waste was sent to the sort-house tailings stockpile. There was a problem, though, with the sorter's settings. Sometimes the machine gun misfired. The largest clear stones fluoresced so brightly that they gave a strong signal to the sensor, which in turn released a large air-blast, one that was out of proportion to the stones' weight. The gust blew the clear diamonds off course. They hit the wall of the sorter and ricocheted into the tailings channel. In this way, many of the best diamonds were thrown out of the sorting stream and into the rubbish.

The glitch was so severe it affected the average size distribution of diamonds recovered from the Northern Bowl of AK1, which had been conspicuously short of large, clear stones. Once the mine operators realised what was happening, they told Tyler and other members of the managing committee, who were both incredulous and relieved that the problem had been detected. The solution was to recalibrate the sorter and go through the rubbish to recover the lost diamonds. As much as 40,000 tonnes of concentrate in the sort-house stockpile had to be scrutinised, in large part by hand. According to a report to the committee, the diamonds salvaged in this way were 'large, well-shaped, clear octahedra in a value range of US$80 to $115 per carat'.

There was another problem, too, with the discarded gravel. As the mining and processing advanced apace, the tailings dam and the terraced piles of tailings grew faster than the cafeteria crocodile. The mine's engineers feared that, in the unlikely event of an earthquake, the precarious piles might liquefy or otherwise collapse. A big effort was made to strengthen the tailings dam and protect the giant mounds of waste.

For what Bailey would later call a 'grossly uneconomic cost', the two biggest Argyle partners set up a sales channel for rough diamonds via Antwerp's diamond district, just as Northern Mining had done. In that district, the Australians were greeted with open arms. Argyle was 'the new mine in town', and a very big one at that. The Australian diamonds electrified the diamond district. Dealers queued up to work with the Australians, but there was an immediate problem. 'They all insisted on dealing only in cash,' Bailey said, 'and CRA couldn't do that.' Nor could Ashton Mining. Transacting exclusively in cash just wasn't an option for a modern, listed, regulated corporation.

A solution was found. The Australians met a specialist rough diamond dealer, Isi Horowitz, who was willing to transact on normal commercial terms and to defensible corporate standards. He would then engage with other dealers and wholesalers on terms he could tolerate. In 1964, at the age of fifteen, Isi had started in the diamond trade as an apprentice cleaver. With his brother Dan he was soon dealing in diamonds, and in 1972 the Horowitzes became sight-holders in the De Beers network. Now, in the mid-1980s, the Argyle partners arranged to sell rough diamonds from a counter inside Isi and Dan's Antwerp premises. Argyle accountant Laurie Fitzgerald became the Australians' manager in Belgium, and the flow of Argyle diamonds into Antwerp began in earnest.

The first mega-loads of Australian diamonds have attained mythic status. The sheer quantity was daunting. Antwerp hadn't seen anything like it. The normal practice in the industry was to deliver diamonds in small parcels. For an especially large delivery, a satchel would usually suffice. But the quantity from Argyle was an order of magnitude larger. When the first major shipment arrived, a Belgian customs official telephoned Fitzgerald. 'We can't store this amount of diamonds,' the officer said. 'We're not equipped to secure them. You have to come and get them.' Fitzgerald raced to the customs office. Please, he asked the officials, could they just hold the latest three trunk-loads of diamonds while he arranged secure transport to Argyle's office? 'No,' came the reply. 'It is not possible. You must take them away immediately.' As the Australians later told John McIlwraith, 'Fitzgerald begged for twenty minutes or so of time, hurried back to his own office a few streets away, wheeled a trolley to the customs office and nonchalantly pushed millions of dollars' worth of diamonds through the streets.'

Marianne Georges was one of the first staff members to join Argyle's Antwerp sales office. When the flood of Argyle diamonds began to arrive, she was astonished, and rushed to store the stones wherever she could. There was a big safe in the office but soon it was filling up. Acutely aware that many more diamonds were on the way, Fitzgerald and Georges settled on a solution. The best way to manage this unprecedented flow of precious goods was to start selling them, in bulk and as soon as possible.

On the first day of selling Argyle diamonds in Antwerp, there was brisk demand among Indian buyers. In fact, the value of the Australian goods sold to those buyers in one day exceeded what Argyle had planned to sell in the first three months. According to Rio Tinto's official account of this period, 'So hectic were the sales of parcels of diamonds that [Fitzgerald] decided to close the Argyle office the following day so that the staff could catch up on paperwork.'

On day three, the office reopened and there was another rush from Indian buyers. The prices were probably too low, as Tyler later recalled: they were seen by the Indians as 'very reasonable'. Fortunately for Argyle, the prices quickly rose. Parcels that would have sold on the first day for between US$1.20 and US$2.00 a carat were soon achieving US$3.00 a carat. For Fitzgerald, these chaotic and nerve-racking days in Antwerp were among the most exciting of his career. In real time and by trial and error, Argyle's representatives were learning about the market.

For the Horowitz brothers, the Australians' arrival in Antwerp was an incredible windfall. They couldn't believe their luck. For the Australians, the brothers were a crucial help during the early months and years of selling Argyle diamonds. Isi and Dan understood the market, and they understood what the Australians were hoping to accomplish. 'It was a rewarding relationship,' Tyler said.

With the Horowitzes' help, Fitzgerald and Georges quickly found a rhythm. As Tyler told McIlwraith,

The technique of negotiating with Indian merchants was unusual. They would often arrive in parties of three or four and would all attempt to take part in the discussions, facing only one Argyle negotiator.

Fitzgerald said one had to quickly learn to speak to only one of the merchants, deciding which would be the crucial person in the sale. It was also important to always let the buyers assume they had secured a bargain, for it would be fatal to the sale if the seller showed any sign of satisfaction at the outcome.

Thus a degree of acting skill and theatrical technique became important, and there was also the kind of psychology that would be recognised in any market. For example, if a parcel of diamonds had been seen with little enthusiasm from a succession of buyers, it sometimes helped to produce them in a casual manner, scatter them across the table, apologise that they had not been properly sorted, but if the buyer wished to glance at them before others saw them …

The first sales of Argyle stones made the front page of the *New York Times*. Kimberley diamonds were world news.

John Philpot of Chase Manhattan had asked of Argyle, 'Are there diamonds?' Yes, there were. In its first full year of operation, the mine produced 29.2 million carats. This was an incredible ramp-up rate, one that silenced the sceptics and consigned the early operational problems to history. Within two years, Argyle was producing 20 per cent above its original capacity, and that growth was to continue.

The processing plant had been designed to handle 3 million tonnes of material per annum, but later output reached 7 million tonnes and, with further enhancement, 9 million tonnes. Part of the enhancement was made by investing in a $20 million high-pressure rolls crusher facility at the front end of the processing line. With further incremental investment, annual production exceeded 10 million tonnes when everything was really humming. As Mick O'Leary recalled, it had been anticipated that the project would process about 60 million tonnes of material over twenty years. But production was accelerated to the point where the mine had moved nearly 70 million tonnes by the mid-1990s—just ten or so years after mine operations had started.

A total of $100 million was spent on enhancing the processing facility. Early targets required the mine to recover a million stones a day, but the rate of diamond recovery would almost double. At peak production, the company employed 1000 people, 650 of them at the mine. Twenty per cent of the employees were women, the highest proportion in Australian mining. (In 1993, Argyle Diamonds won a Business Review Weekly Affirmative Action Award.) The number of Indigenous people was also high. According to Bailey, the proportion of Indigenous people working at Argyle was the highest of any mine in Western Australia.

Up until 1996 some management and staff commuted from Kununurra, where around sixty homes had been built for that purpose. From 1996, though, the mine was mostly staffed on a FIFO basis from Perth. Workers lived according to a cycle: two weeks at the mine, two weeks in Perth on leave (and possibly working a second job). The staffing and commuting arrangements were an experiment that was mostly shown to work. Tyler and Jones had been right all along. Argyle never needed a mine town.

28

CHAMPAGNE DIAMONDS

INDIA'S DIAMOND CUTTING tradition stretches back at least as far as the seventeenth century. During the 1980s, diamonds could be cut and polished in Mumbai and Surat for a fraction of what jewellers in Belgium, New York or Tel Aviv would charge. Before contracting with De Beers and the CSO, the Ashton JV had turned down the option of distributing Argyle diamonds via Mumbai merchants. Now, though, under the CSO umbrella, Argyle was feeding some $350 million of diamonds into the world market annually and Indians were buying most of them. Australian diamonds rapidly became the core feedstock for Indian cutters and polishers.

Early in the marketing of Argyle diamonds, mischievous people had spread rumours that the Australian stones were too hard to cut, or too brittle, or even that they were prone to exploding during cutting and polishing. To quickly counter these perceptions, the Australians held workshops and training sessions with diamond cutters in Mumbai and Surat on how to work with Australian diamonds and how to make the types of pieces that would sell well overseas. In this and other ways, the Argyle partners invested in India to further enhance the cutting and polishing of Australian stones there.

As many as one million Indians would work on cutting and polishing Kimberley diamonds for the world market. In the Indian factories and workshops, Argyle stones as small as 1 millimetre across would be cut with eight facets. These little gems, known as 'single cuts', were sold mainly for use in the 'affordable fashion jewellery sold in American shopping malls'. Though diamonds continued to be perceived as a luxury good, the combination of India and Argyle would help make them vastly more accessible.

In the valuing of diamonds, clarity long reigned supreme. For the main sweep of customers in the mainstream diamond market, the best gems were utterly clear of flaws and also of colour. An appetite for colour was the niche preserve of collectors and connoisseurs. (An exception: blue-white diamonds from Kimberley in South Africa were some of the most sought-after top-end diamonds.) But in the latter part of the twentieth century, tastes and fashions changed. Colour was reappraised: a little was no longer seen as a negative, and a lot—deep reds, blues, yellows—was seen as a major positive. The value of 'fancies' rose exponentially.

Colour in diamonds is largely caused by twisting of the crystal lattice, which makes the carbon refract light in different ways. (Some blue diamonds can also obtain their colour through the addition of boron, and it has been claimed that green diamonds can acquire their colour from exposure to uranium. The Mir pipe alluvials from Siberia—known as 'Russian bears'—have a greenish tinge.) Because diamond colour is mainly due to refraction, diamonds can come in all the constituent colours of visible light—truly all the colours of the rainbow. Diamonds in the full range of colours have in fact been found, including green, blue, yellow and violet ones, and rainbow-coloured diamond showpieces have been made. (Laurie Fitzgerald of Argyle Diamond Sales had a diamond rainbow made: a solid-gold channel shaped as an arch and featuring the full spectrum of Argyle colours.) Diamond colour is fickle. At different stages of cutting and polishing, the intensity of colour can rise and fall. With colour making such a big difference to diamond values, the coming and going of colour can be a tense business.

The Ellendale pipes were remarkable for their beautiful coloured diamonds. At Argyle, too, the partners knew at an early stage that a high proportion of the diamonds weren't colourless. The diamonds in AK1 came in a variety of colours, but the great majority—the 'run of the mine' at Argyle—were shades of brown. Yellow brown, straw brown, ruddy brown, deep brown. In the world of diamond colours, there is a definite hierarchy. Some colours are better than others. Famous and valuable brown diamonds had been found: the unusual 'Earth Diamond' is an example of a valuable brown gem. But notwithstanding that example, brown diamonds weren't well thought of in the diamond world. They were the least desirable of all the coloured stones, usually suitable only as industrials or for the cheapest gem categories. (To make the best of what was seen as a bad situation, very light brown stones were sometimes cut and set in such a way that no layperson could see they weren't white.)

The first bundles of Argyle diamonds were so small and brown in their raw state that they reminded Ewen Tyler of coffee sugar. 'The preponderance of browns was a source of concern,' Bill Leslie said, 'if not embarrassment.' The De Beers people didn't hide their contempt for the 'run of the mine' at Argyle, referring to the brownish and yellowish stones as 'roo poo' and 'frozen spit'. 'They were very dismissive,' Argyle executive Mark Hooper said. 'They'd say things like "Do you call these diamonds?"'

There were several reasons for this disparagement. Apart from the low status of browns, there was an element of old-world diamond people talking down to the new-world interlopers. Also, it was a way for De Beers to come to terms with the extent to which Argyle's enormous supply would affect the market. The massive new mine saw a 100 per cent increase in the supply of diamonds globally. At times, the De Beers people appeared to struggle to accommodate or even to comprehend what was an enormous augmentation of world diamond output. Saying the Australian diamonds were of low quality was a coping strategy, a way to put to one side the impact and the new reality.

◈

Stuart Devlin was born in Geelong during the height of the Great Depression. At a local trade school—the Gordon Institute of Technology—he studied goldsmithing and silversmithing. After displaying a natural talent in those fields, he went on to study at the Royal Melbourne Institute of Technology, and then at London's Royal College of Art and New York's Columbia University. Devlin won a series of high-profile assignments, including the commission to design Australia's first decimal coinage. By the 1970s and 80s, he'd established himself as an acclaimed jeweller and metalsmith, well known for producing limited issue works such as Easter eggs and Christmas boxes. Appointed goldsmith and jeweller to Her Majesty Queen Elizabeth II, he was praised for his creativity and innovation.

Once the leaders of Argyle knew AK1 was a diamond deposit of unprecedented scale, they sought external advice on the likely range of values of the diamonds. They looked to Devlin. Giving him a selection of the most desirable gem-quality diamonds from Smoke Creek, they asked him to cut, polish and assess them, and deliver his findings in a report.

'The cutting and polishing was done in London,' Leslie said. 'When Stuart returned to Argyle's office on Kings Park Road to make his report, in true diamantaire style he unfurled his black velvet swathe and carefully set out the polished white diamonds to show them off to their optimum.' Devlin told a meeting of the mine's leaders that the stones were harder than most diamonds, and some of them were of very good quality. At the end of the meeting, the Argyle principals thanked Devlin for his work. Just as he was preparing to leave, he made an offhand remark. He'd heard that the JV had brown diamonds. Would it be possible, he said, to see a sample of them? 'When Stuart asked about the browns,' Leslie said, 'I felt a bit squeamish. My first thought was to say, "How many bucketloads would you like to take?" But I resisted. Instead he selected a sample and took them back to London to be cut and polished.'

While Devlin investigated the browns, the Argyle partners were confronted with the difficult economics of operating a diamond mine within the embrace of a global cartel. Under the CSO contract, the return on investment was not what the miners and their backers had hoped for. 'Argyle's project managers were struggling to make the mining of AK1 on a large scale profitable,' Leslie said. The JV needed to lift the mine's bottom line.

A year or so after Devlin's previous Argyle meeting, he returned to Perth and again laid out his velvet swathe on the boardroom table. 'Then he rolled out the diamonds he'd just polished,' Leslie said. 'They glittered brightly in the natural light streaming in from Kings Park Road.' Devlin had discovered that when the brown diamonds were set in gold, 'their brilliance and subtle colour produced a wonderfully warm and sparkling effect'.

This led to a turning point in the history of Argyle. 'You don't have brown diamonds,' Devlin said. 'You have *champagne* and *cognac* diamonds.' Inside the diamond world and the jewellery trade, Devlin had heard these labels before, along with amber, mahogany, cinnamon, clove, coffee, chocolate and caramel. But for Leslie and his fellow Ashton Mining directors—who (they were used to being told) 'weren't diamond people'—this terminology was new, and a revelation.

Argyle's leaders would see right away the implications of this change in description and perception. Devlin had shown them a way to regrade a huge part of the mine's output. Leslie later recalled: 'Devlin assured those present at the meeting that with the rebranding and a strong marketing campaign the diamonds would be reclassified in a class of their own and marketed as near gem or better.' If the low-value browns could indeed be sold as higher-value coloured diamonds, there would be an immediate and enormous impact on the mine's economics, as Leslie explained:

> Stones that had been estimated initially in the Ashton Joint Venture's projections at around a dollar a carat could now be classified as cheap gem or near gem and worth many times that figure. Some qualities of the brown goods rose in value by as much as tenfold. To be able to reclassify much of the mine's production as cheap gem or even gem made a big difference to the cash flow projections.

The rebranding of the 'run of the mine' at Argyle would sound throughout the global diamond market and ultimately change consumers' tastes and buying behaviour. Terminology that had been used in a limited way among specialist jewellers and diamond industry insiders would now be used on a massive scale in an unparalleled exercise in rebranding, one of the most astute and audacious instances of product repositioning ever conducted in the entire history of commerce. (As audacious as the rebranding of 'leveraged buyouts' as 'private equity', or Lake Argyle's 'shovel-nosed catfish' as the 'silver cobbler'.)

With the cooperation of shoppers, Argyle would be able to reclassify millions of carats of brown industrials as cheap gem or 'Indian goods', and millions of carats of browns as higher-quality gem diamonds, even as fancies. Immediately, millions of carats of diamonds were worth more, and estimates of the mine's lifetime revenue increased commensurately. But for these estimates to be achieved, the mine partners had to overturn entrenched attitudes and deep conservatism among jewellery manufacturers, wholesalers and retailers.

The Australians embarked on a vigorous, worldwide 'champagne and cognac' marketing campaign. Their strategy was to focus on the top end of the jewellery market rather than the mass-market 'mall jewellery' retailers. The hope and expectation was that the new fashions would spread outward from the apex jewellers and taste-formers in the major cities. In the US, therefore, the Argyle partners held presentations on champagne and cognac jewellery for influential customers. These were a great success. According to Rio Tinto's official record of the campaign, 'there was a "ripple effect" when the ... influential jewellers began to attract attention from other jewellers in a particular city. For a relatively modest outlay in marketing, Argyle reached the maximum number of retailers and, indeed, jewellery buyers.' Argyle's investment went a long way towards cementing champagne diamonds in the American jewellery market.

Small Argyle browns were ideal for mixed pavé settings that brought out the contrast between the different shades. For exhibition around the world, Devlin designed striking showpieces that featured brown diamonds in gold settings. In the words of Argyle's marketing people, the 'Champagne Diamonds [were] displayed to perfection against white diamonds and warmly enhanced by yellow gold'. Placed in major jewellery stores, the showpieces attracted great interest—and eventually sold for extraordinary prices.

One signature Devlin piece is a diamond-studded champagne flute. Another is the 18-carat-gold automated Carousel Egg, which is set with 3039 champagne and cognac diamonds and 600 white diamonds. Twelve centimetres tall and built from four segments, the egg opens to reveal a revolving carousel of eighteen horses that rise and fall under miniature lights. (When the egg was first exhibited, the notorious spendthrift and playboy Prince Jefri of Brunei snapped it up with relish.) Designers such as David Yurman also created special sample pieces using Argyle stones.

Other highlights of the champagne diamonds campaign included an exhibition of 200 pieces of champagne diamond jewellery and *objets d'art* (1986–87); promotion of coloured diamonds at Brisbane's World Expo (1988); the US Champagne Diamond promotions (1991); the International Coloured Diamond Awards (1992); a $20 million exhibition of coloured diamonds, jewellery and *objets d'art* in the Australian Pavilion at the Seville Expo (1992); and, in conjunction with De Beers, a 'Diamonds for Your Man' advertising campaign. A competition sponsored by Argyle and aimed at jewellery designers throughout the world, the International Coloured Diamonds Award competition offered US$250,000 in prize money. In a short space of time, trade awareness of Argyle's champagne diamonds rose from 6 per cent to 90 per cent of jewellers.

To convince smaller-scale local retailers to carry champagne and cognac diamonds, the Argyle JV engaged MVI Marketing of Southern California. In 1989, an Argyle delegation flew from Australia to America to meet MVI principals Liz Chatelain and Marty Hurwitz. The Australians brought diamond samples along with the brand 'Champagne Diamonds'. Speaking to author Rachelle Bergstein, Chatelain recalled the moment when she first heard the concept:

> My partner and I looked at each other and said, wow, this is going to be difficult. Only because, one, the trade didn't even know that diamonds came in different colours—they knew the Hope Diamond was blue—but not at this magnitude of quantity were

coloured diamonds ever exposed to the market … and the second issue was that, historically, browns were industrial, and we had that issue to get past with traditional jewellery store owners and retailers.

Many diamond people had been trained to disregard browns as 'off-colour'. 'We had a joke for twenty years that we don't use the B-word,' Chatelain said, 'because that was a significant barrier.' In its initial market analysis for the diamond venture, the Boston Consulting Group had considered the potential for selling coloured diamonds. (They had also considered the importance of colour in other gemstones, such as sapphires, and had analysed the different markets for natural and synthetic diamonds.) Would Americans, the strategists asked, buy the Argyle diamonds? Devlin showed it was possible, and the marketing consultants now provided further confirmation of consumers' responses to this kind of jewellery. The marketers were confident: 'In no uncertain terms, the American shopper would buy it.' As Bergstein explained in her book *Brilliance and Fire: A Biography of Diamonds*,

> MVI set up the Champagne Diamond Registry, a trade association funded by Argyle, and introduced a champagne colour chart, which provided categories of stones from light champagne to medium to cognac. Then MVI rallied [the Gemological Institute of America] to endorse it, thus standardizing the vocabulary describing brown diamonds and giving everyone in the business a fresh way to talk about them.

MVI persuaded retailers to host champagne diamond events at their stores. Some jewellers remained sceptical, but customers 'proved to be much more open-minded'. According to Bergstein, MVI also took out ads in magazines such as *Town & Country* and *Vanity Fair*.

> MVI's objective with brown diamonds was quite similar to the mission De Beers had with white diamonds in the late 1930s and early 1940s. Just as with NW Ayer, the concept was generic diamond marketing. MVI was promoting not Argyle or any particular designer or brand, but rather the idea of the champagne palette.

The success of the campaign was soon reflected in the price of brown diamonds. In 1991, champagne diamonds were worth as much as 70 per cent of white gems of equivalent size and quality. Bergstein described how the jewellery industry had not just accommodated a new product category, it had embraced the new gems as the basis for a new way of buying and wearing jewels: 'Fashion jewellery—less expensive items that a woman might buy just because, or a man might buy her for a Christmas or birthday present—made use of these tiny, lower-value stones.'

Another feature of the champagne and cognac campaign was its encouragement of the Indian diamond jewellery industry. As Ewen Tyler told journalist John McIlwraith, this was 'a logical sequel to the close relationship built up between Argyle and the Indians in the trade of rough stones'.

◇

Leading diamantaires were fascinated by the Argyle output, and especially by the rare fancies: blues, yellows, greens and some spectacular pinks. Thanks in particular to the pinks, which ranged from rose to a rich burgundy red, Argyle fancies were quickly famous for their brilliant intensity of colour. The saturated colour was almost magical, something to be felt, tasted, bathed in. Bergstein called it an almost purply shade, reminiscent of an orchid petal. CRA's Robyn Ellison called it a fabulous fluke of nature. This fluke was ideal for jewellers: they proved they could do marvellous things with Argyle pinks, whose shades resonated perfectly with the market positioning of diamonds as signifiers of love.

In Africa, the Williamson mine at Mwadui had produced pink diamonds. The Doc himself gave one of the most beautiful pinks to Britain's royal family. Two other famous pink diamonds, the Daria-i-Noor ('Sea of Light') and the Noor-ul-Ain ('Light of the Eye'), are part of the Iranian crown jewels. The two may have come from a single stone, the legendary 'Great Table', described by Jean-Baptiste Tavernier in *Les Six Voyages*. The colour of the 32.24-carat Agra Diamond has been described as a light, slightly orange-tinged blush. In 1990, it sold at Christie's in London for US$6,959,780.

Many other mines, too, have produced pinks, though stones of that colour are nowhere more than a small proportion of the mined diamonds. But at Argyle, the enormous volume of diamonds meant that even a tiny proportion of the output corresponded to a substantial quantity of pinks. Less than a hundredth of 1 per cent of Argyle's annual diamond output were fancy pinks, but in some years that still amounted to 1000 carats, sometimes more. As Bergstein wrote,

> Argyle's production wasn't considered ideal, but it came with a silver lining—or, in this case, a mesmerizing fuchsia one. As it turned out, Australia's earth had more to offer than just an overwhelming number of low-value brown stones: it was the first mine in history to consistently produce gorgeous pink diamonds, in small but steady batches.

(Broadly speaking, Argyle's special pinks and 'run of the mine' browns are part of the same colour family. They both have elements of red, and some browns have a pinkish tinge.)

Under the CSO contract, CRA and Ashton Mining could retain up to 60,000 carats per year for local processing, to help develop the local industry. Thus empowered, the Argyle partners picked out and held back as many pinks as they could, along with rare blue, green and violet diamonds, and high-quality white ones. From this slice of Argyle's output, most of the pinks were cut and polished in Perth. The terms of the contract put Argyle in a position to control most of the distribution of pinks. The Australians therefore put those gems at the centre of their marketing efforts. This helped the JV build the international market for Australian fancies, and it helped establish the global brand of Argyle pinks.

Most of the gems held back by Argyle under the CSO contract were sold through local jewellers. But beginning in 1985, the main Argyle partners held annual 'tenders' to sell the best of the pinks from their share of the mine's output. As few as 50 or 60 carats were offered per tender. The pinks were displayed at invitation-only viewings in major cities around the world. The exclusivity of the events, their sales approach, the colour of the stones, and the fact that the stones were diamonds—all these elements added up to a glamorous and enticing picture. The Argyle tenders earned a strong following among the jewellers, collectors and investors who were willing to pay more than US$100,000 per carat for fancy pink diamonds. According to the miners' own marketing,

> The Argyle Pink Diamond Tender soon became a leading event on the international diamond calendar, with a special selection of outstanding pink diamonds for sale every year. After displays in Tokyo, Hong Kong and Geneva, those invited to tender make sealed bids on the pink diamonds of their choice.

The tenders fuelled a worldwide craze for pinks. One sale of sixty-seven polished pinks in Geneva brought nearly US$8 million. At a Sotheby's auction, a flawless purplish pink of 10.83 carats (not an Argyle gem) sold for US$4.1 million, or more than US$379,000 per carat. As Bergstein noted, another milestone in the mania for pinks was the Harry Winston engagement ring Jennifer 'I'm still Jenny from the block' Lopez received from Ben Affleck in 2002. The ring, 'with a stunning 6.1 carat light pink square stone and two white baguettes flanking it, [was] worth an estimated US$1.2 million'.

The very best loose or unset pinks have brought US$1 million per carat after cutting and polishing.

Argyle pinks appeared in showpiece items, such as the US$300,000, 10-carat pink diamond watch handmade by Bosshard & Co. of Switzerland, and the 23-kilogram, $12 million 'Argyle Library Egg', which features 24,000 pink diamonds, amounting to 348 carats. Top jeweller Paul Kutchinsky made the egg with a team of craftspeople. An object in the tradition of Fabergé's Russian imperial Easter eggs, the Library Egg became a focal point whenever it was displayed. According to Rio Tinto's official record of the marketing campaign, the egg's first appearance in Antwerp in 1990 'caused a sensation'.

Back at the East Kimberley mine site, the processing plant continued to smash the largest of the mesmerising fuchsia and orchid stones.

29

FALLING OUT

O NCE THE CSO contract was signed, diamonds began to flow from the alluvial deposits and then from the main pipe. 'Unhappily,' Ewen Tyler said, 'this did not in itself ensure cordiality in the early years of the agreement.'

The suspicions and tensions that were evident between the two parties during the negotiations did not end with the commencement of the marketing arrangement. A frequent reproach from the De Beers side was 'You are not diamond people.' In this and other ways, the Australians were for De Beers a new kettle of fish. When CRA and Ashton entered the CSO, it was the first time in living memory that De Beers had tied up with commercially savvy people who were in a wholly private enterprise. Most of the other deals had been with mines either co-owned by De Beers or primarily state-owned. Argyle was the first time De Beers had to deal at arm's length with a fully commercial mine, in a country that was politically stable and where overt corruption was hard to pull off.

Argyle hired Robyn Ellison as an analyst to support the agreement with the CSO. 'It was a very fractious relationship,' Ellison later said. 'You're selling the majority of your diamonds to your biggest customer and your biggest competitor. So we were in bed with the enemy.'

The diamond industry is a game of arcane knowledge, secret margins and hidden value. Estimating the worth of any individual diamond is inherently subjective. The process of 'rough sorting' is difficult. It involves a lot of manual work, with rooms of people looking through hand lenses to separate diamonds into categories based on their weight, shape, colour and clarity. Sorting and valuing over 100 million tiny diamonds a year (hundreds of thousands a day)— stones that hover on the borderline between industrial and near-gem quality—is a mammoth undertaking. As Tyler told John McIlwraith,

> Traditionally, hundreds of people had pored over small piles of stones, painstakingly making judgements on each stone's quality in a series of steps that made the classifications more refined. 'Price books' could have thousands of such classifications.

The subjectivity and opacity of the sorting was soon a sore point. During the negotiations before the CSO agreement, some De Beers people had felt the terms were too generous towards the Australians. Those feelings were softened by quiet, reassuring words shared among the CSO camp. Yes, they'd given too much away in the negotiations, but now they would 'get it back on the tweezers'. The Australians overheard a CSO representative saying precisely those words, that De Beers could claw back 'on the tweezers' what their chairman had given up in the negotiations. The meaning was clear: by valuing Argyle's diamonds 'with some frugality', the CSO could make up for their leader's generosity. What was envisaged was a tactical type of deflation. During their careful, quiet, subjective work, the sorters would assign a lower quality to the stones. The CSO would then buy them wholesale at that quality before reclassifying them in order to sell them at a higher price.

Argyle was vulnerable to this kind of chicanery. Australia had few experienced sorters. After the CSO agreement was signed, De Beers offered to send people who could help classify the Argyle diamonds into the different value categories. 'We had to engage sorters from De Beers', Tyler said, 'to teach our own people how to sort.' The CSO seconded twenty experienced staff to Argyle's Perth office. The Australians would rely on the secondees' expertise and goodwill. For the sorters, working in Perth promised to be a pleasant and rewarding interlude. Positive reports were relayed to London. The visitors were enjoying the sun and the sport. As McIlwraith noted, though they found aspects of Australian life baffling, 'in broad terms it was almost a paid holiday'.

As soon as the secondees got to work, however, there were disagreements over the sorting results. 'We started to fear', Tyler said, 'that the De Beers team were undervaluing our product … There were regular debates about where the diamonds would sit in the categories, so there was back-and-forth between Argyle and De Beers and fundamentally De Beers was better at this game. Argyle smelled a rat.'

All around the world, De Beers was forever reclassifying diamonds and creating new categories. The company seemed to be using the complex system of diamond qualities the same way it used its complex corporate structure: as a smokescreen. In Australia, the Argyle team concluded that parcels of diamonds being sold to the CSO were not valued fairly, and that, in Tyler's view, 'the use of the organisation's sorters made it difficult to establish this case'. From Argyle's perspective, the secondees from De Beers were recovering too much 'on the tweezers'.

The terminology in the trade was that the sorters had been 'pushing the categories'. De Beers had previously faced allegations of pushing, including in the 1950s from Edward Wharton-Tigar of Selection Trust. De Beers, it seemed, had form. But the CSO still bridled at the accusation of bad dealing, retorting that the real problem was the Australians' lack of experience. That, combined with the unique nature of Argyle production, 'had lowered average values from the mine'.

The Argyle JV and De Beers were indeed engaged in a game, and De Beers was very much the better player. It had been playing the game for a long time, and had in fact written the game's rules. But the Argyle partners were far from helpless. In the argument over values, they were well equipped to defend themselves. They set up an important experiment, as Tyler explained:

Over five sales, the prices of Argyle goods declined substantially, so that by the end of the cycle they were averaging 25 per cent less than they were at the beginning. The CSO executives rejected any protests about this with the claim that the quality of Argyle's diamonds [was] declining.

There followed a stratagem which while it might have been said by the CSO to show that Australian miners were not 'gentlemen', also demonstrated that they were not easy targets either.

Throughout that cycle, random samples from each sale of goods had been held back, and they were then offered to the CSO's sorters to value, but in a random order—that is, nobody except an independent firm of accountants, Coopers & Lybrand, knew in which order they had been mined and offered for sale.

The result was that there was no discernible difference in the quality of the diamonds, as shown by the random set of five sortings, and the CSO could not identify from the valuations what order they had been originally offered to them.

This was a strong test of the process, and a blunt message to De Beers. The results showed that the Australians were right to be suspicious. Some people at De Beers were indignant about the results. Others, though, were realistic and candid about what had happened. They knew they'd been found out.

The audit results precipitated the sudden return to London of the seconded British sorters. The two parties to the contract characterised this event differently. Did Argyle CEO Mick O'Leary send the sorters away, or did the CSO recall its personnel to London? Either way, the sorters had only a couple of days' notice. Their 'paid holiday' was abruptly over. Though the marriage between Argyle and De Beers had started well, it quickly became prickly, and was now demonstrably at a low point. As a result of the audit and the sorters' return, Argyle and the CSO were on the verge of a formal contractual dispute, and the prevailing atmosphere between them was 'unpleasant'.

In practice, the contractual dispute had already arrived. For three or four months there was a stalemate in which Argyle sold no diamonds through the CSO. As a consequence, Argyle had to stockpile stones while it recruited senior sorters, largely from Belgium and South Africa, and recruited and trained young Australians to work under the seniors. 'There followed a rapid learning experience', Tyler said.

'Training and learning on the go. Working hard to refute the criticism "You are not diamond people".'

In addition to recruiting new sorters, Argyle looked for ways to speed up and streamline the sorting process. Part of the solution was mechanical. Tyler later described how electronic sorting machines were developed to 'classify the stones by colour and clarity, replicating the arduous hand-sorting that so fatigued the sorters. The machines replaced 90 per cent of the hand-sorting previously required.' This was one of many instances in which technology would come to the rescue for Argyle.

When later asked about the early collaboration between the Australians and the CSO, Harry Oppenheimer conceded there had been 'considerable tensions' in the first two years of the relationship. After the audit and exit there were ongoing disagreements about values and marketing but relations gradually improved, and the parties to the diamond marketing agreement settled into a new equilibrium. That equilibrium, however, was inherently unstable.

The inaugural Argyle–CSO contract ran from 1983 to 1985. (It initially covered only the sale of diamonds from alluvial mining and the testing of AK1.) The agreement's provisions allowed for a formal stage of renegotiation at the end of the contract period. But in 1985, despite the earlier tensions, the agreement was renewed, for the most part unchanged, and for a longer period, to 1990.

During the second contract period (in September 1986), David Karpin moved from an executive position at Hamersley Iron to become chief executive and managing director of Argyle. The diamond mine's profitability was disappointing. How, Karpin asked, could Argyle's profits be improved? The basic economics of major mines are well understood. Big mines have high fixed costs, so increasing throughput has the effect of reducing average costs and lifting profit. Another way to boost profit is to reduce costs by mining more efficiently and less extravagantly. A third route is harder and less well travelled: increasing the value of the output.

In 1987 there was a significant meeting of executives at the mine site. According to Rio Tinto's official account of this period,

> At that meeting it was confirmed that the project was returning less than 4 per cent profit to CRA, and George Gauci reported that production would fall from 32 million carats a year to 22 million carats annually in the following five years unless remedies were found.

For Karpin, this lent a sense of urgency to the problems facing the JV. Expert help was sought in several areas, with the goal of lifting the return from the project to between 10 and 12 per cent, which was still marginally below CRA's target rate. According to the official record, 'One result was that a new mining plan was prepared and there were also proposals drawn up to improve the marketing of the project's output.' Under the mining plan, production from Argyle would rise from 3.5 million tonnes a year to 6 million tonnes. Under the marketing plan, the Argyle partners would continue with the 'champagne diamonds' strategy and would seek to improve the prices achieved via both the CSO and Antwerp sales routes.

The profitability drive succeeded. The average wholesale price rose from US$6 a carat in 1986–87 to US$10 a carat in 1991. As McIlwraith heard from the Australians, 'This was partly due to an improvement in the demand for diamonds throughout the world, but also partly to higher prices being paid by the CSO.' Renewal of alluvial production at Argyle was another plank in the strategy. Could the old alluvial plant be freshened up so the mine's output might again be augmented with wild alluvial stones? A feasibility study showed a $1.5 million refurbishment would be enough for mining of the creek beds to restart. In the first year of the alluvial revival, wild diamonds contributed $25 million to revenue and helped enhance the whole mine's bottom line.

In 1989, on the tenth anniversary of the AK1 discovery, the Argyle partners sold a record weight of diamonds to the CSO: 9.7 million carats, or almost 10 per cent of annual world production, in a single sale. The following year, the CSO contract was renewed. But soon after, the Argyle people were again unhappy with the efforts of De Beers and the CSO to sell Argyle diamonds. They did not feel that goods of the Argyle qualities were receiving a fair share of the cartel's marketing effort or budget. 'De Beers was underselling the Argyle diamonds,' Tyler said, 'especially the coloured gems.' It seemed as though the CSO wasn't fully comfortable with the Argyle stones, especially the browns, even though Argyle itself was marketing them with vigour.

The treatment of brown diamonds was the strongest evidence that the interests of Argyle and De Beers were divergent and potentially in conflict. Argyle had shown it could successfully market diamonds on its own. The rebranding and promotion of champagne diamonds was a spectacular example. Even before Stuart Devlin introduced the champagne and cognac terminology at Argyle, De Beers people had encountered these labels among specialist jewellers, but the cartel showed little interest in marketing Argyle's diamonds to their full potential. De Beers took few steps to market the best browns as fancies, for example.

Concerns persisted, too, about diamond values and pricing. In July 1995, the CSO decided to cut the prices of smaller stones. This hit Argyle especially hard. John Robinson was CEO of Ashton Mining. As mining author and journalist Ross Louthean wrote,

> Robinson made no secret that he found it a double blow, because Argyle, like all producers selling to the CSO, was already subject to the 15 per cent reduction on quotas which was imposed precisely to help prices. 'It is therefore a contradiction,' he argued, 'when deferred purchases are in place to defend prices, that prices are then reduced.'

As Louthean noted, Argyle responded by tilting its production towards larger diamonds:

> It introduced larger screens at its ore treatment plant through which tiny, low-value stones of less than 1.5 mm will escape. Although this reduces annual production by 15 per cent, down

to around 34 million carats, extra ore will actually be treated, providing more large stones, thus raising revenue at the AK1 pipe by 10 per cent.

Apart from the impact of overt CSO pricing decisions, the Australians also had a lingering suspicion that they were still losing out 'on the tweezers'.

The next renegotiation of the CSO contract was scheduled for 1996. In the years and months leading up to that moment, the economics of the mine were again finely balanced. The project's profitability was again disappointing. To improve the financial return from the mine, Argyle needed to negotiate better contractual terms. But De Beers was offering a deal that was only marginally more attractive than the status quo. In earlier renegotiation stages, Argyle had looked at alternative options only in a half-hearted way. This time would be different. Ashton Mining's Mark Hooper helped lead the negotiations for the Australians. He knew his negotiating position was only as good as his best alternative. In preparing for the renegotiation, the Argyle JV people therefore did a lot of work to make the alternative options credible, including the option of walking away altogether from the marketing agreement.

Since the beginning of mining from AK1, Argyle had sold a substantial quantity of diamonds through its own channels. Retaining the right to market some of the Argyle diamonds directly had proven to be a crucial move by the JV. The cost of the Antwerp operation might have been exorbitant, but this selling channel was invaluable. It created an alternative to and a benchmark for the De Beers contract. 'It helped keep the CSO honest,' Doug Bailey said, 'and it gave Ashton and CRA a priceless window on the market.' The Antwerp sales channel provided vital information and a direct foothold at the diamond industry's coalface. It was crucial insurance should the Argyle miners ever decide to go it alone, outside the De Beers infrastructure.

The Australians had proven they could market their stones. They had shown they would not be passive participants in the world industry. The champagne and cognac campaign in particular demonstrated that Australian diamonds were a formidable force, and that the newcomers could influence tastes and affect the global market in ways that were traditionally the province of the CSO itself. In the run-up to the 1996 renegotiation, the Australians had the knowledge and confidence gained from ten years' experience in selling diamonds.

Thus armed, the Argyle team now approached people in other potential distribution channels, including in Cape Town and Hong Kong, as well as local sellers in Perth. Argyle did a lot of preparatory work particularly to build the alternative option in India, with Indian cutters and polishers. The pre-work continued for around eighteen months, and then the negotiations proper began.

As with previous contract periods, negotiating with De Beers was difficult and peculiar. For De Beers, Nicky Oppenheimer was in charge but Tim Capon mostly led the negotiations on Oppenheimer's behalf. Capon and his colleagues were sure they had the supreme position; they adopted a commensurately high-handed and standoffish approach. 'There was minimal engagement through the negotiation,' Hooper said, 'and that made it difficult to pin De Beers down on any possible improvements to the contract terms.'

It was evident to the Australians that the De Beers people did not seriously think Argyle would walk away. And the Australians saw the De Beers tactic as running down the clock so the negotiation period would come to an end and Argyle would be forced to make a deal. For the Australians, though, the option of going it alone was a real one. In principle, it could give the Argyle team a way to optimise the mine and its output and marketing. A commercially optimised mine promised better returns. And leaving the CSO would mean escaping contractual terms, such as the reduced purchases clause, that the Australians felt were onerous and one-sided. All these considerations led the leaders of the Argyle JV to a tectonic conclusion: they could do better outside the agreement.

In June 1996, Ashton Mining took this option up with its bigger partner at Argyle. CRA's leaders, though, were hesitant to make the jump from the CSO. Could the Argyle partners really afford to leave the De Beers universe? Plenty of people inside CRA answered no. They knew at the very least it was a big step and a big risk. But a key Rio Tinto executive, Gordon Gilchrist, saw the merits of going it alone. He had the courage to undertake what threatened to be a career-limiting move, and pushed his colleagues inside CRA to agree to the exit.

For Ashton Mining, leaving the CSO contract would be a 'Bet the business' decision. Argyle was Ashton Mining's sole source of income, and the company's loan facilities were predicated on it dealing with De Beers. No one at Ashton Mining wanted to see their financial facilities blow up. Both Ashton and CRA would need to convince their banks that valid commercial reasons were behind the idea of a De Beers divorce.

To square everything away, the executives of both businesses made presentations to their boards and banks. When the bankers first heard of the exit plan, the colour drained from their faces. But then they heard some of the stories about life under the CSO agreement, and of the partners' successes with their own marketing, particularly of Argyle pinks and browns. The bankers were convinced: this big step could improve the mine's viability and profitability.

The Australians informed De Beers of their decision. The CSO contract would not be renewed. As of 1 July 1996, Argyle Diamonds would market all its production through its European sales office in Antwerp. The Argyle partners continued their own marketing—using a simplified set of diamond categories—and continued to benefit to some extent from De Beers' wider efforts to promote diamonds, but the CSO was no longer a sales channel for Argyle diamonds.

The De Beers camp was far from happy with the Australians' decision. Payback came swiftly. The diamond cartel emptied its stockpiles and 'surge bin', flooding the market with stones in an effort to drive down prices. But just as swiftly, the attempt at retribution backfired. Instead of clogging up the works, the torrent of diamonds nourished the market and helped it grow. Perversely, the flood was a boon for the Indian polishing and cutting industry. As Hooper said, the De Beers deluge 'just provided fuel for what the Indians were hoping to do. It gave them the volume they needed and they ran with it.' With Indian buyers taking up the slack, diamond prices soon recovered. De Beers had underestimated the capacity and ingenuity of India's merchants and diamantaires.

In other ways, however, the Argyle exit and De Beers' response had profound and lasting effects. The Argyle contract had been a first for the CSO, and now the Australians' decision to leave it was another. (Other suppliers had left the CSO fold, but not in this way or on this scale.) More cartel members would decide to break away from the De Beers network. Argyle's decision disrupted the cartel and changed the whole industry. Those impacts would play out in unexpected ways. Right now, in the big game that is diamonds, Argyle was one up on De Beers. But the industry's biggest player had other cards up its sleeve.

30

A CLEAN SWEEP

IN 1985 OR thereabouts, Ashton Mining director Bill Leslie had received a phone call out of the blue from Julian Ogilvie Thompson, the recently appointed chairman of De Beers. The matter was highly sensitive. Ogilvie Thompson was taking a confidential sounding on whether Malaysia Mining Corporation's shareholding in Ashton Mining might be available to purchase. As Leslie later recalled,

> In the course of our conversation I was left in little doubt that the suggestion had come from Richard Wiesener, a Monaco-based director of Elders IXL, which was then Australia's largest brewing group. At the time I was dealing with another director of Elders on an unrelated matter and in casual conversation he made the comment that they thought Ashton was undervalued and asked whether I thought MMC were long-term holders in Ashton. I made some ambivalent response and thought nothing more of it. Elders had run the numbers and were of the view that MMC's Ashton shares were a way into Argyle. Wiesener, whom I knew, had sounded out De Beers to see what their attitude would be to such a move, and whether they might support it.

De Beers was running a multi-pronged strategy to control the international diamond market. Helping to finance an Elders acquisition of part or all of Ashton Mining was potentially very attractive, as Leslie explained:

> What Elders needed was support for the funding. I believe they had in mind a structure somewhat similar to the corporate engineering they used when they spent $2 billion on acquiring a 20 per cent shareholding in BHP, Australia's largest mining company. This was done with BHP board encouragement to fend off Robert Holmes à Court, a well-known share-market raider. BHP had taken up preference shares in Elders to effectively help fund the acquisition. This was cleverly done in a way not to trigger a compulsory takeover bid for BHP and not to be treated as BHP financing the buying of its own shares, which of course was and is illegal. I imagine with De Beers and Elders, De Beers would have given some kind of financial support for Elders to acquire the MMC shares in return for gaining negative control. The profit from a 15 per cent interest in Argyle would be neither here nor there in De Beers terms. Guaranteeing the right to purchase the Argyle production was their key interest.

Soon after this, Elders started to unravel and the Elders deal was no longer feasible. De Beers acquired a shareholding in the Argyle owners directly. The shareholding was modest but, as later events would show, highly strategic.

In 1995, Britain's RTZ Corporation and Australia's CRA were unified as a single corporate entity that maintained dual listings in London and Australia. Two years later, the RTZ Corporation was renamed Rio Tinto plc, and CRA Limited became Rio Tinto Limited.

At the same time, the Ashton Mining board was thinking seriously about the company's long-term future. Open-cut mining at AK1 couldn't go on forever. It was estimated that by 2005, above-ground mining would no longer be tenable at the site, and the miners would have to go underground. The miners knew, moreover, that that would be expensive. The alternatives to underground mining included redefining the project entirely or walking away from it altogether.

For the board of Ashton Mining, this thinking was especially acute: the stake in Argyle was still their main revenue source. A train of thought led to an audacious idea. If Rio Tinto decided Argyle was too expensive or too difficult, was there a chance that Ashton Mining could buy out its larger partner and go it alone at Argyle? Could it develop, for example, an underground mine below the open-cut, even if its senior partner chose not to participate?

In July 1997, this speculative train of thought evolved into the candidly named 'Project Hope'. Malaysia Mining Corporation owned 49.94 per cent of Ashton Mining. With the support of MMC, a proposal was devised to acquire Rio Tinto's 60 per cent interest in the mine.

Argyle had only recently left the CSO's orbit, but in an extraordinary turn of events, Ashton Mining discussed Project Hope with De Beers. Might the diamond behemoth be prepared to help finance the acquisition, if Rio Tinto was prepared to sell? De Beers showed more than a little interest in the plan, which offered a backdoor way to return Argyle to the De Beers universe.

As a result of these discussions, Ashton Mining and the Argyle mine were now very much 'in play'. By March 1998, several new permutations had emerged. There was a possible bidder from Israel. And there were rumours that De Beers was interested in financing an acquisition not just of Rio's stake in Argyle, but Ashton Mining's as well, possibly in a new permutation of the abandoned Elders deal. This was something the Ashton Mining board was not prepared for, or enthusiastic about.

In June 1998, Rio Tinto indicated it might be willing to sell its controlling interest in Argyle. The diamond market was tough. Rio was unsure if it wanted to be in that business at all. For Rio, precious stones were an outlier, even an anomaly, in its mining portfolio.

Later in 1998, Rio Tinto briefed Ashton Mining on a new plan for building an underground mine. Expensive drilling would be needed to prove there were enough diamonds in the pipe to make underground mining worthwhile. Rio wasn't enthusiastic, and Ashton still harboured the hope that its senior partner would sell its interest. With Rio facing an expensive new phase of diamond mining, Ashton

Mining convinced its larger partner to sell its 60 per cent of the mine. Ashton Mining's Doug Bailey and Mark Hooper succeeded in driving the purchase price down to $200 million. The idea was that the new entity would be run by Hooper out of Perth. Rio's board approved the sale, and the sale price.

The Ashton Mining team won the support of their bankers to buy out Rio Tinto's interest. At the eleventh hour, however, MMC stymied the deal. Concerns had emerged that the Malaysian company could not afford its share of the likely acquisition price. Perhaps even more decisive was an innocent incident in which Ashton Mining's CEO, John Robinson, was perceived to have insulted one of his Malaysian directors.

Relations between the Ashton Mining board and its major share-holder deteriorated noticeably. Some of the local board members felt betrayed by those from MMC, who very probably knew their company would be unlikely to support the attempt to buy Rio Tinto's stake. The Australian directors reflected that MMC, ultimately controlled by the Malaysian Government, would not have been allowed to participate in Argyle to such an extent because, among other things, the then prime minister of Malaysia, Dr Mahathir, had long nursed an overt antipathy towards Australia. Looking back on Project Hope and the Malaysians' decision, the local Ashton Mining directors would speak ruefully of a lost opportunity.

On 21 July 1999, MMC's financial controller, Phan Leong Kim, received a telephone call. It was from Rosnah Omar, a Singapore-based director of NM Rothschild & Sons. Omar was hoping to put together some kind of deal. Would MMC be receptive, he asked, to a cash offer for its Ashton Mining interest? Kim didn't tell Omar to go away. Maybe a deal was possible. MMC wasn't in a hurry to sell its stake, Kim said, but would consider offers above $1.40 per share.

By March of the following year, MMC had firmed in its plans to sell its Ashton Mining stake. Omar and Kim spoke again, and Kim dropped a fresh bombshell: in the marketing of its interest, MMC would be prepared to talk to De Beers. Through intermediaries, contact was made between the Malaysians and the international diamond cartel. Then in May, Ollie Oliveira of De Beers wrote directly to MMC proposing a characteristically complex transaction structure, and offering $1.20 per share. (The proposal was that De Beers would acquire a 19.9 per cent interest in Ashton Mining from MMC, then make a full takeover offer for the junior Argyle partner.) Kim wrote back. MMC didn't understand the proposed transaction structure; and a price of $1.20 per share did not reflect the true value of Ashton Mining. In fact, a substantially higher price could be justified. The two parties were a good distance apart, but they agreed to enter further discussions that might 'bridge the valuation gap'.

(While these soundings were underway, other parties came forward to express interest in Ashton Mining, and there was an unexpected uplift in Ashton's share price. On 26 June 2000, Kim wrote to Oliveira to assure him MMC was not responsible for the rise in the share price to $1.09.)

In July 2000, Oliveira and Kim met in Singapore. Kim outlined MMC's price expectations: $1.50 to $1.80 per share for its interest in Ashton; discussions of a price below $1.50 per share would not be entertained. De Beers for its part signalled that $1.80 was an absolute upper limit, but there was room for a deal in the indicated range. MMC agreed to go forward with De Beers as per its proposed transaction approach, including the pre-offer acceptance agreement. A full-blown takeover battle ensued.

At the end of July, the international diamond syndicate announced it had reached a pre-offer agreement with MMC (based on $1.62 per share) to acquire 19.9 per cent of Ashton Mining Limited, and that it would now seek to acquire the remaining shares. De Beers offered the same price, subject to conditions, to Ashton's other shareholders. One condition was that De Beers had to obtain the approval of Australia's Foreign Investment Review Board. The old issue of Australian controls on foreign-capital flows was again at the centre of Argyle's story.

The Rio Tinto camp viewed the De Beers strategy with some alarm. Upon reflection, Rio wasn't ready to leave the mine after all, and didn't relish the idea of partnering with De Beers on the next phases of the project. Rio countered the syndicate's bid with an offer at the top of MMC's specified range. Amid the offers and counteroffers, the directors of Ashton Mining held a modest sweep. A pot of $50 was staked on what the final price would be, and on who would win the takeover battle.

Ewen Tyler bet on the Israelis coming forward and snaffling up Ashton Mining. At several points in his journey, Israeli interests had been in the mix: as potential lenders; as a possible distribution channel; and as potential investors. This moment, Tyler reasoned, might very well be the time for those interests to finally step forward.

Tyler kept a sheet showing who held what in the office sweep. It listed the participants, the expected acquisition price, and the expected victor in the takeover battle.

Tan Sri Khalid	1.90	Rio Tinto
Ewen Tyler	2.85	Israelis
David [Baithover]	2.27	De Beers
Robert [Rae]	2.38	Rio Tinto
Barry Jackaman	2.45	Rio Tinto
Doug Bailey	2.40	Rio Tinto
Markus Ziemer	2.26	De Beers
Alison Lansley	2.30	Rio Tinto
Samed	2.25	De Beers
Phan	2.40	De Beers
TS Ibrahim	2.38	De Beers
Neil Johnson	2.31	De Beers

The final bid from the De Beers side was $2.28, still with significant conditions. After much thought and some hesitation, Rio Tinto lifted its offer to $2.20 a share, including a special dividend.

De Beers' offer was therefore higher than Rio's, but there were other factors for investors to consider. De Beers needed FIRB approval, and getting that was going to take at least a month. Rio didn't need FIRB approval, and it used this fact shrewdly. The Anglo-Australian miner was able to make its $2.20 offer firm, and subject to a time limit that was shorter than the FIRB approval period. Though the offer was incrementally lower than the De Beers bid, it was less subject to conditions. And the time limit made the decision urgent.

The Ashton Mining board was concerned that De Beers would not be able to meet the conditions of its offer by the deadline for the more certain Rio bid. But could the board really recommend that shareholders accept the lower offer? In the office sweep, one of the Malaysian directors, Samed, had the closest price ($2.25) to the Rio bid. In that light, he spoke enthusiastically in favour of the Rio offer. Among other things, if the board formally accepted that offer, he would win the sweep. After further deliberations, the board recommended the Rio offer. Rio therefore ended up with complete ownership of the Argyle mine, and a $50 sweep influenced the fate of a multi-billion-dollar project.

The company that had bought out Tanks and Jennings, and that had helped steer the unsuccessful Ellendale project and the successful Argyle one, ceased to exist as a separate entity. Its assets and legacy were now part of the Rio Group. At the St Kilda Road office, Tyler and Hooper packed up all the plans and other documents, and they worked with Rio to effect its transition to complete ownership of Ashton Mining and therefore Argyle.

After the acquisition there was one loose end: the Western Australian Diamond Trust. Since the 1980s, that entity had held the original Northern Mining stake in Argyle. A strange artefact of the WA Inc. era, the trust had given its retail investors a reliably high return. Tyler remained on the trust's board until, two years after Rio Tinto acquired Ashton Mining, Rio also acquired the trust, giving the original unit holders what Brian Burke described as 'a nice profit on their investment'. The trust ceased to exist, and Tyler was no longer a member of any boards or committees formally connected to the Argyle mine.

◈

When the main Argyle partners were operating under the CSO contract, it appears De Beers didn't seriously contemplate Ashton Mining and CRA getting out. That decision seemed like too much of a risk. But when the Australians did in fact walk away, De Beers had to grapple with a new reality. The market arrangements that had been so remarkably resilient throughout the twentieth century came unstuck. Making a play for Ashton Mining was a last-ditch attempt to re-establish the old order, the old diamond industry model in which De Beers could substantially control the supply of diamonds.

When that attempt failed, De Beers had to reposition itself. The cartel had long dominated both supply and distribution in the diamond market. Now, its role as a producer was weakening but it was still a major player on the selling side, controlling as much as 40 per cent of diamond sales worldwide. Having experienced the shake-up in supply, De Beers reoriented itself towards driving demand for diamonds. The first step was to do some legal tidying-up.

De Beers had been under intense pressure from antitrust and securities market regulators in the US, the UK and Europe. These watchdogs placed it in significant peril and under numerous restrictions. As part of the new reality, De Beers cleaned house, concluding several cases in the US. In 2004, as part of an agreement with the US Department of Justice, it pleaded guilty to price-fixing and paid a US$10 million fine. In 2013, it paid US$295 million to settle multiple class-action lawsuits relating to misleading advertising, human rights violations (including in relation to 'blood diamonds'), price-fixing and monopoly conduct.

These steps fundamentally changed De Beers' commercial possibilities and profile. The group's corporate structure was still far from transparent, but it could now trade more safely and overtly. It opened retail stores in New York and other cities, and settled into life as a luxury brand and respectable corporate citizen. At the time of leaving the CSO contract, the Argyle team could never have foreseen that their decision, about a remote Australian mine, would transform the global diamond industry.

31
SPIDERS, BANDICOOTS, COCKATOOS AND PIGEONS

E VERY DAY OF the week, diamond workers face enormous tempta-
tions. Most are honest but a significant minority are not. There
were thefts right back to the first modern diamond mines in India,
Brazil and Africa. Security is understandably a prominent feature of
all stages of diamond handling, but there will always be an element
of pilfering: security can only go so far. Stamping out every kind of
theft is more expensive than it is worth, and there are limits to the
levels of security employees will put up with. The effectiveness of security is limited, too, by the ingenuity of diamond thieves. As mining
and security methods have changed, ingenious diamond thieves have
innovated. Perpetually fighting that ingenuity, diamond businesses
are engaged in what author Ion Idriess called 'a constant battle of wits
between the stealers and management'.

At the offices of diamantaires, parcels of diamonds are weighed
before and after they are handed to clients for inspection. In some
sorting rooms, there are cameras on the ceiling, and sorters must
wear shirts and pants that have no pockets. Other security measures
have already been mentioned, such as random full-body searches, and
surveillance of staff in their private quarters.

In the history of diamonds, there is a colourful vocabulary of
stealing. Popular modes of theft have included 'switching', 'lousing'

and 'bandicooting'. In principle, switching is child's play. A high-value stone is replaced with a lower-value one that the sorter has brought along for the purpose. In reality, this crime is a specialised art. The deft movements of the most talented switcher can foil even the most diligent observer. As Matthew Hart notes in *Diamond: The History of a Cold-blooded Love Affair*,

> The switcher flicks a diamond into his cuff and replaces it with a cheaper one of the same weight. Out comes a half-carat top colour, in goes a half-carat of lesser colour. The packet is handed back, weighed, and because the weight tallies, put back in the safe. The story is told of an Antwerp trader who had a tiny rubber tube in his sleeve. It attached to a rubber bulb under his armpit. First he would expel the air from the line by squeezing the bulb with his arm, then place his cuff near the stone he wanted and raise his arm. Air whooshed back into the line and so did the diamond.

Switchers also take advantage of imprecision in the recording of diamond weights, by swapping smaller stones for incrementally larger ones. (This is called 'switching up'.) Switching happens mostly in the sorting halls, but other styles of theft occur further up the production chain. In *Stone of Destiny*, Idriess described how, at the alluvial diamond mines of New South Wales, 'lousers' would swing into work when a rich patch of diamondiferous gravel was struck underground:

> When the last layer of gravel was loosened and moved by the pick then down there in the dark the brighter diamonds would glint in the candlelight. These shinies were thus easily picked out by aid of the 'spider', by 'lousing', and by sharp, quick, experienced eyes.
>
> The spider is the short iron spike that holds the candle, the flame of which was slowly moved over the wash-dirt. In lousing the fingers of the hand carefully claw through the gravel and spread it out on the stone floor of the drive. As the louser slowly ran his fingers through the gravel his mate bent over him with the candle and a shiny displaced from the gravel by the fingers rolled over and glinted in the candlelight.

Usually, tight supervision of miners is an antidote to 'lousing'. 'Bandicooting', though, can be more difficult to detect and prevent. In New South Wales, miners worked in small tunnels or drives that branched from the main shafts, and tunnels that were constructed to reach the richer gravel. According to Idriess,

> Two men would work at the face of a drive, sitting generally upon crossed legs as they swung their picks … Sooner or later one of these drives would strike a rich patch of wash-dirt. That is, two men working in that drive would one day bore into part of the ancient bed where diamonds were thickly concentrated. A patch!
>
> Swiftly, by sign or signal, probably under the very nose of the shift boss, word would go around to the drive or drives where friends of the stealers were working. The men who originally struck the rich patch would secrete their pick of the rich gravels that were visible. Then would come a friend from an adjoining drive with a bucketful of gravel that is wash-dirt from the unproductive face at which he was working. Hurriedly he would scoop out a bucketful of the rich wash. In its place he would leave the worthless gravel from his bucket, taking back to his mate in their drive the rich dirt.

In this way, the expected quantity of wash-dirt would be sent up from the mine face. A mate on the surface would look after the stolen wash-dirt. At a safe moment in a quiet place it would be put through sieves and the diamonds would be extracted. Idriess found that the 'bandicoots' worked 'very cunningly, very daringly, very unobtrusively':

> Many a miner when working below never knew that the man beside him was in league with the stealers. They were almost impossible to catch, let alone secure a conviction against. The police set traps, but 'cockatoos', night and day, were watching the police.

One way to catch them was to post guards. Another was to block prospective tunnels with iron doors. That worked only sometimes:

One night a 'lone wolf' prised open the door to such a tunnel, but by some means the iron door swung to and locked him fast by the neck. When the management found that ingenuity can find a way to open most locks, they put on a guard, not knowing that the bandicooters were joking hilariously as they worked hard, deep within the mine. They had simply entered with the day shift, then hidden in the dead-end drives—in some cases with a week's tucker.

Idriess tells the story of a congenial woman from Boggy Creek. Capable of sieving 'with the best of them', she'd won the miners' respect:

Yes, she could sieve all right, and her luck! Diamonds simply seemed to come to her sieve. The miners' somewhat grudging admiration was tinged just a little with envy. 'Yes, she's a good diamond getter,' they sighed enviously. They did not know that her boyfriend was a cart driver employed by one of the good mines. And every morning his cart loaded with bags of rich, diamond-carrying wash-dirt was driven past her claim *en route* to the washing machine at the creek, where the diamonds would be separated from the dirt. And each day as the driver drove past the woman's claim he would manage to drop a bag of the rich dirt from the cart.

A more recent story comes from a De Beers mine in South Africa where a man was stealing diamonds using carrier pigeons. He would take a pigeon to the site in his lunchbox, then parcel up a quantity of good-quality diamonds, load them on the pigeon and let the bird fly home. He was caught only when he got greedy. Mine security found the bird weighed down and struggling on the ground, inside the mine site's fence. Swapping the diamonds for a tracker, they followed the bird to catch the thief.

⬨

The Argyle legislation, and accompanying amendments to the West Australian *Crimes Act*, established tight security for the mine site and the distribution of Kimberley diamonds. Just one example: it became a criminal offence to sell or distribute rough diamonds in the entire state of Western Australia. (That rule caused unexpected problems. When participants in an Argyle financing deal were given plastic 'tombstone' mementoes that contained low-value rough, the gifts were a technical breach of the Act, and the company needed special permission.) Despite the tight arrangements, though, in the early years of the Argyle mine there was a culture of petty theft. As with elsewhere in the diamond world, this was regrettable but tolerable up to a point. What wasn't tolerable, though, was theft on a grand scale, and especially substantial thefts of the most prized goods, such as Argyle pinks.

In a career with Victoria Police, Barry Crimmins built a strong reputation as a dogged enemy of crooks and an effective antidote to wrongdoing. When CRA appointed him to a senior operational role at the Argyle mine, security improved somewhat. Crimmins reviewed and tightened the mine's anti-theft measures, which included multiple checkpoints and zones within the mine site that had escalating levels of security. People passing between the zones had to consent to the possibility of cavity searches and other scrutiny. Because of the risk of smuggling in water bottles and food containers—it is easy to hide diamonds in water and waste—no food or water was allowed to be taken away from the site.

Robust rules were followed, too, for transporting diamonds away from the mine site. They were delivered from the site to the airstrip in an oldish, boxy-looking, two-tone LandCruiser that bore a passing resemblance to the Leyland Brothers' Land Rover. The Argyle vehicle was fitted with bulletproof glass, just in case a band of determined diamond robbers ever tried to hold up or hijack the LandCruiser during one of its many trips to the Argyle airstrip. To further improve the odds, the drivers took other precautions, such as making random and phantom deliveries to the airstrip, and maintaining a cloak of secrecy. Even the pilots and crews of the waiting planes didn't know whether any given delivery was of real diamonds or not.

With controls such as these, the mine was well protected from external threats and from the more likely forms of internal stealing. But the thefts continued, perpetrated by an unexpected culprit.

◇

Raw diamonds are like fine wine. Stones from any given region have a distinctive character. Specialists and connoisseurs can tell where a particular piece of rough has come from. In the late 1980s, diamonds recognisably from Argyle, but from outside the normal distribution channels, turned up in Antwerp. The JV thought at first they must have come from WADT's 'roulette wheel', but inquiries confirmed they had not. Argyle's executives reached a troubling conclusion: large quantities of high-quality Argyle diamonds were being stolen. But how? The miners tightened security even further, but the thefts continued.

Then, in 1989, a breakthrough. Richard 'Dick' Corfield, formerly of Scotland Yard, was chief of security for Argyle. Late in that year, he saw rough diamonds at the offices of Noel Newton, a Perth-based jeweller. Just like the stones that had been seen in Antwerp, these diamonds were recognisably Argyle rough. With Newton's consent, the stones were taken away so Argyle's scientists and diamantaires could test them. The testing confirmed that at least some of the diamonds had come from AK1. Furthermore, it showed that some of the stones were 'pre-acid'—they'd not yet been cleaned in acid at the mine's processing plant. No pre-acid diamonds were in legitimate circulation. Somehow, therefore, these stones had been extracted from the production process in an unusual way. It all looked very suspicious and concerning.

Newton had received the diamonds from a customer, Lindsay Roddan, who wanted to have them cut and polished. Formerly a school-teacher, Roddan was now a businessman of sorts. Though he'd acquired interests in real estate and thoroughbreds, the 1989 stock-market crash had left him facing financial ruin. Convinced that Roddan's diamonds were stolen, Corfield contacted Superintendent Brian Illingworth, who put him in touch with Detective Graeme Castlehow. Corfield still had the diamonds when he received a telephone call from Newton. 'You've got a leak,' Newton said. 'Roddan knows you've got the stones and he's coming round to do a check on them.' The diamonds were quickly returned, but when Roddan visited Newton's offices he somehow knew someone from Argyle had been 'looking at his diamonds'.

Corfield gave Detective Castlehow a list of suspects: people at Argyle who might be stealing diamonds, and who might have tipped Roddan off. The detectives now grappled with a matter of tactics. Should they take out a search warrant and collect the diamonds from Newton, thereby confirming to Roddan and perhaps others that police were involved? Or, to allay suspicions on the part of the thieves, should the police allow Newton to return the diamonds to Roddan? They decided to give the stones back. 'If the police hand had already been shown,' Castlehow said, 'then that would have been a compromised inquiry.' According to the subsequent Kennedy royal commission, which inquired into the theft of diamonds from Argyle,

> The intention was that the diamonds would be recovered at a later stage by means of a search warrant. In fact, no warrant for their recovery was executed for several months. In the intervening period, some of the more significant diamonds were cut, with the consequence that any evidentiary value they might have had was lost.

After further inquiries, the detectives concluded that a ring was stealing pink rough from the mine site and selling it in Antwerp and Geneva. The case passed from the bureau to the main force. Detective Senior Sergeant Robin Thoy was tasked to lead the investigation, with the assistance of Sergeant Clayton Gwilliam. As the royal commission report noted, 'Thoy asked Corfield to identify an [Argyle] employee involved in operational security at the mine site who could be trusted. The person identified was Mr Barry Crimmins.' Crimmins was the onsite security manager working under Corfield, who as overall head of security was based in Perth. Corfield briefed Crimmins and told him Roddan was the chief suspect. Crimmins was now in a position to obtain information about the investigation. There was an important piece of information, however, that he did not share with the police. Roddan had a contact at Argyle: none other than Crimmins himself. The two men had been associates for years, and among other things had bred dogs together.

Thoy threw himself into the task, but it was tilted against him. Predictably, the investigation failed. A senior officer reportedly said,

'Police cannot find any evidence that Argyle diamonds have been smuggled out of the country.' Thoy believed Roddan had knowledge all along of where the investigation was up to; and he would later tell the royal commission into police corruption that he believed senior officers had pressured him to drop the inquiry.

Argyle's auditors, Coopers & Lybrand, also looked into the case. They verified the loss of Argyle diamonds, and concluded a key diamond register had been improperly maintained. Argyle's executives pressed the police to reopen the case. There were other grounds, too, for police to look again at the matter, as the royal commission found:

> In June 1990, Ms Rae-lene Shore, Roddan's former de-facto, approached police regarding a separate matter. In the course of discussions, she revealed that Roddan and Crimmins were known to each other and that Crimmins had been at Roddan's home in recent times. This raised an obvious line of inquiry, as it provided a means by which Roddan might have obtained possession of stolen diamonds. Crimmins was confronted by Argyle as to why he had not earlier revealed this connection, and he was forced to resign from his position in operational security at the mine.

A second investigation was launched, led by Senior Sergeant Jeffrey Noye, but it, too, could not reach a satisfactory conclusion. The police said there wasn't enough evidence to bring a prosecution.

The case went back to square one, to the first parcel of diamonds that Newton had received from Roddan. Ownership of that parcel remained in dispute. The executives at Argyle continued their own investigations, and launched a civil action to recover the diamonds. The executives also continued to engage with police, in order to share new evidence and to press for a third investigation.

On 18 January 1993, things came to a head. Crimmins' wife, Lynette, 'attended at the home of Roddan'. This visit would later be described vividly in the royal commission report by the Hon. GA Kennedy AO QC:

> She was in a drunken state and was seeking, according to her, the repayment of money that she had lent to Roddan. She tried to effect

an entry by 'bashing' on the door. She broke a side window, crawled into the house, gashing herself in the process, and was physically removed from the house by Roddan. She suffered a broken finger as a consequence. The police were called and she was taken to the Warwick Police Station. These events caused Mrs Crimmins to make admissions about her own previous activities and allegations regarding those of Roddan.

Lynette alleged that Noye and Roddan had formed a corrupt relationship that compromised the second Argyle investigation. Details of the main conspiracy also came out. Around 1989, Lynette said, she'd begun an affair with Roddan, and they had set out to convince Crimmins to steal Argyle diamonds, especially pinks. All Crimmins had to do, Roddan allegedly said, was to remove diamonds from the mine site, then Roddan would offload them without a trace. For this to work, the former policeman and current security man had to turn thief. As diamond historian Matthew Hart described it,

> Crimmins's 'moment of madness', as he called it, arrived when four quart-sized containers of pink rough landed on his desk … Argyle's sorters in Perth had sent back containers of high-end goods, including pinks, asking that they be washed again. When the rough went out to the cleaning plant … the couriers somehow forgot one of the containers. When Crimmins discovered the mistake, he checked the courier's manifest. There was no mention of the forgotten container. He stole it, and the robbing of Argyle got underway.

Of the many stolen diamonds, it appears some were concealed in tubes of pinkish toothpaste and bottles of pinkish shampoo. Others would be hidden in other ointments and lotions. According to Hart,

> Roddan paid Barry Crimmins in cash, sometimes as much as US$10,000 at once. Some of the pinks went straight out of the country. Others were polished in Perth, then smuggled out by a network of airline employees, who hid the diamonds in jars of face cream and carried them overseas in their personal luggage.

The total value of the stolen diamonds is unclear. Estimates of between $30 million and $50 million have been put forward. Theft on such a scale required multiple hands. As many as seventy people may have been involved in the conspiracy to steal from Argyle. One key participant in the scheme was reportedly known in the Perth underworld as 'The Jeweller'.

The case of the Argyle thefts is one of the murkiest episodes in the history of Australian mining. It had everything: jilted lovers, bugged phones, false identities, international intrigue and far-reaching corruption allegations. When the case reached court, Lynette Crimmins recounted a tragic tale of 'a love affair that had degenerated into hatred'. Hart tells it this way:

> When she appeared in court to plead guilty to conspiracy charges, her lawyer said Lynette Crimmins had been forced into prostitution by Roddan when the money from the diamond thefts dried up. Barry Crimmins, who pleaded guilty alongside his estranged wife, said he had been driven into crime by her greed.

A judge of the Perth District Court sentenced Barry Crimmins to four years in prison. Having cooperated with police, and having arguably suffered enough, Lynette was freed on a good behaviour bond. Roddan was later sentenced to three years jail. The Kennedy royal commission did not uphold Detective Senior Sergeant Robin Thoy's allegation of improper pressure to end the first investigation. Charges were ultimately prepared in relation to Roddan and Senior Sergeant Jeffrey Noye for conspiring to pervert the course of justice in the second investigation, but those charges were not pursued, in part because the principal Crown witness, Lynette Crimmins, was judged to be unwilling and unreliable.

32

AFTER ARGYLE

S OME PEOPLE NEVER really bought the story of John Collier's 1976 diamond find near Morelli's Fox on the King George River. As Ewen Tyler recalled, 'For years, up to the time of his death, Russ Madigan would joke with me about "Paltridge's Plant"!' Tyler, though, accepted the truth of the find. 'It was clearly a Kimberley King George River stone,' he said.

Tyler might have accepted Collier's story, but he and Alan Jones were sceptical about the earlier discovery, in 1969, of nine diamonds at Police Camp Pool on the Lennard River. Nine seemed like an odd number, Tyler said, especially as no diamonds would be found there in subsequent searches. And the diamonds themselves looked odd. They were octahedrons and cubo-octahedrons, very different from other rough diamonds found in the West Kimberley. Jones and Tyler suspected, moreover, that the Police Camp Pool diamonds had been polished by a diamantaire.

But there were certainly genuine finds to be made in the Kimberleys over and above Argyle, even at places where CRA and Ashton Mining had already looked. Ellendale (whose stones were predominantly dodecahedron) was an example. CRA and Ashton Mining had assessed the yields at Ellendale as too low for a large-scale mining operation, but the Ashton JV partners always believed the field could be a viable prospect for a smaller miner. Such a miner would indeed try to make Ellendale pay. De Beers, too, would look closely at the field and its vicinity. To the north-west of Ellendale, the cartel pegged a large area and spent around $20 million on exploration before surrendering the tenements in 1992. Ultimately, a very different team would mine the Ellendale pipes.

Graeme Hutton was born in Mullewa, near Geraldton, in 1943. In the 1960s, he completed an honours degree in geology at Tyler's alma mater, the University of Western Australia. During his treasure-hunting career, Hutton gathered pearls at Broome and gold from the desert. In the 1970s, after the Ellendale discoveries, he and his prospecting friend Terry Allen were among the optimists who pegged Kimberley sheep and cattle stations. Helicopters were not for Hutton and Allen. In methods that harked back to the first European explorers and prospectors, they searched overland by Land Rover and on foot. On account of Allen's 'unconventional and daring exploits', he was profiled in *Time* magazine as 'King of the Kimberley'.

Early in 1993, Hutton and Allen approached Miles Kennedy to raise $5 million to fund a diamond search. Kennedy had recently sold out of the Macraes Mining company, which he'd created to develop a New Zealand gold deposit. Now, Hutton and Allen sought to interest him in the Calwynyardah diamond field, to the west of Ellendale. Calwynyardah consisted of seven main pipes, plus a small one called Avocado. In their pitch to Kennedy, Allen and Hutton said the Ashton JV had done insufficient work on the field in 1978 and had therefore underestimated its potential. Kennedy later recalled: 'Both of them felt that with the advances in diamond exploration over the past fifteen years, these pipes were definitely worth revisiting.' Amused by the *Time* profile, Kennedy liked Hutton and Allen's style of prospecting. 'These guys were actually walking and driving and going in all sorts of ways,' he later said.

Kennedy bought the pitch, and in September 1993 the trio set up Kimberley Diamond Company NL (KDC). Geologist Chris Jennings was KDC's chairman; Kennedy was deputy chairman and executive director. Allen and Hutton subscribed 24 per cent of the stock and retained 20 per cent of the leases on Calwynyardah and the neighbouring Blina cattle station. The company acquired the tenements from De Beers and assembled a crack team. David Jones was exploration manager, and John Pettigrew would look after the prospecting and camp operations. In January 1994, the company was listed on the ASX.

A headline in the July 1995 edition of the mining magazine *Australia's Paydirt* described the KDC team as having 'Stout hearts ... pumping with anticipation'. In Perth, instead of company cars, KDC's leaders rode Harley-Davidson motorcycles. The company spent $2.6 million on its 1995 field season. It was burning through money fast. According to Ross Louthean,

> The initial focus through 1995 was primarily on the main lamproite pipe at Calwynyardah itself, the fourth largest identified in Western Australia, with an area of 124 hectares. When this was originally drilled by the CRA/Ashton joint venture in the 1970s, they recovered 48 micro-diamonds per 100 kilograms. KDC's first intensive and deeper drilling in 1994 produced micro-diamonds from every hole and revealed that kimberlite-related tuff material was more concentrated on the western side of the pipe than previously thought.

In 1998, KDC established a camp on the northern side of the Gibb River Road, 90 kilometres from Derby, and began following trails of diamonds. As Hutton recalled,

> We discovered the Terrace 5 ancient river system and tracked it upstream, covered by up to 10 metres of wind-blown desert sand, for over 40 kilometres. By 1998, we had traced diamonds in Terrace 5 almost right up to the Ellendale Field boundary, still owned by Argyle. Graeme never even entertained the idea of mining this big alluvial system. He was absolutely convinced the diamonds in this ancient river were sourced from a pipe or pipes that had not yet been discovered. It came as a bad shock for us to now realise that these pipes probably lay just across the border on the Argyle ground.

At this point the infamous 1940 *Mining Act* again figures prominently in the Argyle story. Under the Act, the Ashton JV had as many as 104 leases at Ellendale. KDC decided to launch a legal challenge to Argyle's ownership of the leases. To do so, it needed someone who held a miner's right under the old Act. Graeme Hutton did, on account of his earlier prospecting, and he was the one who formally launched the challenge. In 2001, KDC and Argyle reached a legal settlement. KDC would acquire the leases and reimburse the Argyle partners' Ellendale exploration costs, amounting to around $51.5 million, which were incurred between 1976 and 1981.

On 25 February 2002, the Argyle Diamond Mines JV policy committee met to discuss the settlement. All conditions of the sale agreement between Argyle and KDC had been satisfied, and they'd been ratified by the West Australian parliament. KDC's sampling and evaluation activities revealed there were indeed higher diamond grades at Ellendale than previously thought. According to Hutton and Allen,

> We processed the material through our little diamond recovery plant, recovering about 10 tonnes of fine-grain concentrate. For the next ten days everyone in the company, including office girls from Perth and David Jones's wife and sister-in-law, worked around the clock at Kimberley's camp on the Gibb River Road hand-sorting diamonds from the concentrate.

KDC's total estimate for the Ellendale 4 and 9 pipes was 33.9 million tonnes at a grade of 7.7 carats per hundred tonnes, compared to Argyle's estimate of 58.1 million tonnes at a grade of 5.8 cpht. The bad news, though, was that the average value was lower. Nevertheless, KDC established a mining operation with three diamond plants processing more than 7 million tonnes, and a village housing 450 people. Over the past two decades there have been several changes in the mine's ownership. Many of its magnificent yellow diamonds were sold directly to Tiffany & Co.

◈

In the late 1980s, Ashton Mining refinanced its debt on terms that were more flexible than those of the original Chase Manhattan syndication. Argyle now had an admirable financial track record—the mine was generating a lot of cash—and lenders were happy to join in. But the flow of cash did have an endpoint. Production at Argyle had risen quickly and it looked as though the mine would shut in the 2000s. Against this backdrop, Ashton Mining pursued a new strategy, increasing its exploration spending and seeking offshore acquisitions. The company would become a 'three-legged stool', and the legs would be diamonds, gold and platinum.

For gold in particular, Ashton Mining's new CEO, David Tyrwhitt, went on a buying spree, acquiring interests in remote Kalimantan and sundry other places. As Tyler recalled,

> In 1988 Ashton purchased a major stake in Carr Boyd Minerals, which at the time appeared to be a skilled gold explorer and modest producer. It was active in Western Australia, owned the Harbour Lights Mine, and had extensive exploration ground in the Leonora and Laverton greenstone belts. At a 30 per cent level this might have proved a sound investment—it had a good gold exploration group, and was active where Granny Smith and Sunrise Dam were to be found—but Ashton sought to increase its holding to 100 per cent—a move which was dictated by corporate politics rather than ore reserves. This investment ultimately became Aurora Gold Ltd, and the Mt Weld Rare Earth Deposit.

Efforts to find diamonds in Indonesia and platinum in Canada would yield mixed success. Tyler described the company's platinum experience in these terms:

> In platinum exploration we scoured North America and found an evaluation/development project at Goodnews Bay in Alaska, and Helix Resources NL who had made—what was thought at the time—a significant platinum discovery at Fifield in NSW. Goodnews Bay became Badnews Bay, but Ashton exited Helix in 1997 for a net gain of $17.8 million.

The lack of progress at Carr Boyd, plus the failure of the platinum search, turned investors against the 'three legs' strategy. Ashton Mining was urged to return to its core business: diamonds. In response, in 1993–94 its gold interests were bundled up and sold off as a new entity, Aurora Gold. Aurora raised $122 million from the stock market, and Ashton Mining retained a 30 per cent interest.

The re-emphasis on diamonds involved exploring overseas, on continents whose 'cratons' were promising for diamond exploration. (A craton is a thick part of the continental crust.) Building on its Argyle experience, Ashton Mining joined the forefront of the world-wide diamond search. There was a great flowering in its exploration efforts, according to Tyler:

> We had been moderately successful in Finland, and to guard its eastern flank, we arranged, in 1995, exploration rights with the Russian Government in Karelia. West Africa was also selected, and work carried out in Burkina Faso, Mali and Mauritania. For a time we worked in Uruguay. Ashton Canada had been established in 1993, riding on the crest of the Canadian diamond boom, following major discoveries in the Slave craton. Ashton secured its position, trading on its reputation, and raised an initial $30 million from the Canadian market.

Late in 1996, Ashton Mining bought into an Angolan company, SDM, which soon gained access to a vast concession along the diamond-rich Kwango River. With SDM, Ashton Mining looked for Kwango diamonds, both alluvials and pipes.

Tragically, in 1998 the SDM mine manager was killed in a guerrilla attack. 'Following the murder,' Tyler wrote, 'Ashton made a careful onsite assessment of the security arrangements using an Australian SAS colonel as its adviser. The resurgence of the civil war, and the need to maintain a large security force, has made it very difficult for SDM to explore in more than a small part of the concession.'

In 1999, Ashton Mining turned its attention to Australia, seeking to find a successor to Argyle in the northern Australian craton. Some years earlier, the diamond trail had led east of Argyle, to Bow River (of the Cold Chisel song) and across the border into the Northern Territory. In the mid-1980s, Gem Exploration & Minerals discovered mineable concentrations of Bow River alluvial diamonds just 30 kilometres east and downstream from Argyle. The alluvial deposits yielded around 1 million carats annually from 1988 to the early 1990s. Gem Exploration became a takeover target, and the Normandy group bought it in 1989. The operation closed in December 1995.

As well as being a source of diamonds, Bow River was an important signpost on the diamond trail across northern Australia. Tyler was Ashton Mining's exploration director when the company entered a new JV with Aberfoyle Ltd and AOG Minerals Ltd. Ashton Mining was lead partner in the new venture, which was called Australian Diamond Exploration NL (ADEX). Tyler was chair. ADEX followed a micro-diamond trail to a remote corner of the Northern Territory, about 80 kilometres south of the legendary McArthur River town of Borroloola. CRA had already found the Emu Pipes in the McArthur River basin, but had walked away after thorough testing. Australian geologist Tom Reddicliffe was Ashton Mining's exploration manager in the Northern Territory. In 1992, surface sampling on what Louthean described as 'an endless plateau of sand and spinifex', around 10 kilometres south of the Emu Pipes, revealed extensive chromite indicators along with concentrations of micro-diamonds and even some macro-diamonds. On one visit to the site, Tyler himself found a 2.5 carat stone. There would be other discoveries, too, as Tyler recalled:

> Tom Reddicliffe negotiated access to the lapsed CRA titles with Bob Biddlecombe, a local property developer and prospector. There he found two unexplained chromite anomalies and identified a fine, north-trending fracture that had chromite and micro-diamonds. Reddicliffe, following the fracture, found two breccia pipes and an amphitheatre [a level area surrounded by upward-sloping ground]. Following another CRA indicator trail on Abner Range, Reddicliffe recognised another breccia pipe. Its peripheral breccias, concentric fracturing and huge sandstone blocks prompted him to re-examine the amphitheatre, which he

drilled to 20m in 1991 without sign of kimberlite. Redrilling to
26m in 1993, Reddicliffe found kimberlite rich in diamonds.

This became Excalibur, the first of twelve small pipes in a newly
discovered kimberlite field. After detecting 'a sense of magic' in
the vicinity, Reddicliffe christened the field 'Merlin'. In addition
to the great sword Excalibur, the pipes were named after Arthur's
knights. The field was on a pastoral lease; ADEX bought half the lease,
and after negotiating with the traditional owners, a mining lease was
granted on 15 June 1998. Trial mining of what was Australia's third
field of diamondiferous pipes began in late 1998.

In the first years of mining, the best-performing pipes were
Palomides, Ywain and Excalibur itself. The mine continued to operate
until mid-2003. The mined diamonds were sold via Argyle Diamond
Sales, but Merlin was not another Argyle. A London mining analyst
said of its stones: 'not bad, classic small kimberlite but not world
beaters'. Total production was around 500,000 carats of smallish but
high-quality diamonds. (The average size was around seven stones to
the carat, but one spectacular Merlin diamond measured 104.73 carats
or 20.946 grams, making it Australia's largest. Once valued at over
US$525,000, the stone was named Jungiila Bunajina, 'star meteorite
dreaming stone'.) After Rio acquired Ashton Mining, it sold the Merlin
mine and mining rights to Striker Resources, which became North
Australian Diamonds and operated the mine for a short period in 2006.

For over a billion years, the Argyle pipe had been shedding diamonds
through natural erosion. Many of them were washed downstream and
into the ocean. With knowledge of that seductive fact, people have
tried to recover diamonds from off the Kimberley coast.

The cliffs and waters there are dangerous, and searchers have had
to resort to such extreme protections as shark-proof and crocodile-
proof cages. In 1995, from the crane barge Java Constructor off the
mouth of the Berkeley River, Cambridge Gulf Exploration drilled
large-diameter holes 50 metres apart and lined with steel to hold back

the mud and gravel. Bad weather and high tidal ranges bedevilled the drilling, but the company's 'feisty deputy chairman', Brian Conway, was undeterred. He applied for twenty-one mining leases within the Berkeley tenements, remarking, 'My conviction is stronger than before that we will be successful in recovering international gem-quality diamonds from the operation.'

The promise of ocean-bed riches in the Cambridge Gulf also attracted CRA-Rio and WMC (formerly Western Mining Corporation). The prize was especially alluring, as Louthean described:

> Up to 90 per cent of marine diamonds are usually of gem quality, because of the inevitable filtering and loss of small stones and fragments during the journey from original pipe to the sea. Since the problem for the onshore Argyle has always been a high proportion of near gem or industrial goods, the attraction offshore may be that natural selection has already taken place. Whatever you get is going to be mostly gem.

So far, the oceanic diamond concentrations have been low, and the northern ocean hasn't turned out to be a diamond bonanza. But the prospect of finding a Kimberley treasure of marine diamonds is still a real one.

In the 1980s, after the Argyle mine had begun production, Chris Smith moved on, joining Rio Tinto's diamond exploration activities in Zimbabwe and then India. For his services to Australian mineralogy, he received the prestigious Gibb Maitland Medal from the Geological Society of Australia.

CRA and Rio had entered the diamond search almost by accident—after a doubtful yarn with Rees Towie at a barbecue. Argyle, though, cemented Rio as a major world producer of diamonds. As well as chasing prospects in Africa and northern Australia, it would acquire interests in Canada, Russia and elsewhere, and on the strength of what it first learnt in Australia, diamonds would become a central part of its global mineral portfolio.

33

A JOINT ADVENTURE

F OR HIS FIRST job, Harold Tyler spent a year smelting base metals at Namtu in Burma's Shan States. Returning to England, he married Ethel Matthew on 6 June 1925. Shortly after the wedding, the pair were set to return to Burma. This time, Harold wouldn't be smelting base metals. He'd be working as a geologist, helping to develop the Mawchi tin mines. But Ethel developed appendicitis and her departure was delayed by more than a year. Harold had to go on without her.

When she was well again, Ethel travelled solo to Rangoon. Harold met her there, and together the pair spent what was effectively their honeymoon on a difficult seventeen-day journey, on horseback and by punt, up the Salween River to Mawchi. Ethel recorded the outbound leg:

Native boats 6 o'clock in the morning; 2 boats, one for us the other for stores and servants. Keep to side of river, 4 men dig poles into bottom of river, heave boat on bamboo poles with iron spikes; they push, they run with their poles to centre of boat—constant din, rapids a nuisance always against the stream. 6 days in this boat, rest houses at night; wildest men. Around of clock [12 hours] to travel 20 miles [32 kilometres]. Papun. 3 days riding before next river—delayed, lack of fodder for 5 bullocks to carry our luggage-carts. Mounted to 2000 ft [600 metres] that day each 9 miles; each day rained heavily, horses tails in mud. Rest houses each night. Two boats this time. Shans wilder than last. Sacrifice to gnats and smoked opium. 6 nights on this stretch—no rest houses. Finally got to Kemapuy and only an 18 mile ride to Mawchi.

After Mawchi, the Tylers returned to London, but Harold soon left again, this time for Africa. In August 1928, Ethel gave birth to Ewen at the Sharrow Lane Nursing Home in Sheffield. At that time, Harold was in southern Sudan. Beginning in Kisumu, Kenya, a company of the King's African Rifles flashed the news of Ewen's birth from hilltop to hilltop by heliograph. In April 1930, Harold was back in London and met his son for the first time.

On a second trip to Africa, in 1931, Harold went mapping in southern Sudan for the Nile Congo Divide Syndicate. He examined chromite deposits near Kassala and copper deposits at Hofrat el Nahas. On a normal working day, he would march 50 kilometres with a hundred porters. Working in this way, he was the first geologist to explore and map the Congo-Nile divide in northern Uganda and southern Sudan.

Due to a bad case of 'Nile boils', Harold had to leave Sudan. His next role would be in East Africa. In July 1935, Ethel was again pregnant when Harold travelled to Kampala on Lake Victoria. Kentan Gold Areas, a Tanks Group company, had an office there. From Kampala, Harold explored the Kakamega Goldfield in Kenya and later the South-West Mwanza goldfield in Tanganyika.

Over subsequent years, Ewen Tyler rarely saw his father. And when he did, it was often near a mine, and the topic of conversation was usually mining. Ewen heard the foundational stories of mineral discoveries in southern Africa and Malaya and British India. Romantic tales of legendary mines and deposits. 'Ridge 8', 'Prospect 30', 'Mawe Meru'. He came to know the language and rhythms of mining. The sense of adventure and the lure of discovery. Later he would add his own iconic names to the list. Morelli's Fox. Pteropus Creek. Skerring. Geebung.

The modern diamond industry began in Africa. Harold Tyler was one degree of separation from the pioneers of South African diamonds, and Ewen was two degrees away. Together, Ewen and Harold were a link between the 1870s and the 1970s. In the mining industry's early decades, there was little emphasis on geology and methodical exploration. Geological mapping, to the extent there was any, was mainly undertaken by state and national governments. Mines were usually purchased from freelance prospectors or small syndicates. This was the era of 'hero prospectors' who mostly worked independently of big mining groups. Together, Ewen and his father are part of the bridge between that era of the solo adventurer and the modern age of corporate, industrial, scientific mining.

In many ways, the Argyle story is Ewen Tyler's story. It was he who first convinced Lord Colyton to shift Tanganyika Concessions' focus to the New World. The idea of finding valuable minerals in Australia was very much an outside chance. Colyton could easily have said no. Once in Australia, Tyler was the one who insisted on using geologists in field sampling. And in a thousand other ways he helped shape and steer the story of Australian diamonds. He remained as chairman of the Ashton Exploration Joint Venture until he retired from Ashton Mining in 1990. In June 1991, he was awarded membership of the General Division of the Order of Australia for services to the Australian diamond mining industry and the wider community. The following year he was awarded the Clunies Ross National Science and Technology Award. He has since been rightly recognised as the father of Australian diamond mining.

In their day-to-day work, Tyler and his colleagues experienced the grain and texture of diamond exploration. Dropping helicopter crews at remote sites. Making dangerous trips up Kimberley waterways in second-hand prawn boats. Avoiding crocodiles in water and on land. Meeting bankers in plush clubs and offices. Meeting chain-smoking, manspreading miners in cramped motels in Kununurra and Halls Creek and other towns scratched from the bush. Solving legal, managerial and operational problems at remote mine sites. Behind it all was the thrill of exploration and discovery. There is something deeply gratifying about acquiring a body of knowledge, then going out into the field to demonstrate it by extracting treasure. Even better if others had sought the treasure and failed to find it.

Modern mines can be very large: some really are visible from space. In the present scientific and industrial era, mining is an enterprise of awe and wonder. But it is also an enterprise of people. Even when workforces are industrially large, they depend on small teams and personal networks. Decisions, relationships and serendipities at a human scale are what drove the Argyle story, just as they drove other turning points in the history of mining. Miners use big machines and dig large holes, but the success of Argyle depended on a series of discrete decisions and transitory interpersonal moments. Small teams have, it seems, a special power and magic. 'You have to ask,' mining journalist Doug Wilkinson said, 'is there a critical field organisation and laboratory structure which is possible in the smaller company and not in the behemoth? Is there an intimacy, an excitement, that does not translate into the bigger structures? The smaller companies breed diamond people.'

Tyler's respect for Robert Roberts, and Mick O'Leary's for John Toby, was crucial for the diamond search, as was Alan Jones's ability to keep his team together. Tyler's personal network and determination were more important than a hundred helicopters or mineral labs. The respect that Russ Madigan and others at CRA had for Tyler and Jones was a large part of why Ashton Mining was able to remain an independent entity for so long. Looking back, people saw the joint venture as a model of commercial cooperation. There was genuine communication between the main Argyle partners. Issues were dealt with quickly. A principal cause of the mine's success was the smooth and speedy manner in which it was brought to its design capacity.

If mining is driven at a human scale and in small teams, then human conflicts will naturally loom large. In the 1970s, the process of assembling the Kalumburu JV felt like choosing musicians for a rock band. And when the members were ready to pulverise each other with furniture, it felt like the band was imploding. Looking back on the disputes and tensions with Rees Towie and Northern Mining, Tyler reflected on a misalignment of values and objectives. 'All along, their goal was less in the establishment of a mine,' he said, 'and more in the successful marketing of their interest.' Towie's game was less about long-term mineral development than about pumping up his stocks. To some extent, the conflict reflected differences in the mining cultures of Canada and Australia. In Canada, small explorers generally sold out after they found something important, whereas in Australia, the more common mentality was for small explorers to want to become big. The goal was to transform from explorer to miner. 'That process,' Doug Bailey reflected, 'was seen as coming of age.'

The discovery of diamonds in the Kimberleys was the result of a ten-year search that touched every drainage system in the region. The field crews made 35,000 helicopter take-offs and landings. One find led to another. The West Kimberleys led to Ellendale in November 1976, and the East Kimberleys to Argyle in August 1979. The methodical approach over a vast area is why AK1 was discovered. And the difference in results between Ashton and De Beers is telling.

Notwithstanding hundreds of millions of dollars spent exploring, De Beers failed to find a commercial diamond deposit in the southern continent. Globally, the group's exploration successes would be concentrated in southern Africa, such as at Orapa, Jwaneng and Venetia. Tyler reflected on De Beers' performance as an explorer: 'Their success has been in their own continent, just as Ashton Mining's has been in Australia. This, I believe, is no coincidence.' Despite superficial similarities in the Australian and African botany and topography, the Kimberley geology proved to be very different from the African mineralisation known to De Beers. Differences in method were also important. Kalumburu was the first venture to explore systematically and with geologists. De Beers instead used helicopter pilots and field assistants to collect samples. This probably accounted for much of their failure in the Kimberley. 'Having geologists in the field teams made a big difference,' Tyler said.

At the beginning of mine operation, Argyle was slated to yield 20 to 25 million carats a year, making it the world's biggest producer, singlehandedly eclipsing De Beers' South African mines. To get a sense of the scale of the output: in just four days in 1989, Argyle produced more diamonds than the Copeton and Bingara fields produced in their best forty years. The initial estimates of Argyle's grades and yields were exceptionally accurate. Through a series of investments, output was increased until, in the 1990s, Argyle produced up to 40 million carats per year. That's around 8 tonnes of diamonds or 40 per cent of world production. The venturers had come a long way from the days when they used plastic rubbish bins and kitchen strainers to search for billion-year-old diamonds.

For more than twenty-five years, Argyle in carat terms was by far the world's biggest diamond mine. It increased Australian exports by billions of dollars at a time when the West Australian economy was growing rapidly and the Australian economy as a whole was becoming more open to the world. The Argyle profit royalty delivered more than $1 billion to the state of Western Australia. At the height of mine production and sales, gross returns were between 30 and 40 per cent. The Ashton name, haphazardly selected from a mining map, became famous in Australian business history.

Argyle was more than just a mine. It brought a new industry to Australia and changed the world diamond market. Hundreds of Australians were trained as diamond sorters. Thousands of people worked in the development and operation of the mine. Millions of carats of Australian diamonds were sold through Antwerp and processed in India. The venture established global sales channels for champagne and cognac diamonds. Regular tenders for Argyle pinks fed demand for Argyle's signature stone, and established a powerful Australian brand.

The history of Argyle is a collage of firsts and biggests and bests: the first Kimberley diamond search report, the unprecedented sampling program, the biggest diamond laboratory in Australia, the first large-scale helicopter sampling with geologists, the first time diamonds were found in lamproite, the first time chromite was used as an indicator mineral for diamonds, Australia's first mineable diamond pipe, the first external financing of a diamond mine, the first Australian diamond mine, the first Australian member of the CSO, the world's leading producer of rare and valuable pinks.

The Argyle project was built on a collection of innovations—in searching, sample analysis, deposit assessment and mineral extraction, and then in sales and distribution. From the moment Tyler persuaded Lord Colyton to look for valuable minerals in Australia, he was leaving behind the old-world ways of mining and investment. The Kalumburu and Ashton partners broke new ground in mine logistics and workforce management, including FIFO commuting, now a pillar of Australian mining. Other innovations were made in mining law and regulation. Argyle is a case study in how matters of business and commerce are inextricably intertwined with matters of politics and government. The Argyle story is a series of challenges and negotiations, with breakthroughs and lessons at every stage.

Australia's sparkliest start-up grew to become a multi-billion-dollar enterprise that transformed a global industry—and a local community. In the early stages of planning for Argyle, consultants Dames & Moore produced an environmental review and management program. The review found that within the Kimberley region, the impact of the project 'may be seen as quite considerable'. By bringing an enormous engineering project to the East Kimberley, the diamond miners would change the region forever.

'For Europeans,' the review concluded, 'the project is likely to facilitate the fulfilment of values they believe important. For Aborigines, by and large, the benefits are less certain.' Writing in *The Age*, journalist and broadcaster Phillip Adams said the miners were prepared to give the Indigenous owners only 'a pitiful barter of pocket knives, mirrors and beads for perhaps the richest piece of real estate on earth'. The diamond search pre-dated a strong legal framework in Australia for Indigenous rights, and it took place on a bedrock of criminal dispossession. Adding injury to injury, Charles Court and other politicians deliberately blocked a fair settlement with Indigenous people in the Kimberleys.

There were retrograde attitudes among the miners, too, but also some good intentions. The leaders of the Ashton JV felt they were at the vanguard of reaching a just compact with Australia's Indigenous people for mineral exploration and mine development. According to Ashton Mining director Bill Leslie, 'We always had a philosophy of working with the local people. We always had a commitment to fairness and to approaching Indigenous rights in a positive and collaborative way.' The Good Neighbour Policy and other Argyle investments transformed Glen Hill and other communities in the vicinity of the mine. At Kununurra, Argyle funded civic facilities such as a library, a community centre and a school, and otherwise helped make the town a major centre in the East Kimberley. Unquestionably there were direct and indirect economic benefits for the whole region. Yet what was at the time a landmark agreement now seems outdated, ill-conceived and inadequate.

The three Kija women who turned to stone at Cattle Creek are still there today, as three formations overlooking the waterway. But Indigenous fears about site protection around Argyle were well founded. Sugar Bag Yard, formerly a favourite swimming hole and place of cultural importance, was 'grossly disturbed' and became an 'unattractive location'. Flying Fox Hole and Wesley Springs are other examples of important areas lost to local people through displacement and overuse. More serious losses, too, were experienced. In 1982, the Western Australian Museum was notified that the miners had damaged two sites of mythological and ritual significance, in addition to the site that coincided with AK1. This was confirmed after discussions with the JV. In all, as many as five areas of deep cultural importance were destroyed, along with seventeen archaeological sites. According to Curtin University anthropologist Will Christensen,

> What this damage has given rise to is a profound sense of loss, a sentiment which has not lost force over the years ... For example, personal and social troubles (including the flooding which has occurred during the past two wet seasons) are attributed to desecration of the Barramundi site. The perceived complicity of some Aboriginal people in the destruction of this site is, in turn, the cause for continuing tension and ill-feeling within the Aboriginal community. More broadly, and perhaps more insidiously, the damage to this site has reinforced a sense of powerlessness and alienation within the community, and undermined the fragile

movement previously in train toward increasing self-confidence and autonomy in managing community affairs.

Of the mine's total revenue, the share spent on Indigenous programs and projects was small. The workforce legacy may be more enduring, but even that will erode without more projects in the region, ones that are properly driven by local people and that reflect their needs. The scheduled closure of the Argyle mine will leave a big hole in the community and an urgent need for further investment and opportunities.

The Good Neighbour Policy was founded on a lack of understanding, a clash of values, and a failure to recognise the burden of past injustices. Despite the good intentions, it is impossible not to conclude that the Indigenous people of the East Kimberley were forced into a terrible trade-off, between a meagre, short-term gain on the one hand, and invaluable, inviolable traditions on the other. Ewen Tyler believes there will be other major diamond discoveries on the Australian continent. Next time round, he hopes, the country as a whole will apply the lessons from Argyle. (Rio Tinto's recent destruction of important cultural and archaeological sites in Western Australia's Pilbara region to make way for an expanded iron-ore mine is further evidence that our companies, parliaments and regulators still have a lot to learn and big changes to make.)

Dedicated powerlines now connect the Argyle mine to the Ord River hydro scheme, saving millions of dollars and millions of litres of diesel. The mine site also has a gift shop, where visitors can buy tiny pieces of clear or coloured carbon at an eye-watering mark-up. There is a stylish gallery telling aspects of the Argyle story and showing some of the largest stones along with images of the ghostly Argyle pipe.

In the main pit, the stepped walls are as steep and tall as the Great Pyramid of Giza. A decade ago, fears about the safety and stability of the open cut forced the miners to go underground. Deep drilling of the pipe showed it retained its width and grades a long way down. Hundreds of metres below the bottom of the open-cut mine, underground mining commenced using a method called 'block caving'. Two sloping entrances, wide enough for heavy vehicles, led to the underground mine. From the surface you could hear the block caving far below, and you could see periodic landslides on the walls of the open cut. The decision to go underground meant some diamondiferous 'blueground' had to be left unmined on the sides of the main pit. That purplish rock stands out on the terraced slope against the ordinary reddish-brown Kimberley ground.

From the peak of around 40 million carats per year, Argyle's annual output fell to less than 12 million carats. That decline was behind the decision to end mining in November 2020, and the intention to end processing in mid-2021. In advance of that event, Rio is grappling with questions of remediation. Vast terraced piles of gravelly spoil surround the site like the trapezoidal battlements of a medieval star fort. Rio has established a plant nursery and is experimenting with different plantings and other methods of softening the spoil mounds and reuniting them with the Kimberley terrain.

When Argyle closes, the open cut and the underground mine will both need to be fenced off or filled in and otherwise made safe— because the site and its leftover diamonds are magnets. Remediation also means removing the processing plant, the powerlines, and possibly the offices and the 'Club Argyle' village. Unless, that is, new uses can be found for these facilities. An ideal scenario for Rio would be to sell the site, perhaps for redevelopment as a desert resort. Or the whole site could be sold to another miner, one lithe and nimble enough to go after diamonds in the sides of the pit, at the bottom of the pipe, in the vast mounds of tailings, under the diamondiferous runway, in the diamond-studded highway and, as gently as in a dream, in the roots of the Kimberley boabs.

ACKNOWLEDGEMENTS

M OST OF THE events described in this book took place in north-western Australia on the lands of the Gija and Mirriwung people, whose rich culture and traditions stretch back more than 70,000 years. The modern history of Indigenous Australians is marred by crimes and injustices, including corporate theft and state-sponsored dispossession on a vast scale. I acknowledge that history, and pay my respects to the Gija and Mirriwung people, their elders past, present and future, and their fellow Indigenous people near and far.

The research for this book was very much a collaborative effort. Bill Leslie, Ewen Tyler and Alan King Jones had long hoped that the Argyle story, with all its impossible twists and turns, would one day be told. I spent many fascinating hours with Bill, Ewen and Alan. I am deeply grateful for their generous collaboration: apart from sharing their memories and their archives, they introduced me to other key people in the Argyle story.

Sadly, on 13 July 2020, Alan Jones passed away, at the age of 94. Alan was a gentle and humane person who made important contributions in multiple fields, including but not limited to mineral exploration and mine development. It was a privilege to capture part of Alan's story in the writing of this book, which Alan read in pages but not in its printed form.

My friend Leon Morris shared crucial insights and stories about the culture of the Kimberleys in the 1980s and 1990s. I also thank and acknowledge the generous and valuable input of Elizabeth and Louise Lane, Doug Bailey, Andrew Berry, Mark Hooper and Ian Warner; several anonymous mentors and reviewers; and the miners and other personnel from Tanks Australia, the Kalumburu JV, the Ashton JV, CRA, Ashton Mining, Malaysia Mining Corporation and Rio Tinto, including the managers and workers at the mine site in 2019.

I am grateful to Andrew Barker of the Kununurra Museum and Historical Society; and to the librarians and other staff of the state libraries of Western Australia, Victoria, New South Wales and Queensland; the City of Perth Library; Kununurra School & Community Library; Broome Public Library; the Geoffrey Blainey Mining Collection at Federation University Library, Ballarat; La Trobe University Library; the University of Melbourne Library; the Australian Institute of Petroleum; and the Argyle mine-site museum.

Apart from being a collaborative project, this book was also a family project. My wife, Fiona, and my daughters, Thea and Charlotte, travelled with me to Perth and the Kimberleys. There and in Melbourne, Fiona helped find key documents, assisted with referencing, read multiple drafts of the manuscript, and—as she has with other research and writing projects over many years—otherwise assisted in dozens of practical and essential ways.

I am indebted to Professor Geoffrey Blainey for his generous foreword to this book, and for his extensive contributions to the history of Australian mining and business. I also acknowledge the prior work of other authors and journalists, especially John McIlwraith, Rachelle Bergstein (*Brilliance and Fire: A Biography of Diamonds*, New York: Harper, 2016), Nick Norman (*The Extraordinary World of Diamonds*, Auckland Park: Jacana Media, 2010), and Matthew Hart (*Diamond: The History of a Cold-blooded Love Affair*, London: Fourth Estate, 2003).

The monograph *Aborigines and Diamond Mining: The Politics of Resource Development in the East Kimberley, Western Australia* (Nedlands: University of Western Australia Press, 1990), edited by RA Dixon and MC Dillon, was immensely valuable in picturing the lives of Indigenous people in the East Kimberley in the 1980s. The editors of and contributors to that volume captured important oral accounts and other evidence that was crucial for my chapters relating to John Toby, the Glen Hill community and the 'Good Neighbour' agreement.

It was a pleasure to work again with the marvellous editor Katie Purvis and the whole team at MUP, especially Nathan Hollier, Cathryn Smith, Ikumi Cooray, Brian MacDonald and Sarah Valle.

NOTES

1 Breaking out of the Congo

'always ensured that the Prince's girlfriend was doing well': Enrico Carisch, 'The unusual suspects: Africa, parapolitics and the national security state complex', in Eric Wilson (ed.), *The Dual State: Parapolitics, Carl Schmitt and the National Security Complex* (London & New York: Routledge, 2016), p. 125.

'scandalously rich': Carisch, p. 124.

'quite against': Ewen Tyler, *Ewen William John Tyler: His Story*, unpublished memoir, n.d., Ewen Tyler archive.

'An independent Africa would be better for Africans': Tyler, ibid.

'wistfully longing for the old days': Author interview with Ewen Tyler.

'7.45 p.m. for 8.15 p.m. ... Piccadilly entrance ... No black tie necessary': Charles Waterhouse, letter to Ewen Tyler dated 28 March 1969, Ewen Tyler archive.

'It was immediately apparent that Union Minière's money and expertise would be most welcome': Tyler, *Ewen William John Tyler: His Story*.

'It was natural that in Australia they should be invited to participate in uranium exploration and mining': Tyler, ibid.

2 A dual role

'Conventional wisdom in Belgium didn't think Australian uranium prospects ... Who wanted Australian iron ore?': Ewen Tyler, *Ewen William John Tyler: His Story*, unpublished memoir, n.d., Ewen Tyler archive.

'They had no experience in nickel but rapidly, because of Western Mining Corporation's ... nickel. It's amazing how sheep-like corporate culture can be': Tyler, ibid.

3 The allure of diamonds

NSW Geological Survey: Garry Lowder, cited by David Duval, Timothy Green & Ross Louthean, *New Frontiers in Diamonds: The Mining Revolution* (London: Rosendale Press, 1996), p. 133.

'were probably formed much later, as Australia drifted eastwards … the surface by some magma other than kimberlite': Nick Norman, *The Extraordinary World of Diamonds* (Auckland Park: Jacana Media, 2010), p. 189.

'I resolved this was not for me': Ewen Tyler, *Ewen William John Tyler: His Story*, unpublished memoir, n.d., Ewen Tyler archive.

'For a time we had a Jewish German housemaid … to Hitler's broadcasts and shout at the wireless': Tyler, ibid.

'Sea trunks had to be bought. We were limited … then Irish maid, Kitty, to wash up, close the house and give the key to a neighbour': Tyler, ibid.

'There were some European children, mainly girls … Malay boys, Sinawie and his younger brother Sibawie, sons of the museum's principal taxidermist': Tyler, ibid.

'*Tuan Kitchie*. Little master, that is a diamond': Tyler, ibid.

'Chemistry was to be my major subject, with physics … no real interest, I chose geology, because my father was a geologist': Tyler, ibid.

'We used chains and compasses, plane tables and levels, to create our own maps and cut our own rock slices': Tyler, ibid.

'He interested me in mineral grains. … I knew something about the recovery of heavy minerals from rocks and sands and gravels': Author interview with Ewen Tyler.

'The volcanics are obvious. The vents and plugs rise conspicuously above the surrounding plains': Author interview with Ewen Tyler.

'What an unimpressive lot they were. Mostly weathered, difficult to section': Rex Prider, quoted in Norman, *The Extraordinary World of Diamonds*, p. 190.

'consanguineous': Author interview with Ewen Tyler.

'There were many … if they don't find a diamond in them it won't prove I was wrong': Rex Prider, quoted in Norman, *The Extraordinary World of Diamonds*, p. 190.

4 Tyler's mining start-up

'So instead of going to London to become an accountant, I went to Malaysia and became a miner. It was one of the best decisions of my life': Author interview with Alan Jones.

'listening post': Ewen Tyler, *Ewen William John Tyler: His Story*, unpublished memoir, n.d., Ewen Tyler archive.

'I was looking for diamond hunters and AO and … they had to do now was persuade their boards': Author interview with Ewen Tyler.

'I had a fear of the ship's doctor … The wound eventually healed': Ewen Tyler, *Ewen William John Tyler: His Story*.

'He was a couple of years older than me, but I remembered him well … He ended up reading engineering at the University of Western Australia': Tyler, ibid.

'At school I'd had almost no contact with … was an Old Guildfordian made him OK': Tyler, ibid.

'He had several appealing things in his bag. Some iron, some gold, copper': Author interview with Ewen Tyler.

'That obscure name was an ideal choice for what was of necessity a clandestine activity': Ewen Tyler, quoted in Nick Norman, *The Extraordinary World of Diamonds* (Auckland Park: Jacana Media, 2010), p. 194.

5 Looking for diamonds in Australia

'People saw through … and the extraction costs were higher': Alan Kohler, *It's Your Money* (Melbourne: Black Inc., 2019), p. 172.

'In 1972 it was the end of the nickel boom and there were lots and lots of geologists out of work': Maureen Muggeridge, quoted in 'Geologist left no stone unturned in quest for glittering prize: Maureen Muggeridge, 1948–2010', *Sydney Morning Herald*, 26 November 2010.

'with nothing more than £10 and a degree in geology': 'Geologist left no stone unturned', ibid.

'Australia was famous for gold, base metals and iron ore, but not diamonds': Maureen Muggeridge, quoted in 'Geologist left no stone unturned', ibid.

'flying over the outback in a helicopter looking for diamonds': 'Geologist left no stone unturned', ibid.

'It all had to be hush-hush … I felt like a character in a James Bond movie or a Wilbur Smith novel': Maureen Muggeridge, quoted in 'Geologist left no stone unturned', ibid.

'gravel gatherers': John McIlwraith, unpublished manuscript, c.2007, drawing on interviews with Ewen Tyler and other key Argyle participants; Ewen Tyler archive.

'We would put out fuel dumps … require fuel drums to be airlifted in by helicopter': Chris Smith, quoted in Nick Norman, *The Extraordinary World of Diamonds* (Auckland Park: Jacana Media, 2010), p. 195.

'the rugged terrain meant that you could not always land next to … get to them and carry heavy samples back out to the chopper': Chris Smith, quoted in Norman, p. 195.

'One geo and one fieldie would be put down ... the chopper would return to the second pair': Chris Smith, quoted in Norman, ibid.

'Then we noticed it was full of crocodiles ... had come for him': Chris Smith, quoted in Norman, p. 196.

'I *sail* Diamonds': Ewen Tyler, *The First Twenty Years*, unpublished memoir, n.d., Ewen Tyler archive.

'I spent my fourth year at the university doing just that': Ewen Tyler, *Ewen William John Tyler: His Story*, unpublished memoir, n.d., Ewen Tyler archive.

'Imagine examining an eggcup full of pinpoint-sized sand-grains ... what the mineral observers had to do': Author interview with Ewen Tyler.

'The observers resorted to whatever worked ... reduce the volume of the concentrates prior to observing': Author interview with Ewen Tyler.

6 M109

'a hole in the ground with a liar sitting on top': Ewen Tyler, 'Ethics and the mining industry', unpublished speech, n.d., Ewen Tyler archive.

'Where are we going to get a chairman for Northern?': Author interview with Ewen Tyler.

'The upshot was that my chairman in London ... My chairman became irritated with me': Ewen Tyler, *Ewen William John Tyler: His Story*, unpublished memoir, n.d., Ewen Tyler archive.

'He was an eccentric Englishman': Author interview with Ewen Tyler.

'suitable for shooting bustards in India': Author interview with Ewen Tyler.

'in an orderly manner': Ewen Tyler, *Ewen William John Tyler: His Story*.

'Australia was now considered entirely expendable': Author interview with Ewen Tyler.

'Union Minière in Australia was going nowhere ... had elected a "socialist government"': Ewen Tyler, *Ewen William John Tyler: His Story*.

'A brief reply to your letter of 7th May ... with that because it is the only exploration project which has clearly proved successful': Ronny Medlicott, letter to Ewen Tyler dated 14 May 1973, Ewen Tyler archive.

'Mad Colonial': Doug Wilkinson, 'Veteran diamond seeker is still in the hunt', *Australia's Paydirt*, February 2002, p. 40.

'My chips were at a low ebb': Author interview with Ewen Tyler.

'My heart leapt': Chris Smith, quoted in Nick Norman, *The Extraordinary World of Diamonds* (Auckland Park: Jacana Media, 2010), p. 197.

'We've found the lot. Pyrope, picroilmenite, chromite, kimberlitic zircon, and a diamond!': Chris Smith, quoted in Norman, ibid.

'Are you sure?': Norman, p. 198.

'I said I knew it was definitely a diamond, but he insisted the joint venturers would require separate proof': Chris Smith, quoted in Norman, p. 198.

'It was hard to believe, and we didn't. We thought someone in the sampling and processing chain was having us on': Ewen Tyler, 'Argyle Diamonds', unpublished speech (delivered to Rotary Club of Heidelberg, 15 March 2010), Ewen Tyler archive.

'We were elated ... looking at something having shed from a kimberlite that wasn't very far away': Tyler, 'Argyle Diamonds', ibid.

7 Opposite sides

'Now we are in elephant country!': Author interview with Ewen Tyler.

'They were as excited as I was': Author interview with Ewen Tyler.

'Now we are on opposite sides': Author interview with Ewen Tyler.

'He was mercurial, passionate, sometimes over the top. A master of brinkmanship': Author interview with Ewen Tyler.

'He became almost paranoid that Mitchell Cotts or one of the other investors would buy him out, and he'd be cheated again': Author interview with Ewen Tyler.

'We were constantly being probed. We lived in fear of John Byrne, who seemed to take a keen interest in our activities': Ewen Tyler, 'The Australian diamond industry: The creation of the Argyle diamond project—A chairman's perspective', unpublished speech, c.1983, Ewen Tyler archive.

'I was looking for ways and means to transfer myself and my organisation ... in spite of Tanganyika': Ewen Tyler, Ewen William John Tyler: His Story, unpublished memoir, n.d., Ewen Tyler archive.

8 The price of silence

'The West Australian mining law ... all of which merit careful consideration': AC Veatch, quoted in M Hunt, 'The Mining Act 1978 of Western Australia', *Australian Mining and Petroleum Law Association Yearbook*, 2:1, 1979, p. 2.

'Provisions for the issue of Temporary Reserves had been introduced ... before a discovery could not only be made, but proven to be commercial': Author interview with Bill Leslie.

'The present Act is not only outmoded in its concept but it is ambiguous ... trying to fulfil the needs of a mechanised and sophisticated industry': M Hunt, 'The Mining Act 1978 of Western Australia', pp. 2–3.

'Officially, no one outside the JV knew of what had been found. I was apprehensive about disclosure to anyone, and especially to the state government': Author interview with Ewen Tyler.

'What should I tell the government about the diamond discovery?' ... 'Vamp in G,' Court explained. 'That's what the pianist does whilst waiting for the Fat Lady to come on stage': Author interview with Ewen Tyler.

'This suited my timing. No more fieldwork ... start to rain, and there was no money left in the budget for further work anyway': Ewen Tyler, *Ewen William John Tyler: His Story*, unpublished memoir, n.d., Ewen Tyler archive.

'Your excellency': Author interview with Ewen Tyler.

'Under the normal rules, our annual rental ... We proposed a hundredth of that, which was $19,600': Author interview with Ewen Tyler.

'The government tried to help but the *Mining Act* defeated them': Author interview with Ewen Tyler.

9 To Oombulgurri

'The Aboriginal Affairs Planning Authority ... grant entry permits, provided the Aborigines agreed': Ewen Tyler, *Ewen William John Tyler: His Story*, unpublished memoir, n.d., Ewen Tyler archive.

'white advisers': Tyler, ibid.

'It seemed straight out of fairyland': Ewen Tyler, *The First Twenty Years*, unpublished memoir, n.d., Ewen Tyler archive.

'You whites must think we are mad. Why would a sane person hunt kangaroo with a boomerang if he could use a rifle?': Robert Roberts, conveyed by Ewen Tyler in an interview with the author.

'Because we had no mineral title in the A Class reserve ... describe our interest as being for minerals generally': Author interview with Ewen Tyler.

'Toohey believed Oombulgurri lands ... for 25 years, to allow the people time to adjust': Ewen Tyler, *The First Twenty Years*.

'There was a corroboree at which John Toohey and I ... would be welcome to explore the Reserve': Ewen Tyler, *Ewen William John Tyler: His Story*.

'We thought that, with its exclusivity ... we proposed a joint venture with the Oombulgurri': Author interview with Ewen Tyler.

'Such an arrangement appealed to the Commonwealth Department ... but it became abundantly clear that we were offending the government': Author interview with Ewen Tyler.

'The idea had to be canned': Author interview with Ewen Tyler.

'Often reluctant contributors anyway, they now started to feel even less welcome in Australia': Ewen Tyler, *Ewen William John Tyler: His Story*.

'Aboriginal fuss', 'They were cannibals a hundred years ago': Ronny Medlicott, quoted by Ewen Tyler in *Ewen William John Tyler: His Story*.

10 Steel balls

'That area was so cold it ... could work in there for any length of time': Author interview with Ewen Tyler.

'The new laboratory was divided into processing facilities ... with an engineering facility for vehicle maintenance': Author interview with Ewen Tyler.

'Apart from a secretive De Beers laboratory in Melbourne … It was the first of its kind here': Author interview with Ewen Tyler.

'I used my own daughter, then a university student … working there, and the distribution of the sexes': Author interview with Ewen Tyler.

'It was as though only my technical team … been only local success and no grand picture emerging': Ewen Tyler, *Ewen William John Tyler: His Story*, unpublished memoir, n.d., Ewen Tyler archive.

'For years these names of airstrips … would nonchalantly say they were going to Mumbo Jumbo': Author interview with Ewen Tyler.

'up the pole': Author interview with Ewen Tyler.

'All parties had become instant exploration experts': Author interview with Ewen Tyler.

'Exploration is an expensive business … often doesn't yield commercial results': Author interview with Alan Jones.

'It's a common thing in mining. As soon … need to put cash in to get cash out': Author interview with Ewen Tyler.

'*Ah, nous avons le renard par la queue!*' 'Ah, we have the fox by the tail!': Ewen Tyler, 'Mines and tribulations: Searching for Aussie diamond mines', *Jeweller*, 23 August 2016.

'[Bruno] spent some hours digging out crevices …There are diamonds here. Why don't you dig them up?': Chris Smith, quoted in Nick Norman, *The Extraordinary World of Diamonds* (Auckland Park: Jacana Media, 2010), p. 200.

'Ah, Smith, you never find the kimberlite. And if you find him, he will have no diamonds': Bruno Morelli, quoted in Norman, ibid.

'It was a concept for which I held … of the joint venture, making my position as manager more difficult': Author interview with Ewen Tyler.

11 A new partner

'At one stage it looked as though the overseas companies wouldn't … There were a lot of sleepless nights': Ewen Tyler, 'The Australian diamond industry: The creation of the Argyle diamond project—A chairman's perspective', unpublished speech, c.1983, Ewen Tyler archive.

'The Kalumburu parties were losing patience … agree, but Northern would always seek alteration': Author interview with Ewen Tyler.

'As if the problems of five parties had not been enough!': Ewen Tyler, *Ewen William John Tyler: His Story*, unpublished memoir, n.d., Ewen Tyler archive.

'Peko had considerable skill … and it seemed that we would be a good match': Tyler, ibid.

'I struck oil with Peko. … Their first payment of $250,000 was virtually in the bank': Ewen Tyler, 'The Australian diamond industry: The creation of the Argyle diamond project'.

'Rees had been asking … much for confidentiality!': Author interview with Ewen Tyler.

'We did not see how we could … sensing a lack of joint venture cohesion, might walk away': Ewen Tyler, *Ewen William John Tyler: His Story*.

'CZC had Broken Hill … cashed in its Spanish interests, had the cash': Bill Leslie, email to the author dated 1 June 2019.

'They were big, with plenty of muscle': Ewen Tyler, *Ewen William John Tyler: His Story*.

'Although I knew them well … the foreign companies' preferred position': Author interview with Ewen Tyler.

'Their money was in the bank … because they were all well known to me from my London days': Author interview with Ewen Tyler.

'It had been promoted by Northern … have some commitment to it': Ewen Tyler, *Ewen William John Tyler: His Story*.

'I was powerless to exert … of us could tame him': Author interview with Ewen Tyler.

12 A long-term perspective

'Collier beat us down … of Mr RFX Connor and the election of Malcolm Fraser': Ewen Tyler, email to John McIlwraith dated 18 October 2007, Ewen Tyler archive.

'It was the Kalumburu Joint Venture funding … only this time CRA paid the bill': Ewen Tyler, *Ewen William John Tyler: His Story*, unpublished memoir, n.d., Ewen Tyler archive.

'Inducting the new staff was not … follow Chris and Maureen's meticulousness': Author interview with Ewen Tyler.

'a highly skilled field observer and … nothing more than being out in the bush': Chris Smith, quoted in Nick Norman, *The Extraordinary World of Diamonds* (Auckland Park: Jacana Media, 2010), p. 202.

'He was an excellent geologist … He had excellent eyes': Author interview with Ewen Tyler.

'If I could persuade CRA of the technical …. diamond vision might still become a reality': Author interview with Ewen Tyler.

'The emphasis on Kimberley gravels was very much reduced': Author interview with Ewen Tyler.

'Broken Hill spawned many … five directors who'd been underground managers at Broken Hill': Bill Leslie, email to the author dated 1 June 2019.

13 The great explorer

'We realised we were close to more bodies': Ewen Tyler, *Ewen William John Tyler: His Story*, unpublished memoir, n.d., Ewen Tyler archive.

'I've got it': John Collier, quoted in John McIlwraith, unpublished manuscript, c.2007, drawing on interviews with Ewen Tyler and other key Argyle participants; Ewen Tyler archive.

'It seemed too good to be true ... And an amazing coincidence': Author interview with Ewen Tyler.

'*Vous êtes le grand explorateur*', 'You are the great explorer': Author interview with Ewen Tyler.

'Morelli nearly had a fit ... He was absolutely deflated': Author interview with Ewen Tyler.

'strange-looking depression': Frank Hughes, quoted by Robyn Ellison, email to Ewen Tyler dated 13 October 2011, Ewen Tyler archive.

'There was a gentle mound in the middle ... see the microscopic crystals of chromite in the sand': Robyn Ellison, email to Ewen Tyler, ibid.

'The chromite was the first thing I found. The second was a peg belonging to Mt Isa Mines': Frank Hughes, quoted in McIlwraith.

'CRA's instant success led to the belief ... young CRA fieldie say, "Just collect bags of sand in creeks"': Ewen Tyler, *The First Twenty Years*, unpublished memoir, n.d., Ewen Tyler archive.

'There was no doubt CRA had the bit ... more money than their partners are, and gradually to increase their interest"': Ewen Tyler, *Ewen William John Tyler: His Story*.

'Bruno Morelli still wasn't happy ... he must also have been under some other spending constraints': Author interview with Ewen Tyler.

'fed up with Northern Mining', 'put control firmly into the hands of CRA': Ewen Tyler, *The First Twenty Years*.

'Uncontrolled spending was not permitted ... seemed to escape Morelli and Medlicott': Ewen Tyler, *Ewen William John Tyler: His Story*.

14 Ellendale

'Hopes were raised even further ... when Frank Hughes picked up a 1.76-carat diamond that was just lying on the surface': Author interview with Ewen Tyler.

'Hughes was so surprised at how ... discovered it glittered enough to be easily sighted again': John McIlwraith, unpublished manuscript, c.2007, drawing on interviews with Ewen Tyler and other key Argyle participants; Ewen Tyler archive.

'Once all the pipes were under mineral ... 25-tonne-per-hour heavy media separation plant': Author interview with Ewen Tyler.

'We would receive weekly telexes ... lustrous, well-shaped stones, often of good size': Ewen Tyler, *The First Twenty Years*, unpublished memoir, n.d., Ewen Tyler archive.

'the mouse house': Author interview with Doug Bailey.

'I believe we can now say ... international significance which could rival South Africa': Ewen Tyler, letter to Bruno Morelli dated 24 August 1978, Ewen Tyler archive.

'Sir Philip nearly fell over': Author interview with Ewen Tyler.

'Everyone knew that the ... evaluating Australia's first diamond field': Ewen Tyler, *The First Twenty Years*.

'We literally pegged sheep stations ... throughout the west and into the east Kimberley': Graeme Hutton, quoted in David Duval, Timothy Green & Ross Louthean, *New Frontiers in Diamonds. The Mining Revolution* (London: Rosendale Press, 1996), p. 128.

'technical skill and dedication', 'comparable ... to the best and largest pipes in South Africa': R. Baxter Brown, 'Consulting Geologist's Report', in *Ashton Mining N/L Prospectus* (Melbourne: Potter Partners, 1978), p. 11.

'At last we could ... for the previous ten years': Ewen Tyler, *Ewen William John Tyler: His Story*, unpublished memoir, n.d., Ewen Tyler archive.

'The diamonds were beautiful, ... any of the pipes to justify a major mining operation': Author interview with Ewen Tyler.

'By the middle of 1979, things were starting to look gloomy': Ewen Tyler, *Ewen William John Tyler: His Story*.

15 The jewel box

'For reasons of sample complexity ... we had identified the Wilson River as a kimberlite district': Ewen Tyler, *Ewen William John Tyler: His Story*, unpublished memoir, n.d., Ewen Tyler archive.

'We've done it!' Frank Hughes, quoted in John McIlwraith, unpublished manuscript, c.2007, drawing on interviews with Ewen Tyler and other key Argyle participants; Ewen Tyler archive.

'One diamond was exciting enough', 'phenomenal': Maureen Muggeridge, quoted in Tony Thomas, 'Argyle: The gleam in Ewen Tyler's eye', *Business Review Weekly*, 7 June 1991.

'Finding diamonds was no longer ... Smoke Creek could be something very special': Author interview with Ewen Tyler.

'The system was that you had a sieve ... It was like a jewel box': Russel Madigan, quoted in Amanda Hooton, 'Diamonds aren't forever: The party's nearly over for Australia's most successful luxury export', *Sydney Morning Herald*, 6 May 2019.

'Frank raced down to Ellendale with a piece of the tuff to show me. You could see likely olivine pseudomorphs in it': Chris Smith, quoted in Nick Norman, *The Extraordinary World of Diamonds* (Auckland Park: Jacana Media, 2010), p. 203.

'They had one, and now we had one': Author interview with Ewen Tyler.

'One of the first things we saw was a small diamond embedded in an anthill. We saw several of those': Warren Atkinson, quoted in McIlwraith.

'Very satisfying, very interesting': Frank Hughes, quoted in McIlwraith.

'It was outcropping and diamonds were everywhere': Ewen Tyler, 'Challenges for mining companies in the new millennium', unpublished speech (delivered at Australian Resources Conference, 4 November 1998).

'It was like Ellendale all over ... went away and we were able to apply for the ground we wanted': Author interview with Ewen Tyler.

'If this had been seen by a competing company the implications would have been obvious. A major discovery had been made': Ewen Tyler, quoted in McIlwraith.

16 Jumped

'In all equity we were the rightful ... for ten years to find this promising deposit': Author interview with Ewen Tyler.

'Afro-West claimed the CRA miner's right was defective, and they challenged our right and title': Author interview with Ewen Tyler.

'Partly as a result of an omission ... the miner's right used by CRA at Argyle was in fact defective': Author interview with Ewen Tyler.

'Appearing in the Warden's Court, CRA's counsel said ... Afro-West was not a bonafide prospector': John McIlwraith, unpublished manuscript, c.2007, drawing on interviews with Ewen Tyler and other key Argyle participants; Ewen Tyler archive.

'It would be utterly unjust ... the original claims were invalid': Author interview with Ewen Tyler.

'[The JV's mineral claims] were being challenged ... "So the answer is no"': Ronda Jamieson, *Charles Court: I Love This Place* (Osborne Park, WA: St George Books, 2011), p. 356.

'The title issue was dragging ... end up with an appeal to the Privy Council in London': Ewen Tyler, *The First Twenty Years*, unpublished memoir, n.d., Ewen Tyler archive.

'It could've deferred development for years': Ewen Tyler, 'The Australian diamond industry: The creation of the Argyle diamond project—A chairman's perspective', unpublished speech, c.1983, Ewen Tyler archive.

'Sir Charles had known from the outset ... about the discovery of our first diamond on my birthday': Ewen Tyler, email to John McIlwraith dated 18 October 2007, Ewen Tyler archive.

'We've got this problem ... Supreme Court is the WA Parliament': Author interview with Ian Warner.

'We were going to need a state agreement … package of legislation that the state parliament would pass?': Author interview with Ewen Tyler.

'He had a can-do reputation. He knew about making decision': Author interview with Ewen Tyler.

'The pressing need for secure title was a strong bargaining chip for Sir Charles': Author interview with Ewen Tyler.

'Rees continued his great performances … that meant Argyle had a perceived value far greater than reality': Ewen Tyler, email to John McIlwraith dated 18October 2007, Ewen Tyler archive.

'Because of the expectation … thought the joint venture was sitting on a bonanza … our secret affairs were now becoming major public issues': Ewen Tyler, *Ewen William John Tyler: His Story*, unpublished memoir, n.d., Ewen Tyler archive.

'The media had taken up the issue … that charged to the iron ore industry, an industry well established': Tyler, 'The Australian diamond industry: The creation of the Argyle diamond project'.

'the sequestration of a major part of the Joint Ventures assets': Ewen Tyler, *Ewen William John Tyler: His Story*.

'The profit-related royalty was set … was giving itself a 22½ per cent interest in the deposit': Ewen Tyler, 'The Australian diamond industry: The creation of the Argyle diamond project'.

'We paid dearly for the lack … royalty and also a township requirement': Ewen Tyler, *The First Twenty Years*.

'milking the cow before it was born': Ewen Tyler, 'The Australian diamond industry: The creation of the Argyle diamond project'.

'We were smarting about some … make a profit for the Joint Venturers and the government alike': Tyler, ibid.

'We brought in a special Bill which had special conditions in it so far as the title and the responsibilities and the role of Argyle Diamonds were concerned': Jamieson, *Charles Court*, p. 356.

'That's exactly what we did, and it was appropriate': Author interview with Ian Warner.

'You can charge anything for this': Author interview with Ian Warner.

17 A major force

'It is probably no coincidence that there … and the geologist left. The Kalumburu JV's cover had been blown': Nick Norman, *The Extraordinary World of Diamonds* (Auckland Park: Jacana Media, 2010), p. 200.

'It was obvious at the outset … that the diamonds were not of top quality': Ewen Tyler, *Ewen William John Tyler: His Story*, unpublished memoir, n.d., Ewen Tyler archive.

18 Distribution is everything

'Selling the product is always the key to a successful mine, however excited the miners might get about finding it': Russel Madigan, quoted by Bill Leslie in email to the author dated 1 June 2019.

'Neither CRA nor Ashton Mining had any ... that bought at least 80 per cent of all diamonds mined': Bill Leslie, email to the author dated 2 April 2019.

'over a drink in the long room at the Australian Club ... purchased will not go down the minute he walks out of the shop': Bill Leslie, email to the author, ibid.

'The buyer states the quantities, shapes and sizes he requires ... the stones he does not want': Eric Bruton, *Diamonds* (London: NAG Press, 1978), p. 170.

'feeding the ducks', 'The ducks come paddling over and you throw them the bread and they eat what you throw': Richard Wake-Walker, quoted in Matthew Hart, *Diamond: The History of a Cold-blooded Love Affair* (London: Fourth Estate, 2003), p. 138.

'with its anticipated production, Australia ... think, the site could produce 40 million carats a year': Pamela G. Hollie, 'Australia's diamond debate', *New York Times*, 4 December 1981.

'With a stable cash flow from a blue-chip ... best blue-chip companies in the world': Bill Leslie, email to the author dated 23 April 2019.

'Occasionally [the Russians] would sell a large quantity direct ... get approval and come back down again': Bill Leslie, email to the author dated 2 April 2019.

'Our research indicated that De Beers ... Better to be with them than against them': Author interview with Bill Leslie.

19 An astonishing sight

'There he arranged a job for his favourite ... there was a glow in his eyes as he explored it': Anthony Hocking, *Oppenheimer and Son* (New York: McGraw-Hill Book Co., 1973), pp. 17–18.

'I recall the day I first saw Ernest ... terribly shy, and he doesn't seem to be very bright': Emily Hahn, quoted in Hocking, p. 22.

'strange and impelling form of humility', 'It was not an abasing form of humility ... flowed inevitably from the logic of his responses': John Cope, quoted in Hocking, pp. 132–3.

'I hardly think so': John McIlwraith, unpublished manuscript, c.2007, drawing on interviews with Ewen Tyler and other key Argyle participants; Ewen Tyler archive.

'holy of holies', 'An astonishing sight', 'As well as being a gesture ... showing the strength of their hand': Author interview with Bill Leslie.

'a slight and dapper man, well-tailored', 'He had a firm but warm ... ability to maintain control of his empire': Bill Leslie, email to the author dated 19 July 2019.

'extremely polite and courteous but hard to read', 'One knew with the Japanese ... quid pro quo that you gave them something': Bill Leslie, email to the author, ibid.

'you were left in no doubt what they ... reticence to divulge details of the workings of the CSO': Bill Leslie, email to the author dated 23 April 2019.

'He brought people together. That was his special strength': Author interview with Bill Leslie.

'It was extremely difficult for Ashton ... segmented, and if segmented, how the segments interacted': Author interview with Bill Leslie.

'what the immediate purpose of this exercise was', 'Fitzgerald retrieved the worksheets ... matters related to geology and location as much as marketing': McIlwraith.

'These were further uncertainties in the supply-demand equation': Author interview with Bill Leslie.

'Argyle contained more diamonds ... significant position in the world of diamonds': Bill Leslie, email to the author dated 31 March 2019.

'could be predator but not prey': Author interview with Bill Leslie.

'We had to be sure that goods ... activities did not adversely affect our range of goods': Author interview with Bill Leslie.

'probably be absorbed': McIlwraith.

'Well, if we had a mine that required that sort of guarantee, I do not think we would regard it as worth developing': Harry Oppenheimer, quoted in Argyle Diamonds, *Barramundi Dreaming: The Argyle Diamonds Story* (West Perth: Argyle Diamonds, 2011), p. 44.

'If we were being screwed, at least we would know about it': Author interview with Bill Leslie.

'There was a general feeling ... no agreement': Argyle Diamonds, *Barramundi Dreaming*, p. 43.

'De Beers had expected ... would participate in the industry': Geoff Billard, unpublished memoir.

'bloody ridiculous': Argyle Diamonds, *Barramundi Dreaming*, p. 43.

'Harry was always tough but fair, and of course the ultimate gentleman': Russel Madigan, quoted in McIlwraith.

'there was dismay on the part of many De Beers and CSO executives over what they regarded [as] the generous terms agreed to by their chairman': McIlwraith.

'As the US represented a very big market for diamonds, this was a risk that could not be entertained': McIlwraith.

'a good deal of handwringing and various suggestions': Bill Leslie, email to the author dated 29 May 2019.

'Have a reduction in purchases, without actually … DiCorp, which would be credited against the APR': Bill Leslie, email to the author, ibid.

20 A South African monopoly

'We have got to be careful': Rees Towie, quoted in Pamela G. Hollie, 'Australia's diamond debate', *New York Times*, 4 December 1981.

'This is very like South Africa … an elephant walking into view': Author interview with Ewen Tyler.

'In the mind of the prime minister, South Africa was a dirty word': Author interview with Ewen Tyler.

'Doug was on our side. He understood … He promised to get Fraser onside': Author interview with Ewen Tyler.

'I am concerned … 40 per cent below': Bill Hayden, quoted in 'Ashton looking for the best deal', *Canberra Times*, 29 August 1981.

'This is against the national interest and so far the Federal and WA Governments have done nothing to intervene': John McIlwraith, unpublished manuscript, c.2007, drawing on interviews with Ewen Tyler and other key Argyle participants; Ewen Tyler archive.

'was very supportive': Author interview with Ewen Tyler.

'He understood our plans … He had a brilliant brain': Author interview with Alan Jones.

'a matter of national importance': Paul Keating, quoted by Ewen Tyler in 'The mining industry', unpublished speech (delivered to Country Women's Association, Australia Day 1998), Ewen Tyler archive.

'I direct a question to the Prime Minister about South Africa and diamond policy … rendering it less and less competitive?'; 'It is imperative that we do not let Ashton fall into the hands of De Beers': Paul Keating, 'Questions Without Notice: Diamond Production', *House of Representatives: Official Hansard. No. 125, 1981. Thursday, 15 October 1981. Thirty-Second Parliament. First Session—Third Period* (By Authority of the House of Representatives, 1981), p. 2066.

'The honourable gentleman has asked a detailed question … Any examination that we would undertake would be against that background': Malcolm Fraser, 'Questions Without Notice: Diamond Production', ibid.

'I refer the Prime Minister to his answer last week … significant mineral commodities?' Paul Keating: 'Questions Without Notice: Australian Diamond Industry', *House of Representatives: Official Hansard. No. 125, 1981. Tuesday, 20 October 1981. Thirty-Second Parliament. First Session—Third Period* (By Authority of the House of Representatives, 1981), p. 2186.

'A sentence which I did use last week … I do not believe there is any': Malcolm
Fraser: 'Questions Without Notice: Australian Diamond Industry', ibid.

'I desire to put another question to the Prime Minister … guarantee that the
marketing of Australian diamonds proceeds in the national interest?': Paul
Keating, 'Questions Without Notice: Australian Diamond Industry', *House
of Representatives: Official Hansard. No. 125, 1981. Tuesday, 20 October
1981. Thirty-Second Parliament. First Session—Third Period* (By Authority of
the House of Representatives, 1981), p. 2186.

'Concerning the naturalisation of the firms involved with the Argyle diamond
project … until the question of how the diamonds are to be marketed is
put before the Government': John Anthony, 'Questions Without Notice:
Australian Diamond Industry', ibid.

'He saved the day for us': Author interview with Alan Jones.

'We are family now. Whenever you travel to South Africa, you must visit me and
we will have a meal together': Author interview with Bill Leslie.

21 Finding the money

'CRA was left owning less of the project than it would have liked': Author
interview with Alan Jones.

'What I thought was a light … be a train coming the other way': Rees Towie,
quoted by Ewen Tyler in *Ewen William John Tyler: His Story*, unpublished
memoir, n.d., Ewen Tyler archive.

'more English than the English': Author interview with Ewen Tyler.

'surge bin', 'slush fund': Author interview with Andrew Berry.

'What was the mine, at the most … be realised?' 'There was the threshold
question … did you know if there was value there?': Author interview with
Andrew Berry.

'Gold is gold … Diamonds are different': Author interview with Andrew Berry.

'It was an awkward half-hour before then': Author interview with Alan Jones.

'You're mad. You will … ready, come and speak to us': Author interview with
Andrew Berry.

'If Bill didn't like a financing … deal would not be done': Author interview with
Andrew Berry.

'This is a piece of shit', 'I'm in real shit. I beat up the Xerox repairman': Author
interviews with Andrew Berry and Doug Bailey.

'There is no way that I'm going to approve this': Author interview with
Andrew Berry.

22 Are there diamonds?

'Dominique could've made … But he didn't': Author interview with Andrew
Berry.

'I have no idea what this is. I have no understanding of what I'm looking at', 'Are there diamonds there?': Author interview with Andrew Berry.

'You bet there are!': Author interview with Andrew Berry.

'OK. We're in for 175, but I only want to be left with 25': Author interview with Andrew Berry.

'Can this selldown of exposure be done?', 'It will be done': Author interview with Andrew Berry.

'It took six months to get to three minutes': Author interview with Andrew Berry.

'I'll be back in Melbourne in a few days', 'I need to show Sir Leslie ... I need something in writing': Author interview with Andrew Berry.

'Before we have tea, we need to pose for *The Age*': Author interview with Andrew Berry.

'It was a colossal sum at that time': Author interview with Alan Jones.

'If we get this deal done, can you get me a knighthood?', 'Yes. If you do this deal, you will be a knight': Author interviews with Ewen Tyler and Doug Bailey.

'glamour photos': Author interview with Andrew Berry.

'Somebody is in for 25': Author interview with Andrew Berry.

'mail letters over the phone': Author interview with Doug Bailey.

'Intellectually, the financing ... challenging project of my career': Author interview with Andrew Berry.

'Will Bill Mulligan please come up?', 'Kneel before me', 'Arise, Sir William of the Hutt River Province': Author interviews with Ewen Tyler and Doug Bailey.

23 Mandangala

'We used to go down ... day and went back the next day': John Toby, quoted in Bruce Shaw and John Toby, '"We still got the idea": Opportunity, not identity change, in the East Kimberley', in RA Dixon & MC Dillon (eds), *Aborigines and Diamond Mining: The Politics of Resource Development in the East Kimberley, Western Australia* (Nedlands: University of Western Australia Press, 1990), p. 57.

'from round Mandangala ... to a place called Cattle Creek Yard': John Toby, quoted in Shaw and Toby, pp. 57–8.

'They'd say ... through somehow back to the station, sneak away': John Toby, quoted in Shaw and Toby, p. 57.

'and keep, too, like tucker and tobacco': John Toby, quoted in Shaw and Toby, p. 58.

'[no] matter what colour you were': John Toby, quoted in Shaw and Toby, p. 59.

'Well we have the whitefella's ... We still have our own Law, our own way': John Toby, quoted in Shaw and Toby, pp. 62–3.

'I said to them, 'It's the grandfather's ... you can go back any time you want to': John Toby, quoted in Shaw and Toby, p. 63.

'Mandangala is the waterhole right alongside ... where the station Glen Hill was', 'going back to where I started from': John Toby, quoted in Shaw and Toby, ibid.

'I've got no money for it ... way I can get money to run the place': John Toby, quoted in RA Dixon, 'Aborigines as purposive actors or passive victims: An account of the Argyle events by some of the Aboriginal participants', in RA Dixon & MC Dillon (eds), *Aborigines and Diamond Mining*, p. 71.

'These anthropomorphic ancestor beings ... social order prescribed by Aboriginal Law': Rod Dixon et al., 'A preliminary indication of some effects of the Argyle Diamond Mine on Aboriginal communities in the region', in Dixon & Dillon (eds), p. 116.

'They went over to make sure ... gone through and we can't stop them': Rammel Peters, quoted in Dixon, 'Aborigines as purposive actors or passive victims', p. 71.

'It was getting worse ... But they started again', 'When Kingsley and Nancy ... Barramundi sites': Rammel Peters, quoted in Dixon, pp. 71–2.

'I think that place where they ... I'm worried. I think we'll have to stop it': John Toby, quoted in Dixon, p. 72.

24 *Winan*

'That mine's making too many ... what can we do': Bob Nyalcas, quoted in RA Dixon, 'Aborigines as purposive actors or passive victims: An account of the Argyle events by some of the Aboriginal participants', in RA Dixon & MC Dillon (eds), *Aborigines and Diamond Mining: The Politics of Resource Development in the East Kimberley, Western Australia* (Nedlands: University of Western Australia Press, 1990), p. 73.

'With the Liberal Government what ... mean European helpers—but my *own* people': John Toby, quoted in Dixon, p. 74.

'appeared depressed', 'When I left him he was debating ... made and adjoining sites left undisturbed': Bruce Shaw and John Toby, '"We still got the idea": Opportunity, not identity change, in the East Kimberley', in RA Dixon & MC Dillon (eds), *Aborigines and Diamond Mining: The Politics of Resource Development in the East Kimberley, Western Australia* (Nedlands: University of Western Australia Press, 1990), pp. 64–5.

'[Barramundi Gap] was a woman's site. But the women ... I don't want [the miners] to go near there': John Toby, quoted in Dixon, 'Aborigines as purposive actors or passive victims', p. 76.

'"What do you reckon *kangkayi*" ... up and we had no choice except to go along with him': Bob Nyalcas, quoted in Dixon, p. 74.

'The first time when I and John ... a lot of mines in different countries': Peggy Patrick, quoted in Dixon, p. 77.

'We took people out to Glen Hill ... we got up there were the right people':
    John Toby, quoted in Dixon, p. 76.
'John Toby opened the discussion ... they would raise no opposition to the
    development of the Argyle project': Mick O'Leary, quoted in McIlwraith.
'John [Toby] said, "What do you mob want ... from their grandfather, from
    their mother"': Peggy Patrick, quoted in Dixon, 'Aborigines as purposive
    actors or passive victims', p. 76.
'spent two days ... the final signing of the Agreement': letter from Russel
    Madigan to Senator Susan Ryan, 25 February 1981, quoted in Dixon,
    'Aborigines as purposive actors or passive victims', p. 74.
'That's why I was keen ... the chance I missed out on': John Toby, quoted in
    Shaw and Toby, '"We still got the idea"', p. 60.
'tinned meat, blankets, all kinds of tucker': Bob Nyalcas, quoted in Dixon,
    'Aborigines as purposive actors or passive victims', p. 74.
'From this perspective ... the very achievement of these objectives': Dixon, p. 68.
'That money *kartiya* call royalties ... as long as you give something back': Joe
    Thomas, quoted in Dixon, p. 83.
'along *winan* routes for the benefit of "all"': Dixon, p. 81.
'*Winan* is forever ... young people will take it over': Jack Britain, quoted in
    Dixon, p. 84.
'I don't know why ... to go ahead, they got angry at me': John Toby, quoted in
    Dixon, p. 85.
'considerable strife': Shaw and Toby, '"We still got the idea"', p. 56.
'I nearly got my throat cut .... I nearly got a spear right through my guts': John
    Toby, quoted in Dixon, 'Aborigines as purposive actors or passive victims',
    p. 85.
'These meetings called on John ... extension of the Agreement to other
    communities': Dixon, p. 86.
'coming on good again ... demands of Aboriginal custom': Dixon, ibid.

25 Western Australia Incorporated
'Mine towns are difficult enough ... of a diamond mining operation could be
    intolerable': Author interview with Ewen Tyler.
'All things considered, one might ... mine town—a feature of other state
    agreements—would be waived': Author interview with Ewen Tyler.
'The obligation to build a ... town that no-one wanted': Author interview with
    Ewen Tyler.
'We were stunned and angry ... to pay what in my view was blackmail': Author
    interview with Ewen Tyler.
'We were already contributing $160 million ... but that wasn't enough': Author
    interview with Ewen Tyler.

'I will never forget ... driving a Rolls. It felt like Las Vegas': Author interview with Bill Leslie.

'Connell said we had to pay ... should go to the state and not Argyle': Author interview with Bill Leslie.

'This was rejected, and ... how it would be structured': Author interview with Bill Leslie.

'This night, the ministers sat at different tables ... O'Leary replied, "Well, he's just a television journalist really"': Brian Burke, *A Tumultuous Life* (Scarborough, WA: A Tumultuous Life Pty Ltd, 2017), p. 237.

'next year': Author interviews with Ewen Tyler and Bill Leslie.

'That's good, Mick. I'm just a television journalist doing my best': Burke, *A Tumultuous Life*, p. 237.

'The fact that the state already ... agreement, did not seem to matter': Ewen Tyler, *Ewen William John Tyler: His Story*, unpublished memoir, n.d., Ewen Tyler archive.

'This was a bitter pill to swallow': Author interview with Bill Leslie.

'to minimise any political fallout', 'the whole transaction ... in a very different political light': Burke, *A Tumultuous Life*, p. 236.

'The price the Government had paid ... would previously have been granted for no charge whatsoever': Burke, p. 237.

'The fact that Connell had arrangements ... it is something I should have known about': Burke, p. 433.

'The manoeuvre by Brian Burke ... fuel from overseas to meet the mine's power needs': Ewen Tyler, *Ewen William John Tyler: His Story*.

26 The decision to mine

'Forty to fifty years was not an unreasonable expectation': Author interview with Ewen Tyler.

'I felt that I had completed ... my dream had almost become a reality': Ewen Tyler, *Ewen William John Tyler: His Story*, unpublished memoir, n.d., Ewen Tyler archive.

'They didn't want to go ... that could be seen from space': Author interview with Doug Bailey.

'They brought the A Team ... could call on a wide range of expertise in mine development': Author interview with Doug Bailey.

'I believe I assisted in the ... real sense of responsibility in its growing up': Author interview with Ewen Tyler.

'housed in tents and uncomfortably situated in an inhospitable landscape': John McIlwraith, unpublished manuscript, c.2007, drawing on interviews with Ewen Tyler and other key Argyle participants; Ewen Tyler archive.

'The TWU's members … litigation began': McIlwraith.

'This was intended … production phases': McIlwraith.

'More serious, but not in the public … problems and complaints about the structure of its contract': Argyle Diamonds, *Barramundi Dreaming: The Argyle Diamonds Story* (West Perth: Argyle Diamonds, 2011), p. 78.

'a pilot plant', 'a commercial-scale plant by most standards': Author interview with Ewen Tyler.

'The whole of the 4000 tonnes per day … yielded 60 carats of diamonds to the tonne': Argyle Diamonds, *Barramundi Dreaming*, p. 55.

'The higher proportion of gem quality diamonds retrieved … about $20 million was profit': McIlwraith.

'The operation of the alluvial plant … excellent training ground for operations staff': Argyle Diamonds, *Barramundi Dreaming*, p. 57.

'Right from the beginning … we were not, as they would say in the industry, "diamond people"': Mick O'Leary, quoted in McIlwraith.

'From the beginning, it was emphasised … to have a more flexible and self-motivated approach': Argyle Diamonds, *Barramundi Dreaming*, p. 77.

'At one stage, there was a queue … employees lined up to lodge their applications': Argyle Diamonds, ibid.

'The last 600 on the "shortlist" … two weeks of separation out of every four': George Gauci, quoted in McIlwraith.

'the individuality of the worker', 'generous-sized bed': Argyle Diamonds, *Barramundi Dreaming*, p. 81.

27 Digging for diamonds

'It was literally a mountain of … wasn't much overburden': Author interview with Alan Jones.

'No-one could have been more thrilled than me': Author interview with Ewen Tyler.

'We had no interest in such things in production': Author interview with Ewen Tyler.

'The kimberlite ore wore everything … mining techniques didn't work at Argyle': Author interview with Doug Bailey.

'We had to use X-rays … ever processed this many diamonds': Author interview with Doug Bailey.

'large, well-shaped … of US$80 to $115 per carat': Author interview with Ewen Tyler.

'the new mine in town': Author interview with Doug Bailey.

'grossly uneconomic cost': Author interview with Doug Bailey.

'They all insisted on dealing … CRA couldn't do that': Author interview with Doug Bailey.

'We can't store this amount of diamonds … come and get them', 'No … take them away immediately': Author interview with Doug Bailey.

'Fitzgerald begged for … millions of dollars' worth of diamonds through the streets': McIlwraith.

'So hectic were the sales … the staff could catch up on paperwork': Argyle Diamonds, *Barramundi Dreaming*, p. 89.

'very reasonable': Author interview with Ewen Tyler.

'It was a rewarding relationship': Author interview with Ewen Tyler.

'The technique of negotiating … glance at them before others saw them': John McIlwraith, unpublished manuscript, c.2007, drawing on interviews with Ewen Tyler and other key Argyle participants; Ewen Tyler archive.

28 Champagne diamonds

'affordable fashion jewellery sold in American shopping mall': Argyle Diamonds, *Barramundi Dreaming: The Argyle Diamonds Story* (West Perth: Argyle Diamonds, 2011), p. 63.

'The preponderance of browns … if not embarrassment': Author interview with Bill Leslie.

'roo poo', 'frozen spit', 'They were very dismissive … "Do you call these diamonds?"': Author interview with Mark Hooper.

'The cutting and polishing … diamonds to show them off to their optimum': Author interview with Bill Leslie.

'When Stuart asked about … back to London to be cut and polished': Author interview with Bill Leslie.

'Argyle's project managers … AK1 on a large scale profitable': Author interview with Bill Leslie.

'Then he rolled out … streaming in from Kings Park Road': Bill Leslie, email to the author dated 21 July 2019.

'their brilliance and subtle … warm and sparkling effect': Stuart Devlin, *Champagne Diamond Exhibition by Stuart Devlin, Melbourne, Victorian Arts Centre, 8th to 15th December 1987 … Presented by Argyle Diamonds* (n.p., 1987).

'You don't have brown diamonds. You have champagne and cognac diamonds': Stuart Devlin, quoted by Bill Leslie in an interview with the author.

'Devlin assured those present …. marketed as near gem or better': Author interview with Bill Leslie.

'Stones that had been estimated … made a big difference to the cash flow projections': Bill Leslie, email to the author dated 21 July 2019.

'there was a "ripple effect" … and, indeed, jewellery buyers': Argyle Diamonds, *Barramundi Dreaming*, p. 109.

'with Champagne Diamonds displayed ... warmly enhanced by yellow gold':
   A Legend in the Making (Argyle Diamonds, n.d.), p. 15.
'My partner and I looked at each ... traditional jewellery store owners and
   retailers': Liz Chatelain, quoted in Rachelle Bergstein, *Brilliance and Fire:
   A Biography of Diamonds* (New York: Harper, 2016), pp. 238–9.
'We had a joke for twenty ... was a significant barrier': Liz Chatelain, quoted in
   Bergstein, p. 239.
'In no uncertain terms, the American shopper would buy it': Bergstein, p. 238.
'MVI set up the Champagne ... business a fresh way to talk about them':
   Bergstein, p. 239.
'proved to be much more open-minded': Bergstein, ibid.
'MVI's objective with brown ... the idea of the champagne palette': Bergstein,
   p. 240.
'the industry was once ... these tiny, lower-value stones': Bergstein, ibid.
'a logical sequel to the close relationship built up between Argyle and the Indians
   in the trade of rough stones': John McIlwraith, unpublished manuscript,
   c.2007, drawing on interviews with Ewen Tyler and other key Argyle
   participants; Ewen Tyler archive.
'Argyle's production wasn't considered ... in small but steady batches': Bergstein,
   Brilliance and Fire, p. 241.
'The Argyle Pink Diamond Tender ... bids on the pink diamonds of their
   choice': *A Legend in the Making*, p. 21.
'In 2002, Jennifer Lopez ... worth an estimated US$1.2 million': Bergstein,
   Brilliance and Fire, p. 243.
'caused a sensation': Argyle Diamonds, *Barramundi Dreaming: The Argyle
   Diamonds Story* (West Perth: Argyle Diamonds, 2011), p. 108.

29 Falling out

'Unhappily ... this did not in itself ensure cordiality in the early years of the
   agreement': Author interview with Ewen Tyler.
'It was a very fractious relationship. You're selling the majority of your diamonds
   to your biggest customer and your biggest competitor. So we were in bed
   with the enemy': Robyn Ellison, quoted in Rachelle Bergstein, *Brilliance and
   Fire: A Biography of Diamonds* (New York: Harper, 2016), p. 237.
'Traditionally, hundreds of ... have thousands of such classifications': Argyle
   Diamonds, *Barramundi Dreaming: The Argyle Diamonds Story* (West Perth:
   Argyle Diamonds, 2011), p. 63.
'on the tweezers', 'with some frugality' Author interview with Ewen Tyler.
'We had to engage sorters from De Beers to teach our own people how to
   sort': Ewen Tyler, 'Why diamonds?', keynote speech at World Diamond
   Conference, Perth (delivered 2 December 2002).

'in broad terms it was almost a paid holiday': John McIlwraith, unpublished manuscript, c.2007, drawing on interviews with Ewen Tyler and other key Argyle participants; Ewen Tyler archive.

'We started to fear … undervaluing our product': Ewen Tyler, 'Diamonds'.

'There were regular debates … Argyle smelled a rat': Author interview with Ewen Tyler.

'and that the use of the organisation's sorters made it difficult to establish this case': Author interview with Ewen Tyler.

'had lowered average values from the mine': McIlwraith.

'Over five sales, the prices of Argyle goods declined substantially … what order they had been originally offered to them': Ewen Tyler, memo to John McIlwraith, 18 October 2007, Ewen Tyler archive.

'unpleasant': Author interview with Ewen Tyler.

'There followed a rapid learning experience … to refute the criticism "You are not diamond people"': Ewen Tyler, memo to John McIlwraith, 18 October 2007, Ewen Tyler archive.

'considerable tensions': McIlwraith.

'classify the stones by … of the hand-sorting previously required': Author interview with Ewen Tyler.

'At that meeting it was … five years unless remedies were found': Argyle Diamonds, *Barramundi Dreaming*, p. 90.

'One result was that … the marketing of the project's output': Argyle Diamonds, ibid.

'This was partly due to … higher prices being paid by the CSO': McIlwraith.

'De Beers was underselling … especially the coloured gems': Author interview with Ewen Tyler.

'Robinson made no secret that he found it a double blow … "when deferred purchases are in place to defend prices, that prices are then reduced"': Ross Louthean, 'Australia: Any heirs to Argyle?', in David Duval, Timothy Green & Ross Louthean, *New Frontiers in Diamonds: The Mining Revolution* (London: Rosendale Press, 1996), pp. 120–1.

'It introduced larger screens at its ore treatment plant through which tiny, low-value stones of less than … will actually be treated, providing more large stones, thus raising revenue at the AK1 pipe by 10 per cent': Louthean, p. 121.

'It helped keep the CSO honest. And it gave Ashton and CRA a priceless window on the market': Author interview with Doug Bailey.

'There was minimal engagement … improvements to the contract terms': Author interview with Mark Hooper.

'just provided fuel … needed and they ran with it': Author interview with Mark Hooper.

30 A clean sweep

'In the course of our conversation ... and whether they might support it': Author interview with Bill Leslie.

'What Elders needed was support ... Argyle production was their key interest': Author interview with Bill Leslie.

'a nice profit on their investment': Brian Burke, *A Tumultuous Life* (Scarborough, WA: A Tumultuous Life Pty Ltd, 2017), p. 238.

31 Spiders, bandicoots, cockatoos and pigeons

'a constant battle of wits between the stealers and management': Ion L. Idriess, *The Diamond: Stone of Destiny* (Sydney: Angus & Robertson, 1969), p. 197.

'The switcher flicks a diamond ... into the line and so did the diamond': Matthew Hart, *Diamond: The History of a Cold-blooded Love Affair* (London: Fourth Estate, 2003), p. 133.

'When the last layer of gravel was ... fingers rolled over and glinted in the candlelight': Idriess, *The Diamond*, p. 195.

'Two men would work at the face ... taking back to his mate in their drive the rich dirt': Idriess, pp. 196–7.

'very cunningly, very daringly ... but "cockatoos", night and day, were watching the police': Idriess, p. 197.

'One night a "lone wolf" prized ... in some cases with a week's tucker': Idriess, ibid.

'with the best of them ... drop a bag of the rich dirt from the cart': Idriess, pp. 198–9.

'You've got a leak. Roddan knows you've got the stones and he's coming round to do a check on them': Noel Newton, quoted in *Royal Commission into Whether There Has Been Corrupt or Criminal Conduct by any Western Australian Police Officer* (Parliament of Western Australia, 2004), pp. 417–18.

'looking at his diamonds': Noel Newton, quoted in *Royal Commission into Whether There Has Been Corrupt or Criminal Conduct*, p. 418.

'If the police hand had already been shown, then that would have been a compromised inquiry': Graeme Castlehow, quoted in *Royal Commission into Whether There Has Been Corrupt or Criminal Conduct*, ibid.

'The intention was that the diamonds would be recovered at a later stage ... any evidentiary value they might have had was lost': *Royal Commission into Whether There Has Been Corrupt or Criminal Conduct*, p. 393.

'Thoy asked Corfield ... The person identified was Mr Barry Crimmins': *Royal Commission into Whether There Has Been Corrupt or Criminal Conduct*, ibid.

'Police cannot find any evidence that Argyle diamonds have been smuggled out of the country': a senior Western Australia Police officer, quoted in Hart, *Diamond*, p. 178.

'In June 1990, Ms Rae-lene Shore, Roddan's former de-facto, approached police regarding a separate … revealed this connection, and he was forced to resign from his position in operational security at the mine': *Royal Commission into Whether There Has Been Corrupt or Criminal Conduct*, p. 394.

'attended at the home of Roddan', 'She was in a drunken state … allegations regarding those of Roddan': *Royal Commission into Whether There Has Been Corrupt or Criminal Conduct*, p. 397.

'Crimmins's 'moment of madness', … the robbing of Argyle got underway': Hart, *Diamond*, pp. 177–8.

'Roddan paid Barry Crimmins … them overseas in their personal luggage': Hart, p. 178.

'a love affair that had degenerated … had been driven into crime by her greed': Hart, pp. 178–9.

32 After Argyle

'For years, up to the … joke with me about "Paltridge's Plant"!': Author interview with Ewen Tyler.

'It was clearly a Kimberley King George River stone': Author interview with Ewen Tyler.

'unconventional and daring exploits … King of the Kimberley': *Kimberley Diamond Company NL: 2007 Annual Report* (2007).

'Both of them felt that … pipes were definitely worth revisiting': David Duval, Timothy Green & Ross Louthean, *New Frontiers in Diamonds. The Mining Revolution* (London: Rosendale Press, 1996), pp. 128–9.

'These guys were actually … going in all sorts of ways': Miles Kennedy, quoted in Duval, Green & Louthean, p. 129.

'Stout hearts … pumping with anticipation': *Australia's Paydirt*, July 1995, p. 9.

'The initial focus through 1995 … than previously thought': Duval, Green & Louthean, *New Frontiers in Diamonds*, p. 129.

'We discovered the Terrace 5 … across the border on the Argyle ground': *Kimberley Diamond Company NL: 2007 Annual Report* (2007).

'We processed the material … diamonds from the concentrate': *Kimberley Diamond Company NL*, ibid.

'In 1988 Ashton purchased … Mt Weld Rare Earth Deposit': Ewen Tyler, email to Paul McClintock dated 22 June 2000, Ewen Tyler archive.

'In platinum exploration … Helix in 1997 for a net gain of $17.8 million': Ewen Tyler, email to Paul McClintock, ibid.

'We had been moderately successful … $30 million from the Canadian market': Ewen Tyler, email to Paul McClintock, ibid.

'Following the murder, Ashton ... a small part of the concession': Ewen Tyler, email to Paul McClintock, ibid.

'on an endless plateau of sand and spinifex': Duval, Green & Louthean, *New Frontiers in Diamonds*, p. 123.

'Tom Reddicliffe negotiated access ... found kimberlite rich in diamonds': Ewen Tyler, 'Mines and tribulations: Searching for Aussie diamond mines', *Jeweller*, 23 August 2016.

'a sense of magic': Duval, Green & Louthean, *New Frontiers in Diamonds*, p. 123.

'not bad, classic small kimberlite but not world beaters': Duval, Green & Louthean, p. 124.

'feisty deputy chairman': Duval, Green & Louthean, p. 135.

'My conviction is stronger than before that we will be successful in recovering international gem-quality diamonds from the operation': Brian Conway, quoted in Duval, Green & Louthean, ibid.

'Up to 90 per cent of marine diamonds ... Whatever you get is going to be mostly gem': Duval, Green & Louthean, ibid.

33 A joint adventure

'Native boats 6 o'clock ... only an 18 mile ride to Mawchi': Ethel Tyler (née Matthew), biographical note, Ewen Tyler archive.

'You have to ask, is there ... smaller companies breed diamond people': Doug Wilkinson, 'Veteran diamond seeker is still in the hunt', *Australia's Paydirt*, February 2002, p. 40.

'All along, their goal was ... successful marketing of their interest': Ewen Tyler, 'The Australian diamond industry: The creation of the Argyle diamond project—A chairman's perspective', unpublished speech, c.1983, Ewen Tyler archive.

'That process was seen as coming of age': Author interview with Doug Bailey.

'Their success has been ... no coincidence': Ewen Tyler, email to Paul McClintock dated 22 June 2000, Ewen Tyler archive.

'Having geologists ... a big difference': Author interview with Ewen Tyler.

'may be seen as quite considerable': John McIlwraith, unpublished manuscript, c.2007, drawing on interviews with Ewen Tyler and other key Argyle participants; Ewen Tyler archive.

'For Europeans, the project is likely ... For Aborigines, by and large, the benefits are less certain': Dames and Moore, environmental review and management program, cited by John McIlwraith in memo to Ewen Tyler, 18 October 2007, Ewen Tyler archive.

'a pitiful barter of pocket knives, mirrors and beads for perhaps the richest piece of real estate on earth': Phillip Adams, *The Age*, 11 October 1980.

'We always had a philosophy … rights in a positive and collaborative way':
    Author interview with Bill Leslie.
'grossly disturbed', 'unattractive location': Will Christensen, 'Argyle impact:
    Issues and concerns', in RA Dixon & MC Dillon (eds), *Aborigines and
    Diamond Mining: The Politics of Resource Development in the East Kimberley,
    Western Australia* (Nedlands: University of Western Australia Press, 1990),
    p. 96.
'What this damage has … and autonomy in managing community affairs':
    Christensen, ibid.

BIBLIOGRAPHY

Argyle Diamonds, *Barramundi Dreaming: The Argyle Diamonds Story* (West Perth: Argyle Diamonds, 2011).

Ashton Mining N/L Prospectus (Melbourne: Potter Partners, 1978).

Bergstein, Rachelle, *Brilliance and Fire: A Biography of Diamonds* (New York: Harper, 2016).

Bruton, Eric, *Diamonds* (London: NAG Press, 1978).

Burke, Brian, *A Tumultuous Life* (Scarborough, WA: A Tumultuous Life Pty Ltd, 2017).

Carisch, Enrico, 'The unusual suspects: Africa, parapolitics and the national security state complex', in Eric Wilson (ed.), *The Dual State: Parapolitics, Carl Schmitt and the National Security Complex* (London & New York: Routledge, 2016).

Devlin, Stuart, *Champagne Diamond Exhibition by Stuart Devlin*, Melbourne, Victorian Arts Centre, 8th to 15th December 1987 … Presented by Argyle Diamonds (n.p., 1987).

——*From the Diamonds of Argyle to the Champagne Jewels of Stuart Devlin* (West Perth: Argyle Diamond Sales, 1990).

Dixon, RA & Dillon, MC (eds), *Aborigines and Diamond Mining: The Politics of Resource Development in the East Kimberley, Western Australia* (Nedlands: University of Western Australia Press, 1990).

Duval, David, Green, Timothy & Louthean, Ross, *New Frontiers in Diamonds: The Mining Revolution* (London: Rosendale Press, 1996).

Garden, Donald S, *Builders to the Nation: The AV Jennings Story* (Carlton, Vic.: Melbourne University Press, 1992).

'Geologist left no stone unturned in quest for glittering prize: Maureen Muggeridge, 1948–2010', *Sydney Morning Herald*, 26 November 2010.

Hart, Matthew, *Diamond: The History of a Cold-blooded Love Affair* (London: Fourth Estate, 2003).

Hocking, Anthony, *Oppenheimer and Son* (New York: McGraw-Hill Book Co., 1973).

Hollie, Pamela G, 'Australia's diamond debate', *New York Times*, 4 December 1981.

Hooton, Amanda, 'Diamonds aren't forever: The party's nearly over for Australia's most successful luxury export', *Sydney Morning Herald*, 6 May 2019.

House of Representatives: Official Hansard. No. 125, 1981. Thursday, 15 October 1981. Thirty-Second Parliament. First Session—Third Period, [and] Tuesday, 20 October 1981. Thirty-Second Parliament. First Session—Third Period (By Authority of the House of Representatives, 1981).

Hunt, M, 'The Mining Act 1978 of Western Australia', *Australian Mining and Petroleum Law Association Yearbook*, 2:1 (1979).

Idriess, Ion L, *The Diamond: Stone of Destiny* (Sydney: Angus & Robertson, 1969).

Jamieson, Ronda, *Charles Court: I Love This Place* (Osborne Park, WA: St George's Books, 2011).

Kimberley Diamond Company NL: 2007 *Annual Report* (2007).

A Legend in the Making (West Perth: Argyle Diamonds, n.d.).

McIlwraith, John, unpublished oral history manuscript, c.2007, drawing on interviews with Ewen Tyler and other key Argyle participants, Tyler archive.

Norman, Nick, *The Extraordinary World of Diamonds* (Auckland Park: Jacana Media, 2010).

Royal Commission into Whether There Has Been Corrupt or Criminal Conduct by any Western Australian Police Officer (Parliament of Western Australia, 2004).

Thomas, Tony, 'Argyle: The gleam in Ewen Tyler's eye', *Business Review Weekly*, 7 June 1991.

Tyler, Ewen, 'Argyle Diamonds', unpublished speech (delivered to Rotary Club of Heidelberg, 15 March 2010), Tyler archive.

——'The Australian diamond industry: The creation of the Argyle Diamond project—A chairman's perspective', unpublished speech, c.1983, Tyler archive.

——'Challenges for mining companies in the new millennium', unpublished speech (delivered at Australian Resources Conference, 4 November 1998).

——'Ethics and the mining industry', unpublished speech, n.d., Tyler archive.

——'Ewen William John Tyler: His Story', unpublished memoir, n.d., Tyler archive.

——'The First Twenty Years', unpublished memoir, n.d., Tyler archive.

——'Mines and tribulations: Searching for Aussie diamond mines', Jeweller, 23 August 2016.

——'The mining industry', unpublished speech (delivered to Country Women's Association, Australia Day 1998), Tyler archive.

——'Why diamonds', keynote speech at World Diamond Conference, Perth (delivered 2 December 2002), Tyler archive.

Wilkinson, Doug, 'Veteran diamond seeker is still in the hunt', Australia's Paydirt, February 2002.

INDEX